Palgrave Shakespeare Studies

General Editors: **Michael Dobson** and Dympna Callaghan

Co-founding Editor: **Gail Kern Paster**

Editorial Advisory Board: **Michael Neill**, University of Auckland; **David Schalkwyk**, Folger Shakespeare Library; **Lois D. Potter**, University of Delaware; **Margreta de Grazia**, University of Pennsylvania; **Peter Holland**, University of Notre Dame

Palgrave Shakespeare Studies takes Shakespeare as its focus but strives to understand the significance of his oeuvre in relation to his contemporaries, subsequent writers and historical and political contexts. By extending the scope of Shakespeare and English Renaissance Studies the series will open up the field to examinations of previously neglected aspects or sources in the period's art and thought. Titles in the *Palgrave Shakespeare Studies* series seek to understand anew both where the literary achievements of the English Renaissance came from and where they have brought us.

Titles include:

Pascale Aebischer, Edward J. Esche and Nigel Wheale (*editors*)
REMAKING SHAKESPEARE
Performance across Media, Genres and Cultures

James P. Bednarz
SHAKESPEARE AND THE TRUTH OF LOVE
The Mystery of 'The Phoenix and Turtle'

Mark Thornton Burnett
FILMING SHAKESPEARE IN THE GLOBAL MARKETPLACE

Carla Dente and Sara Soncini (*editors*)
SHAKESPEARE AND CONFLICT
A European Perspective

Cary DiPietro and Hugh Grady (*editors*)
SHAKESPEARE AND THE URGENCY OF NOW
Criticism and Theory in the 21st Century

Kate Flaherty, Penny Gay and L. E. Semler (*editors*)
TEACHING SHAKESPEARE BEYOND THE CENTRE
Australasian Perspectives

Lowell Gallagher and Shankar Raman (*editors*)
KNOWING SHAKESPEARE
Senses, Embodiment and Cognition

Daniel Juan Gil
SHAKESPEARE'S ANTI-POLITICS
Sovereign Power and the Life of the Flesh

Stefan Herbrechter and Ivan Callus (*editors*)
POSTHUMANIST SHAKESPEARES

David Hillman
SHAKESPEARE'S ENTRAILS
Belief, Scepticism and the Interior of the Body

Anna Kamaralli
SHAKESPEARE AND THE SHREW
Performing the Defiant Female Voice

Jane Kingsley-Smith
SHAKESPEARE'S DRAMA OF EXILE

Katie Knowles
SHAKESPEARES'S BOYS
A Cultural History

Rory Loughnane and Edel Semple (*editors*)
STAGED TRANSGRESSION IN SHAKESPEARE'S ENGLAND

Stephen Purcell
POPULAR SHAKESPEARE
Simulation and Subversion on the Modern Stage

Erica Sheen
SHAKESPEARE AND THE INSTITUTION OF THEATRE

Paul Yachnin and Jessica Slights
SHAKESPEARE AND CHARACTER
Theory, History, Performance, and Theatrical Persons

Palgrave Shakespeare Studies
Series Standing Order ISBN 978–1403–91164–3 (hardback)
978–1403–91165–0 (paperback)
(*outside North America only*)

You can receive future titles in this series as they are published by placing a stand-ing order. Please contact your bookseller or, in case of difficulty, write to us at the address below with your name and address, the title of the series and the ISBN quoted above.

Customer Services Department, Macmillan Distribution Ltd, Houndmills, Basingstoke, Hampshire RG21 6XS, England

Shakespeare's Anti-Politics

Sovereign Power and the Life of the Flesh

Daniel Juan Gil
Texas Christian University, Fort Worth, Texas, USA

Softcover reprint of the hardcover 1st edition 2013 978-1-137-27500-4

First published 2013 by
PALGRAVE MACMILLAN

Palgrave Macmillan in the UK is an imprint of Macmillan Publishers Limited,
registered in England, company number 785998, of Houndmills, Basingstoke,
Hampshire RG21 6XS.

Palgrave Macmillan in the US is a division of St Martin's Press LLC,
175 Fifth Avenue, New York, NY 10010.

Palgrave Macmillan is the global academic imprint of the above companies
and has companies and representatives throughout the world.

Palgrave® and Macmillan® are registered trademarks in the United States,
the United Kingdom, Europe and other countries.

ISBN 978-1-349-44598-1   ISBN 978-1-137-27501-1 (eBook)
DOI 10.1057/9781137275011

Typeset by MPS Limited, Chennai, India.

Contents

Acknowledgments   vi

Introduction   1

1   The Historical Conditions of Possibility of the
    Life of the Flesh: Absolutism, Civic Republicanism,
    and "Bare Life" in *Julius Caesar*   20

2   The Life of the Condemned: The Autonomous
    Legal System and the Community of the Flesh in
    Measure for Measure   42

3   Unsettling the Civic Republican Order:
    The Face of Sovereign Power and the Fate
    of the Citizen in *Othello*   68

4   Life Outside the Law: Torture and the Flesh in *King Lear*   98

Epilogue: The Afterlife of the Life of the Flesh   124

Notes   130

Bibliography   152

Index   163

Acknowledgments

I would like to thank Alexandra Halasz and Jonathan Crewe for the opportunity to deliver an earlier version of the chapter on *Measure for Measure* at Dartmouth. I would also like to thank Sharon O'Dair for the opportunity to present a version of the *Othello* chapter at a symposium held at the Hudson Strode Program in Renaissance Studies at the University of Alabama. The thoughtful responses of audiences at both events helped me to understand my own argument more clearly. I presented an early version of some of my ideas at a 2005 SAA seminar led by Julia Reinhard Lupton and Graham Hammill, and I appreciate the brilliant feedback both provided. I would also like to thank Jeffrey M. Perl, the editor of *Common Knowledge*, for his help with the shorter version of the *Julius Caesar* chapter that first appeared in *Common Knowledge*. A revised and expanded version of that chapter is reproduced here by the permission of Duke University Press.

At Palgrave, I would like to thank Felicity Plester for her initial interest in the project, and Ben Doyle and Sophie Ainscough for their continued interest. I am deeply grateful for the expert work of Linda Auld and Sally Osborn in getting the book through production. I also want to thank the series editors, Michael Dobson and Dympna Callaghan, and Palgrave's anonymous reader for very helpful feedback and suggestions. Finally, I would like to thank my editorial assistant, Emily Cody, for her help in compiling the bibliographical material.

Through the years spent writing this book I have benefited from many professional and personal friendships. First and foremost, I want to thank Michael Drexler, who has been a steady source of wisdom, encouragement, and happy conversation for the past 20 years. I deeply appreciate Rick Keyser's long-standing friendship. I am fortunate to count Lara Bovilsky and Aaron Kunin as close friends and occasional collaborators. Jonathan Goldberg's kindness, rigor, and brilliance are an abiding inspiration. I also deeply appreciate the friendship of Barbara Correll, Brian Warren, Frances Dickey, and Julie Kimmel.

My biggest debt is to Anne Frey, whose own brilliant work is an inspiration and whose love, generosity, and patience have made this book possible. The book is dedicated to Anne and to our beautiful daughters, Madeleine and Elena.

Introduction

Much of the best Shakespeare criticism over the past decade has explored Shakespeare's attitude toward the political structures of the rising nation-state. While many critics have seen Shakespeare as a political and cultural conservative who celebrates the power of the absolute monarch, an influential number of critics have suggested that Shakespeare champions oppositional civic republican values of citizenship and shared responsibility for governance.[1] In this book I argue that seeing Shakespeare as a partisan of either absolutism or civic republicanism misses the fundamentally anti-political drive in his literary-political imagination. I argue that Shakespeare uses his plays to reveal that all state forms are by their nature vehicles of a sovereign power that seizes the bodily lives of its subjects in order to impose on them a regulated subjectivity and a textured social life. I argue that Shakespeare uses his plays to explore the phenomenological experience of utter subjection to sovereign power. However, I also argue that Shakespeare uses the medium of theater to chart a surprising form of opposition to state power that bypasses the limited terms of the absolutism vs. civic republicanism debate. Shakespeare does not imagine a strategy of direct confrontation with or opposition to the sovereign power of the nation-state. Rather, he imagines using its sovereign power against itself to engineer distinctively theatrical forms of selfhood and relationality. In the plays I discuss in this book—*Julius Caesar*, *Measure for Measure*, *Othello*, and *King Lear*—characters are forced to recognize themselves as utterly exposed to the arbitrary sovereign power of the state, but again and again this recognition leads to a transformation in self and in the links between self and others. The experiences of selfhood and relationality that are energized by an encounter with raw sovereign power are what I term "the life of the flesh," and I see them as the central focus

1

of Shakespeare's theatrical work. As Shakespeare represents it, therefore, the rising nation-state (inadvertently) energizes a life of the flesh that is rooted in the (shared) experience of the body abjectly exposed to sovereign power. I argue that the focus of Shakespeare's art is to bring this life of the flesh to the stage as the object of an audience's aesthetic experience; through Shakespeare's plays, readers and audiences are invited to take aesthetic pleasure in seeing and even fantasmatically participating in a life of the flesh that is an alternative to functional integration into the nation-state.

I.   Sovereignty

I will argue that Shakespeare crystallizes the life of the flesh in his plays by staging a heightened version of the conflict between divine right absolutism and civic republicanism. However, to understand his project, it is helpful to begin with some modern theoretical models, specifically Carl Schmitt's theory of the role of sovereignty in political orders and Giorgio Agamben's development of Schmitt's insights in the direction of an engagement with Foucault's notion of "bio-politics." In essence, I argue that Shakespeare anticipates the Schmitt/Agamben vision and uses it to launch a nihilistic critique of state power and a sustained exploration of a countervailing life of the flesh.[2]

For Schmitt, no matter how democratic or law-governed a political order, it is always underpinned by a sovereign power that is outside the institutionalized political framework. As Schmitt understands it, the normal, constitutionally bounded functioning of a political and legal system is only made possible by a sovereign who sustains a state of affairs that is normal enough for the conventional political and legal system to function. And the sovereign can sustain normality only by maintaining the right to declare an exception, a state of emergency in which the normal procedures are suspended and in which the sovereign may use legally unconstrained violence to restore the normal state. For Schmitt, therefore, normal political life is inconceivable without the in-dwelling potential for a non-normal situation, and the sovereign is the person who is responsible for deciding on when and how violence should be used to maintain or restore a normal state.

For Schmitt, liberal parliamentary democracies (like the Weimar republic under which he came of age politically) are just as much structured by sovereign power as are explicitly authoritarian forms of government. However, whereas authoritarian orders embrace and even celebrate the role of extra-legal and extra-political sovereign power as the

denial of sovereign power

guarantor of the normal political and legal order, liberal parliamentary democracies are uncomfortable with it, even to the point of denying it altogether. For Schmitt, this willful blindness to the structuring role of sovereign power can render liberal parliamentary democracies unable to respond effectively to existential threats. According to Schmitt, an existential threat to the political order requires the sovereign to suspend the normal political and legal systems and declare a state of emergency in which extra-legal violence is allowed in order to address the existential threat. Schmitt believes that parliamentary democracies tend to be unable or unwilling to make this shift to a state of emergency. For Schmitt, liberal parliamentary democracies tend to respond to existential threats by descending into endless procedural quibbling that, according to Schmitt, amounts to trying to deal with an extra-normal situation by normal means.

Despite being tainted by his work as a jurist and apologist under German National-Socialism, Schmitt has become quite popular in recent years, notably in the aftermath of the 9/11 terrorist attack on the World Trade Center. Part of the explanation is that his model seems to provide a good way of understanding the explosion of extra-legal state violence undertaken by the United States and other Western governments in recent years.[3] Whereas liberal political theorists are scandalized and frankly puzzled by the sudden emergence of seemingly arbitrary, executive power in Western democracies in recent years, Schmitt's model suggests that this development is no surprise at all, since it amounts to nothing more than the re-emergence of the principle of sovereignty that is, he argues, always present at the heart of any political order.

A second reason that Schmitt has become so popular today is the way his model has been appropriated and developed in the work of Giorgio Agamben. For Agamben, Schmitt's analysis provides a template for understanding the history of Western political formations from the ancient Greeks to the industrialized mass democracies of the twentieth century. Nevertheless, Agamben believes that Schmitt underestimates the full extent of the effects of sovereign power. Whereas Schmitt is only concerned with the role of sovereign power in the functioning of legal and political institutions, Agamben believes that the effects of sovereign power pervade all of social and subjective life.

Agamben's perspective seeks to merge Schmitt's analysis of the role of sovereign power in structuring institutional legal and political life with the late Foucault's interest in "bio-politics," the state's effort to penetrate and manage the very core of life of all of its subjects.[4] The way Agamben combines Schmitt's account of the foundational role of exceptional sovereign power in *political* communities and Foucault's notion of a generalized bio-politics that pervades social and subjective life is to argue that every political society is founded and maintained by an act of unconditional sovereign will that creates not only (1) a set of political structures, as Schmitt had argued, but also (2) a definition of what counts as human nature and as a valid, legitimately human form of life. In other words, according to Agamben, in addition to instituting political and legal structures, sovereign power also operates at the very roots of life, using violence to create and maintain a demarcation between state-sanctioned forms of life and what is marked as other than state-sanctioned life.[5] For Agamben, therefore, the "normal" state guaranteed by sovereign power is more than a set of institutionalized legal and political procedures (which is as far as Schmitt takes his analysis). Rather, Agamben argues that the "normal" situation that is guaranteed by sovereign power is a distinctive form of state structuration of the very fabric of human life and the whole web of social and relational life that follows from it. Schmitt argues that the political and legal order is structured by the presence of sovereign power that can suspend the constitutional order.[6] But for Agamben, sovereign power is, at the same time, fundamentally bio-political; for him, the whole web of subjective and social life is structured by the presence of sovereign power.

One important implication of Agamben's development of Schmitt's account is that it calls into doubt any notion of a "civil society," a form of social life that is *outside of* or *separate from* the institutions of state power, for Agamben sees all forms of social life as products of primordial sovereign power. Agamben rejects the notion that there could be a community life (rooted in family, civic institutions, faith communities, or local ties) that could exist other than as an effect of sovereign power and, for him, any notion of a pre-political community life is essentially a liberal-communitarian fantasy. As far as Agamben is concerned, the precondition for any social life is a prior sovereign decision about the limits and nature of human being, which is at the same time a decision about who is inside the community and therefore is "us" and who is excluded from the community and is therefore not "us" (what Schmitt, anticipating this portion of Agamben's argument, calls an "enemy" as opposed to a "friend"). By making this decision, sovereign power stamps an existential identity onto some human bodies and thus elevates those human bodies to the personhood that is the precondition for what liberal-communitarian theory misrecognizes as extra-political community life. From Agamben's perspective, therefore, the theory that there is a social and relational life that is genuinely outside of the sovereign power of the state is simply naïve.

Much critical theory has focused on understanding and modeling what appear to be extra-state structures of subjective, relational, and cultural life, starting with psychoanalysis and continuing through to the current focus on cultural and ethnic identity. Yet with the exception of the Marxist tradition (notably in the work of Gramsci and Althusser), twentieth-century critical theory has been largely indifferent to the presence and impact of sovereign power (and state institutions) on the texture of social and subjective life. The challenge faced by critical theory today is to bring together Agamben's understanding of the role of sovereign power in anchoring an essentially bio-political order with our already quite nuanced theoretical accounts of the texture of subjective, relational, and cultural life.[7]

In this book I do not offer such a systematic synthesis, but I certainly start with the assumption that there is a complex link between the structures of subjective, relational, and cultural life of early modern England and the historically new form of sovereign power carried by the rising nation-state. I believe that this basic assumption is shared by Shakespeare, whose drama starts with two premises: (1) that sovereign power structures the political order of the nation-state by being outside of the political order and therefore outside political norms; and (2) that this sovereign power is deeply bound up in defining and maintaining social roles and identities and even personal subjective experiences.

For Shakespeare, these premises open the door to staging a distinctive form of resistance to state power that avoids taking flight into a supposedly pre-political civil society. For Shakespeare, understanding state power in the way Schmitt and Agamben do opens the door to a kind of ju-jitsu in which the bio-political power of the nation-state is used against itself to energize forms of life and subjectivity that escape the orbit of the sovereign nation-state. In his plays, Shakespeare engineers situations in which characters encounter—and are radically transformed by—the raw sovereign power that stands behind structured political and social life. Schmitt's term for a situation in which the sovereign is forced to show his or her hand is a "state of emergency." Seeing Shakespeare as staging states of emergency is a perspective that I share with Lupton, although Lupton argues that a political state of emergency allows a pre-political civil society defined by social norms to appear.[8] This is precisely wrong, at least as an account of Shakespeare's plays. For Shakespeare, a state of emergency does not merely sheer off a superficial layer of legal and political control to allow some pre-political civil society to emerge. For Shakespeare, as for Agamben, when a state of emergency appears in the political domain it also unsettles the whole fabric of subjective, relational, and cultural life. Yet for Shakespeare, this social emergency also opens the door to a countervailing intersubjective experience. When it appears in Shakespeare's plays, sovereign power strips characters of their conventional social roles and identities and transforms them into a new and generative category of the flesh, capable of entering into new kinds of relationship with other flesh.

II.   Absolutism and Civic Republicanism

While the Agamben/Schmitt theory provides a general model for understanding Shakespeare's project, Shakespeare himself theorizes the political/social field and its breakdowns by means of the early modern discursive conflict between divine right absolutism and civic republicanism. Shakespeare does not champion civic republicanism, nor does he champion the absolutism that civic republicanism critiques. Rather, he uses the conflict between these two different visions of how political and social life structure each other to make manifest the arbitrary sovereign power that lies at the very foundation of any structured political and social life.

Schmitt himself admired the absolute monarchs of early modern Europe for their uncompromising affirmation of themselves as the embodiment of absolute, sovereign power. Early modern monarchs were quite happy to see their own power as radically above and beyond the conventional legal and political mechanisms of the state. King James famously believed that his word was law. For James, what created and maintained a nation was the will of the sovereign and his absolute power of life and death over his subjects. Opposing both trans-national religious assertions of collective identity (like Catholicism or Puritanism) and local or regional sources of collective identity (like Welshness or Scottishness), early modern absolute monarchs claimed for themselves the exclusive right to define a national identity and way of life (including a national church) and to define the enemies of that way of life. And even if the collective life sponsored by the absolutist nation-state remained marked by alternative sources of identity (such as region, religion, class, and gender), the absolute monarchs nevertheless claimed the right to override, at least in the limiting circumstances of an emergency, all other sources of identity and to define the existential grouping. Schmitt admired the willingness of early modern European monarchs to take responsibility for the definition of collective life rooted in nothing but their personal fiat. From this standpoint, it is the monarch alone who defines the collective life of the nation as against other national collectives, and who also makes individual members of the nation sacrificeable in the name of defending the whole.[9]

In practice, this theoretical emphasis on the radically exceptional nature of the sovereign who defines and guarantees a way of life is veiled by the early modern development and expansion of quasi-autonomous, bureaucratic administrative agencies that increasingly do the work of government without the actual, personal involvement of the king or queen.[10] On the one hand, the rise of such administrative agencies hides the face of sovereign power; on the other hand, it also attests to what Agamben sees as the essentially bio-political nature of state power, its explicit desire to gain control of and manage the very lives of its subjects, to find mechanisms to penetrate to the minutest levels of daily life. Yet in early modern absolutist theory, the normal, even autonomous functioning of the quasi-bureaucratic administrative apparatuses of the state is only possible to the extent that the king or queen stands above them, authorizing them but also capable of interfering in routine operations for reasons of state.[11]

There can be no doubt that this absolutist perspective (in which the king is outside the institutionalized political order that he also authorizes) is the dominant political framework in early modern England. Nevertheless, this framework is challenged by an oppositional discourse of civic republicanism.[12] At its most limited, civic republicanism affirms only that a privileged elite with roles in the state's growing administrative apparatus have the right to be consulted on decisions that the prince makes. This limited form of elite civic republicanism essentially accepts the exceptional role of the sovereign in maintaining the political community, but affirms that those to whom the king grants offices and responsibilities may play a consultative role in political life.[13]

However, in its more radical form, civic republicanism aims to develop an alternative way of organizing political and social space that would evade any subjection to arbitrary sovereign power.[14] This radical civic republicanism is animated by what Skinner calls a "neo-Roman" theory of liberty that indicts absolute power precisely because of its effects on social and subjective life. For such civic republicanism, any subjection to arbitrary, unaccountable power—even if that power is in fact exercised with restraint—produces slavishness or "obnoxiousness" in its subjects. Such radicalized civic republicanism therefore imagines replacing the absolutist political and social order with a new political order in which the political community is defined not by an external sovereign power but by its own collective decision-making power.

For Shakespeare, this radical civic republican vision is valuable because it reveals and indicts the raw sovereign power that lies at the heart of absolutist political orders. In Shakespeare's plays the civic republican critique forces attention to the full effects of exposure to an unaccountable sovereign power, effects that, according to the neo-Roman critique, pervade all facets of personal identity and subjective life and render persons obnoxious. However, as against recent critics who have seen Shakespeare as essentially a spokesperson for civic republican values, I argue that Shakespeare never allows civic republicanism to escape its own critique.[15] Shakespeare consistently dramatizes the failure of civic republicanism to institutionalize a political and social life that would collectively embody sovereign power rather than being subject to external sovereign power. In Shakespeare's hands, therefore, civic republican discourse is essentially self-annihilating; it criticizes the monarchical order for the demeaning effects of dependence on raw sovereign power without finding a way to define a political and social order that itself escapes being dependent on raw sovereign power.[16]

The way civic republicanism functions in Shakespeare's plays amounts to a distinctively Shakespearean *reading* of early modern civic republican discourse. One especially clear example of how Shakespeare reads civic republicanism in order to heighten its nihilistic power is his approach to Contarini's *The Commonwealth and Government of Venice*, which is one of his major sources for civic republican thought in general and the Venetian context of *Othello* in particular. Translated by Lewis Lewkenor in 1599, with dedicatory poems by Spenser and John Harrington, Contarini celebrates Venice as the best model of a functioning civic republican order that apparently bypasses the need for any unaccountable sovereign power outside the political community. According to Contarini, the way Venice does so is to combine the institutions of a collectively managed public life with a social fabric structured by the virtue of public mindedness. In place of a monarch who is imagined to found, structure, and guarantee the political community, Contarini describes the Venetian republic as the autochthonous, self-generated product of the continuous political and social virtue of its citizens.[17] As it is presented in Contarini, therefore, the Venetian political structure seems to be a counterexample to Schmitt's claim that political communities always rely on arbitrary sovereign power to define and maintain their borders and their institutional procedures. Venetian civic republicanism appears to treat the existential decision that makes "us" who "we" are as one that unfolds in time through citizens acting freely in conjunction with others to determine a collective course of action.[18]

Shakespeare uses Contarini's account for his dramatic vision of Venice, but as I explore in greater detail in Chapter 3, Shakespeare also subjects the fantasy of a truly republican order to a withering critique. As he represents it in *Othello*, the civic republic of Venice is itself necessarily underpinned and guaranteed by a raw sovereign will that is outside the political and social order; this sovereign will is precisely what the character of Othello represents within Shakespeare's Venice. Moreover, it turns out that Contarini's own account of Venice is haunted by this very suspicion. Rereading Contarini after reading Shakespeare's play brings to light how Contarini's account persistently fails to provide a starting point for the political and social life of the republic that does not beg the question of who or what creates and maintains the politico-social community.[19] Contarini's account is, in fact, marked by an infinite regress toward some mythical origin of Venetian political and social structures, an infinite regress that can only be healed by the real exercise of sovereign power.[20] As Shakespeare sees it, civic republicanism reveals the disabling effects of being exposed to sovereign power in monarchical orders only then symptomatically to perform its own inability to escape its own critique. The effect of this discourse in Shakespeare's plays is therefore to teach Agamben's central lesson; namely, that sovereign power stands at the origin of any structured social and political life, that there is no way out of exposure to sovereign power.

III. The Life of the Flesh

Critical efforts to see Shakespeare as a partisan of civic republican values have occluded his distinctive *use* of civic republicanism in his plays, namely to lay bare the inescapable core of arbitrary sovereign power within any political and social order, whether absolutist or nominally republican.[21] But if for Shakespeare there is no way out of subjection to sovereign power, then this revelation is the starting point for a ju-jitsu–like effort to use sovereign power against itself. Once it appears in Shakespeare's plays, raw sovereign power strips characters of their conventional social roles and identities and discloses the substrate on which their socio-symbolic identities are mounted, a luminous fleshliness that is neither "naturally" human nor functionally identical to any social or symbolic identity. Shakespeare treats this fleshly substrate as a starting point for a distinctively theatrical project of reworking and rewiring the basic circuitry of interpersonal connections, and it is this transformed terrain of self and other that arises in the shadow of sovereign power that I term the "life of the flesh."

To explain the core of my argument here, it is useful to return again to Agamben's theoretical language. As I have noted above, Agamben argues that the sovereign power that institutes a political order also institutes a particular form of human life, and it does so by devaluing (or even dehumanizing) other forms of life. For Agamben, the life that is cast away, denied, repressed, or ostracized by the sovereign act that founds a particular political order is "bare life," life that is not raised to the privileges of full membership in the political community.[22] Agamben argues that "bare life" reappears in various symptomatic ways in Western political orders, for example in the ideal of a "natural" good life, but also in the form of ritual scapegoats through whose exclusion the supposed purity of the politically sanctioned community is reaffirmed. However, the fact that sanctioned life (that is, a politically valid subjectivity) depends on arbitrary sovereign power also leaves a mark inside sanctioned life itself, inside the citizen: the haunting awareness that within the citizen is a body that is radically subject to sovereign power, and thus that there is a trace of unsanctioned life within the heart of the socially sanctioned person. It is this trace of bare life *within* the socially valid self that Shakespeare's civic republican critique of sovereign power reveals.

To emphasize the generative, productive potential of the experience of being utterly and inescapably exposed to state power in Shakespeare's plays, I translate the concept of "bare life" into the notion of the "life of the flesh." The difference between Agamben's "bare life" and my "life of the flesh" is precisely that while bare life is repeatedly, though ineffectually, excluded from the political community, the "life of the flesh" is an ever-present potential woven into the very fabric of political life, and as such it can come to be seen as a home away from home, a place where an abiding experience of exposure to sovereign power can be developed into new, often theatrical experiences of selfhood and relationality.[23] As Shakespeare imagines it, the life of the flesh is, by its very nature, potentially social (or better: proto-social), in that it projects a matrix of ties between persons who have been "decommissioned" as persons by an encounter with the raw power of the sovereign. Bypassing any fantasy of a civil society constituted by well-fashioned, conventionally social subjects, the life of the flesh brings together persons who lack the conventional attributes of social identity. Describing the specific morphologies and patterns of the life of the flesh as Shakespeare imagines them in his theater is one of the main contributions of this book, but one important analogue for it is investigations of the experience of togetherness mediated by a sense of corporeal vulnerability undertaken by critics like Agamben, Nancy and Blanchot, and Negri.[24]

One morphology and pattern that plays an especially important role in my discussion is a non-intimate eroticism that appears so frequently in the "anti-political" plays that I discuss here. This non-intimate eroticism is defined by using exposure to sovereign power to drive persons away from conventional social identities and the socially legible ties that bind persons together. I have elsewhere examined a form of early modern sexuality defined by transforming invidious social codes of quasi-biological class difference into a form of theatrical play that creates erotic connections where a functionally social interpersonal connection is impossible.[25] In this book, I see a similar erotic energy triggered by broader political states of emergency in which not only class but the whole spectrum of conventional social identity attributes are unhinged. If raw sovereign power strips persons of their conventional social personas and thus forces them to come to terms with a generative, fleshly life within themselves, then Shakespeare's plays identify a powerful form of pleasure—and a powerful alternative form of intercorporeal glue—in this form of social and personal unmaking. In the perverse glue that connects such characters as Marc Antony and Caesar, Angelo and Isabella, and Othello and Desdemona in the shadows of a breakdown of political structure, we see an eroticism that is built on the recurring experience of being stripped down to a core of bare life.

In the plays I examine in this book, the eroticism of feeling the self unmoored from its conventional social indices comes in two forms. On the one hand, it spans characters who have been equally stripped or decommissioned in the face of raw sovereign power—as happens in *Measure for Measure* when Mistress Overdone's customers all feel themselves driven together in the face of the universal condemnation that Angelo's law imposes on them. On the other hand, an essentially asymmetrical version of eroticism spans characters who embody raw sovereign power and characters who are unmade by it—as with the relationship of Angelo and Isabella or Othello and Desdemona. For the "weak" characters in these dyads, there is a powerful erotic charge in experiencing the self as radically subject to raw power, but alongside it there is a rebound in which the "sovereign" characters recognize a distorted version of themselves in the bodies that are abjectly at their mercy. This reveals an important truth about sovereign power, which is that while it structures a political and social order, it is itself radically undefined within that order; when sovereign power strips others of personhood, it can come to recognize itself as lacking personhood as well.

My claims in this book about an eroticism that is built on the breakdown of conventionally defined persons draw on and develop important theoretical work on the constitutive role of masochism in sexuality. The major theorists here are Bersani and Laplanche, who both argue, in somewhat different ways, that sexuality is not defined by a mutual affirmation of identity, but is rather essentially about shattering the self, about temporarily relieving the self of the burden of being a socially recognized person. This account of sexuality-as-masochism is difficult to apply to early modern culture, because early modern culture does not yet assume the ideal of a well-defined and well-defended self that can be pleasurably shattered.[26] I suggest that Shakespeare locates an early modern antecedent of sexuality-as-masochism in moments in which a stable socio-symbolic identity delivered by functioning state power is theatrically disengaged. Moreover, Shakespeare suggests that this proto-masochistic sexuality is essentially a community-building practice. In framing sexuality in this way, Shakespeare provides a bridge between seeing sexuality as essentially solipsistic—as Laplanche and Bersani view it—to seeing it as the kernel of an alternative community built on the (paradoxically) shared experience of such solipsism.

IV.   Theater and the Aesthetics of the Flesh

One of the animating ideas of this study is that the life of the flesh does not take on institutional forms of sovereign power in a head-to-head assault, as though the flesh had a political party. Direct opposition to an institutional form of state power is as much a move within the game of politics as supporting it is; both take their places in a predetermined universe of political stances within a political community presided over by sovereign power. Nor does the life of the flesh endorse liberal bromides about a civil society of rights-bearing individuals freely engaging in reasoned interactions with one another outside of the state. Instead, the life of the flesh is a "tangential" form of opposition; it opposes the institutional structures of sovereign power by using those structures against themselves, as it were, to energize a theatrical experience of fleshly life that is ultimately not contained by functioning political sovereignty.

By using Shakespeare to recover and reconstruct this tangential path through or beyond the early modern field of sovereign power, I rely on a distinctive literary-historical methodology. Though this book draws on historicist principles, it is also resistant to the way historicism is practiced as a critical norm in much of Renaissance literary studies, and Shakespeare studies in particular. While standard historicist accounts attempt to contextualize the plays by folding them into extra-aesthetic historical discourses, I see Shakespeare's literary/theatrical texts as capable of saying something that cannot readily be said in any other historical discourse.[27] While I argue that early modern observers could envision a life of the flesh founded on a phenomenologically shared experience of subjection to sovereign power, they could not readily articulate this life in any of the political, religious, or social discourses available to them to "think though" social formations. For this reason, the life of the flesh appears in a privileged way in art, and especially in the dramatic art that uses words to set bodies in motion across a stage.

Shakespeare devotes all of his theatrical and discursive resources to making visible, staging, cataloguing, and assessing the implications of the life of the flesh. Part of the goal of this book is to articulate an aesthetic framework that is adequate to the task of seeing, recognizing, and responding to the life of the flesh as it appears on the Shakespearean stage. I argue that the aesthetic framework Shakespeare uses to represent the life of the flesh is built on two distinctive elements: a specialized *discourse* of the humors; and a systematic exploitation of the corporeal theatricality of the *medium* of theater.

First, a discourse of the humors. To describe the phenomenological experience of the life of the flesh, Shakespeare fashions a somewhat eccentric version of the humoral theory of the emotions that has been the subject of much critical attention by literary scholars and historians.[28] What makes humoral discourse valuable as a way of capturing and representing the interpersonal or transpersonal life of the flesh is that from the humoral perspective, bits and pieces of other persons—the humors they emit, their fluids, even the puffs of air that constitute their words— are able to cross the porous membrane of the self.[29] Shakespeare's plays use the discourse of the humors to represent networks of connections between emotionally inflamed bodies that flourish in the shadow of functional state power and the personhood that sovereign power imposes. As the plays imagine them, these proto-social networks are knitted together by bits of humoral matter that cross from one body to another, defining corporeal channels that bypass interactions between socially legible persons. Thus, in *Measure for Measure*, prostitution is metaphorically described as a kind of cannibalism in which bodies nibble on each other and digest bits of one another into themselves. The proto-social network defined in this way undermines (even as it is parasitically animated by) the legal order that both Angelo and the duke wish to impose on Vienna. The bonds on which such fleshly networks are built do not take place in a social vacuum, but neither are they functionally contextualized in the dominant social and political discourses that early modern English society uses to think about itself. Instead, the humorally defined patterns of connection between bodies are a concrete, historically situated alternative to the normative, collective life defined by the rising nation-state.

Second, the distinctively theatrical resources of Shakespeare's medium. Part of the way in which he brings the life of the flesh onto the stage is by drawing on the essentially theatrical and bodily nature of his medium, and its ability to put bodies into gestural interactions with other bodies. Shakespeare's plays draw on social discourses, including discourses of politics, to define characters, but they often elicit a double perspective in which audience members see and respond to the characters, and also to the gestural reality of the actors engaged in corporeal interactions with one another. These gestural interactions are always set in motion by the script, though they sometimes leave the script behind to take on a life of their own. At such moments, the audience *hears* words that bring a character and a story to life, but *sees* a visible life of the flesh take shape on the stage. Especially in my discussion of *Othello* and *King Lear*, I argue that the hybrid entities that are discursively generated characters within the imagined world of the play, yet are also "real" bodies engaged in gestural interactions with other bodies, are capable of presenting a life of the flesh that cannot readily be represented in any early modern social discourse.

Trusting to theatricality to put the life of the flesh on the stage is especially marked when Shakespeare represents forms of state violence like torture, legal condemnation, execution, imprisonment, and war. In his plays, Shakespeare hijacks such forms of violence, re-functioning them into a kind of fleshly play, using them unseriously or theatrically to produce emotionally heightened forms of connection between bodies that transcend any real obedience to the collectivizing power of the state. In other words, in Shakespeare's plays, the sovereign privilege of violence is re-functioned as a theatrical scaffold on which flesh can meet other flesh to experiment with new forms of life together. In *Julius Caesar*, for example, state conflict triggers a "war" that amounts to a campy practice of character-actors theatrically thrusting swords into each other's bodies.[30] These gestural interactions theatrically strip the bodies on the stage of the armor of personhood (that defines characters in the imagined world of the play) and instead join bodies with other bodies at the level of flesh. In *Julius Caesar*, as in the other plays I discuss, Shakespeare uses the civic republican critique of sovereignty to trigger an event on the stage that does not merely *represent* but actually *enacts* the life of the flesh.

And if the script is only a way of putting into play the bodily life of the actors who animate the characters, spectators can respond to those moving bodies, to their gestural and even physical reality. That is especially true when the bodies in motion bring to light an essentially physical cruelty that violates traditional political notions of the dignity of the person, as with the scenes of torture in *King Lear*. In such scenes, Shakespeare aims to shift spectators out of a detached relation to a story or narrative and into a more physically engaged relation with bodies that have been placed in motion on the stage. Thus, Shakespeare's theater moves from *representing* fleshly interpersonal communions seared together by a transformative use of the dark energy of sovereign power to *enacting* such a form of community in the relations of the bodies of the actors, as well as in the relations of the bodies of the actors and the bodies of the spectators.

V. Book Overview

In closing, I want to offer an overview of the structure of the book as a whole and an account of how the various components of the argument work together. Each of the individual chapters of this study focuses on a specific institutional register where the new sovereign power of the nation-state manifests itself: the "public sphere" (Chapter 1); the legal domain and the regulation of sexuality (Chapter 2); the use of military power in times of emergency (Chapter 3); and the use of political assassination, torture, and other forms of state-sanctioned violence (Chapter 4). However, rather than celebrating or naturalizing the power of the nation-state in each of these registers, Shakespeare shows each of them to contain a fault line (essentially, a version of the conflict between absolutism and civic republicanism) that strips sovereign power of its legitimacy by reducing it to brute force, the arbitrary power of life and death over its own subjects, a recognition that, in turn, opens the door to a countervailing "life of the flesh."

In Chapter 1, I show how *Julius Caesar* sets an absolutist perspective embodied by Caesar into conflict with the civic republican rebellion led by Brutus. Rather than framing this conflict as a battle between state power and a civic resistance movement that is outside of state power, Shakespeare designs Brutus's rebellion to undermine any notion of a civil society that supports a public sphere that is outside of the state, as Jürgen Habermas would have it. Following Schmitt and Agamben, I argue that Shakespeare's version of the public sphere is, in fact, not external to state power but a product of it.

In place of a classical public sphere, I see the play sketching a different form of opposition; namely, a collective life of the flesh that is energized by state power and yet also escapes from it. When Caesar's and Brutus's competing visions of the state evacuate each other of legitimacy, characters find themselves ejected from all politically mediated forms of public life. They are plunged, instead, into a life of the flesh that is figured by a theatricalized version of war. After the assassination of Caesar, Marc Antony triggers a civil war that he frames not as "politics by other means," as Clausewitz would have it, but as an alternative to politics. In war, as Marc Antony dreams of it and as the play stages it, clusters of bodies engaged in theatrical violence figure a collective life that is essentially different from any politically mediated public life.

I go on to argue that Shakespeare uses a humoral discourse of the passions as fluids—with an especial focus on blood as the fluid that causes anger—to trace the outlines of concrete, fleshly connections between characters. Almost the first wish that Marc Antony expresses after seeing the body of Caesar is to be stabbed with the swords still covered in Caesar's blood: "If I myself [am going to be killed], there is no hour so fit/ As Caesar's death's hour, nor no instrument/ Of half that worth as those your swords, made rich/ With the most noble blood of all this world" (3.1.154–157).[31] Being stabbed by a sword already "made rich" with "noble blood" points to the fantasy of a transformed relation to the other by means of a direct experience of the body and its fluids. It is a fantasy that reappears toward the end of the play in the rash of stabbings-by-shared-sword that continue to mingle the blood of men in ways that affirm connections between bodies that exceed any loyalty to a functioning political party. I end this chapter by contextualizing the play in the history of civic republican and common law thought, a context that plays a determining role in *Measure for Measure*, the subject of my next chapter.

In Chapter 2, I focus on the legal system that the nation-state uses to project its power into the lives of its subjects. Legal historians and theorists have shown that early modern thinking on the law is deeply conflicted between, on the one hand, celebrating the common law tradition that appears to function autonomously from the will of the sovereign and, on the other hand, emphasizing the prerogative power of the sovereign to modify common law judgments in the interests of "equity." In *Measure for Measure*, Shakespeare uses this conflict to trigger a legitimacy crisis in the system of law. The play tears the veil of legitimacy from the law to reveal it as nothing but the raw personal will of the sovereign exercised on the bodies of his (or her) subjects. And once the law comes to be seen as the expression of an arbitrary and even incomprehensible power that seizes bodies and can kill them at will, the fact that everyone in the play is subject to the law becomes the starting point for a transformed and transformative form of intercorporeal life based on shared abjection before sovereign power. In *Measure for Measure*, this new experience of intercorporeality is figured by the prostitution that the law wants to stamp out but is irrepressible. I argue that the irrepressible, corporeally mediated interpersonal connections defined between characters in the illegal underworld of prostitution sketch the flip side of a legally molded political community. Moreover, as I have already noted, prostitution is figured as a kind of cannibalism through which the citizens of Vienna ingest bits of each other. I argue that this view represents the truth of the humoral model of the emotions, in which the membrane between self and other is always porous and in which people are always ingesting bits of others—their fluids, their humors, their words—into themselves. In the cannibalistic prostitution that is only made more tenacious when it is attacked by the law, *Measure for Measure* systematically explores the subterranean order of life that is paradoxically energized by the law's effort to stamp it out.

Whereas in Chapter 1 I analyze the trouble at the heart of "civil society" and in Chapter 2 I analyze the trouble at the heart of the law, in Chapter 3 I focus on the way in which raw sovereign power unsettles the "citizen" who plays a functional role within the civic republican political order represented in *Othello*. As a political ideal, civic republicanism exercised a deep fascination for many early modern English intellectuals, because it seemed to offer a basis for political order other than the arbitrary will of the sovereign. As Shakespeare depicts Venice, the civic republican order assumes political subjects ("citizens") with stable socio-symbolic identities who are capable of carrying out their duty to the state. Yet the play reveals the reliance of these civic republican subjects on an exceptional person who embodies raw sovereignty and answers to no one. It is Othello—and his army of foreign-born mercenaries—who represents this veiled but nonetheless decisive sovereign power within the seemingly civic republican order of Venice.

I argue that Iago does not unmake Othello so much as force him to be what he truly is; namely, raw sovereign power that answers to no one. And when citizens are exposed to the raw sovereign power that Othello represents, they cease to be discrete individuals with socially legible identities and instead become mere flesh. Iago uses Othello (as sovereign) to reverse engineer persons into mere flesh; he then assembles such flesh into new social patterns. To make these new social patterns visible, I argue, Shakespeare carefully orchestrates a geometry of theatrical stabbings, beatings, and torture that begins in the two riots that Iago triggers on the streets of Cyprus and culminates in the erotic murder of Desdemona, who represents, in its purest form, the life of the flesh that is triggered by an encounter with absolute sovereignty.

Throughout the chapter, I pay special attention to the play's recasting of early modern assumptions about emotional experience. Modifying Paster and Floyd-Wilson's account of the play as fundamentally continuous with humoral thought in early modern England, I argue that Iago undermines the normative early modern humoral understanding of the emotions and how they relate to the self. Whereas the emotional norm in early modern culture is the assumption that the self's inner life is defined by the external social and spacial coordinates of the self, Iago triggers emotional experience based on nothing but inner, cognitive belief, an experience that can therefore be "wrong" in a way that would be impossible for humoral emotions. Though a cognitive understanding of emotional experience is the norm in psychology today, it is profoundly deviant in the early modern context and it opens the door to "theatrical" uses of emotion to define connections between persons stripped of their socio-symbolic identities.

In Chapter 4, I focus on *King Lear's* depictions of extra-legal state violence—and especially torture—as a practice that institutes political power, but also energizes a life of the flesh that transcends functional subordination to political power. As in *Measure for Measure*, the play begins with the resignation of a sovereign. In *King Lear*, this resignation creates a state of emergency in which rival claimants to power frantically attempt to re-institute a sovereign order through exceptional displays of violence. I argue that the torture of Gloucester and the banishment of Lear, Edmund, and Gloucester are attempts to reinstate state power, but that they have the inadvertent effect of foregrounding a form of life that is built on the recurring dissolution of all social identities in the face of sovereign power. Because it is founded on a shattering of social identity, I compare the fleshly life that appears on the stage in *Lear* to the masochistic sexuality theorized by Leo Bersani and Jean Laplanche.

Connecting this argument about sexuality back to the larger concerns of the book, I suggest that sexuality in the play is not conceived of as a private practice, but as a public practice that prefigures a transformation of collective life. In this chapter I also make a second argument focused on theater and theatricality: I argue that the play seeks to shift out of a narrative framework where characters have defined social identities, in order to redirect attention to the gestural level where the bodies on the stage enact (rather than represent) a life of the flesh. I suggest that the play uses gestural violence as a way of deranging audience members' own imbrication in an instituted sovereign political order by forcing them to recognize the fleshly vulnerability that they share with the bodies of the actors on the stage.

I conclude with an epilogue that looks at the afterlife of the life of the flesh. As I understand Shakespeare's project, it is profoundly marked by the discursive world of early modern England. To trigger the life of the flesh, Shakespeare exploits turmoil and conflict between discourses that are quite specific to the time and place of early modern England. At the same time, Shakespeare's vision does have something to offer to us today as we enter the beginning of the end of the era of the nation-state at whose birth Shakespeare was writing. Taking Julie Taymor's brilliant and disturbing film adaptation of *Titus Andronicus* as a case study, I argue that the film updates the crisis of sovereign power that appears in Shakespeare's play by placing it in the context of the massive expansion of state power characteristic of the twentieth century and how this development reveals bare life, something that is made most explicit in the context of European fascism. Looking at it through the lens of twentieth-century fascism, the fleshly life that Shakespeare imagined 400 years ago lives again in ways that pose a challenge to our contemporary norms of political and cultural life.

1

The Historical Conditions of Possibility of the Life of the Flesh: Absolutism, Civic Republicanism, and "Bare Life" in *Julius Caesar*

Julius Caesar appears to stage a conflict between a political tyrant and a public of civic-minded men who do not want power but only want to hold power accountable from the outside. In fact, the play's agenda is much more unsettling. *Julius Caesar* provides an especially clear model of the central discursive conflict that pervades the early modern political field, a conflict between two competing theories of the state and state power, one monarchist and the other civic republican, and both equally committed to expanding the sovereign power of the nation-state. Shakespeare stages this conflict not in order to side with one or the other theory of sovereignty (as some critics have thought), but in order to evacuate the institutional structures of the early modern state of their legitimacy. In Shakespeare's theatrical treatment, the friction between these two competing theories of sovereignty throws off bodies that have escaped from any state-mediated, politically legible form of "public" life. It is in such de-mobilized, de-commissioned, or de-politicized bodies that the play identifies a transformative experience of a collective life of the flesh, a formation that is eminently at home in the medium of theater.

Shakespeare's representation of Brutus's rebellion is sometimes taken as a symptom of the existence of a nascent, early modern "public sphere" capable of criticizing state power from the outside. In his classic study *The Structural Transformation of the Public Sphere*, Jürgen Habermas argues that a public sphere relies on private connections between people who come together outside of the institutions of state power. Focusing on eighteenth-century England, Habermas describes a critical public sphere that is founded on an extra-state civil society that allows private individuals to come together as private individuals and to subject the operations of the state to reasoned criticism from the outside.[1]

A better point of entry into Shakespeare's political project is, in fact, offered by Agamben's critique of the very idea of a civil society that lies outside of state power. In *Homo Sacer: Sovereign Power and Bare Life*, Agamben argues that all political power is "bio-political," in that it seeks to organize and structure the basic, biological infrastructure of human life. Revisiting the notion of civil society from this "bio-political" standpoint, Agamben suggests that civil society is not an autonomous social development, but a product of state power's penetration and shaping of social life:

> It is almost as if, starting from a certain point, every decisive political event were double-sided: the spaces, the liberties, and the rights won by individuals in their conflicts with central powers always simultaneously prepared a tacit but increasing inscription of individuals' lives within the state order, thus offering a new and more dreadful foundation for the very sovereign power from which they wanted to liberate themselves. [...] The fact is that one and the same affirmation of bare life leads, in bourgeois democracy, to a primacy of the private over the public and of individual liberties over collective obligations and yet becomes, in totalitarian states, the decisive political criterion and the exemplary realm of sovereign decisions. (121–2)

Agamben points to the state underpinning of what appears, in liberal political theory, as an extra-state realm of liberty that is anchored in private life. The paradox to which Agamben points is that this extra-state private realm liberates itself from the state only by demanding from the state a charter of rights and privileges that imbricates private life ever more fully in the political order. In effect, Agamben launches a broad attack on any liberal theory that posits a social life preexisting state power and that provides a standpoint from which state power can be criticized from the outside; for Agamben, the very appearance of such an extra-state social life is itself a manifestation of a state power that defines and structures a social life that seems like a non-state realm endowed with liberty vis-à-vis the state. In place of a "public sphere" conceived of as a social formation that precedes the exercise of state power and can critique state power from the outside, Agamben suggests that any public sphere is, in fact, a *product* of state power, depending on the state's ability to organize social space. From this standpoint, any civil society rooted in a supposedly non-state realm of private life and any critical "public sphere" founded on it remain captured by a state framework that they silently affirm, even if they also allow for critical detachment from particular state policies.

In fact, Shakespeare is quite aware of the fact that seemingly extra-state zones of private life or critical public spheres are themselves products of the structuration of social life by the nation-state, just as Agamben argues. However, Agamben's account of state power as essentially bio-political, as always seeking to structure and organize an ambiguous realm of what Agamben calls "bare life," turns out to offer a powerful point of entry into an early modern discourse that bypasses the symbiotic dyad of nation-state and state-mediated civil society.[2] In one form or another, the early modern state's effort to organize the infrastructure of social life is the central concern of much early modern culture. My argument in this book is that theatrically staged crises in the early modern nation-state's grasp on "everyday life" makes "bare life" visible as such, not as a politically hegemonized form of "civil society," but as the basic, historically conditioned biological infrastructure of human life. In Shakespeare's theatrical work, "bare life" dissolves out of political structures; once bare life becomes visible, it becomes the basis for an alternative form of being-together that I call the life of the flesh. Bringing this life of the flesh to the stage is Shakespeare's real aim in *Julius Caesar*, and the resistance movement that Brutus leads is merely the means to that end.

To describe the life of the flesh that is built on bodies that have ceased to be functionally subordinated to the political structures of the nation-state, Shakespeare turns to the contested domain of the passions and humors, which he treats neither as privileged signs of an inner self (as modern psychology does) nor as merely bodily imbalances; rather, he treats humors and passions as defining bodily states that open and close the body to other, humorally or passionately inflamed bodies in recurring patterns. For Shakespeare, in other words, humoral discourse can be used to define a grammar of pre- or extra-social connections between bodies that arise when politically ordered social webs break down.[3] Looked at in this way, the humors and passions provide a discourse for describing recurring, historically conditioned matrices of relationship that constitute a level of social life "beneath" the interplay of state power and institutionalized civil society.

I.   Two Forms of Public Life and Two Forms of Resistance

Julius Caesar does two things at the same time: on the one hand, it registers and theorizes the emerging political framework of the nation-state and its role in defining and structuring social life; on the other hand, however, it reveals a deep-seated impulse to break with this emerging political framework and shift to an alternative life rooted in de-politicized, de-mobilized bodies, a life of the flesh. This is precisely how Marc Antony's rebellion must be understood, a rebellion not for Caesar or against Brutus (conceived as rival political positions) but against politics *as such*, against any state form that defines social life and demands agonizing personal sacrifices in the name of public goods. Marc Antony aims to bypass the nation-state form altogether by shifting to a mode of interpersonal bonding that defines connections between bodies (via emotions conceived as fluids) that colonize and replace any functional, politically mediated public life. Antony's rebellion harnesses the political friction between Caesar and the conspirators to cut beneath politics, as it were, to an emotional terrain that provides the terms for connections between bodies that escape from the gravity of the rising nation-state and of the civil society that the state spawns. From the standpoint of the nascent political field of the nation-state, Antony's oppositional discourse looks irrational, non-pragmatic, or anti-social. But from a standpoint outside this political field, such radical opposition is not anti-social so much as it is anti-systemic, a break from the emerging, modern vision of the nation-state as a fundamental condition of social life.[4]

We can summarize the political field that Shakespeare sketches in *Julius Caesar* by saying that this field is organized around the competing discursive poles of absolutism and elite civic republicanism, each of which generates a specific (state-mediated) form of "public life." Caesar is accused of wanting to become a tyrant, but within the terms of early modern political discourse his reliance on a potent blend of charismatic popularity and canny manipulation of aristocratic elites makes him look very much like an absolute monarch. In order to secure his grip on the state, Caesar brings into existence an abstract public of more or less formally interchangeable individuals who encounter the state as a spectacle that they either applaud or deride. The conspirators are not more public-minded than Caesar's citizens, only differently public, and with a different relationship to state power. The familiar interpretation of *Julius Caesar* is that Brutus and the conspirators represent a kind of nascent public sphere that is outside of the state and that checks the dictatorial state power that Caesar represents. In fact, however, the conspirators do not see themselves as operating outside the state at all, only as embodying a different relationship to the state than either Caesar or the public citizenry Caesar conjures up. As against Caesar's popular absolutism, Brutus and the conspirators view the exercise of state power as an opportunity for their own ethical self-perfection. For the conspirators, possessing state power allows aristocratic elites like themselves to pursue ethical perfection and virtue by providing opportunities for its exercise; this public of virtue-seeking elites, in turn, allows the state to preserve its integrity through time. For Brutus and the conspirators, a public of patrician elites seeking to maximize their honor constitutes the state, and they use this vision to try to de-legitimize the popular public that Caesar has forced into the political field. Yet the fact that Caesar and the conspirators take rival versions of political publicity into account from the start attests to the fact that their differences are essentially local variations within a single political field; what Caesar and the conspirators share is a deep commitment to the public-making power of political forms that structure a nationalized social life. It is precisely this commitment that Antony will transcend.

The conspirators cannot understand themselves and their exercise of virtue at all outside the exercise of state power that Caesar threatens to take away from them. Cassius experiences a loss of political power as a diminution of self, because for him the state is a vehicle to develop and exercise his own virtue. In his initial temptation speech, Cassius reminds Brutus that "I was born free as Caesar, so were you" (1.2.99) and complains that they have both become Caesar's "underlings":

> Why, man, he does bestride the narrow world
> Like a Colossus, and we petty men
> Walk under his huge legs, and peep about
> To find ourselves dishonorable graves.
> Men sometime were masters of their fates.
> The fault, dear Brutus, is not in our stars,
> But in ourselves, that we are underlings. (1.2.136–142)

Cassius sees state power as synonymous with the aristocrats' freedom to exercise their virtue and to act as "masters of their fates" by pursuing honor rather than being condemned to "dishonorable graves." For Cassius, the fundamental problem is not that Caesar wants too much state power, but that he organizes state power on a footing that deprives aristocrats like himself and Brutus of an opportunity to use the state to advance their own honor. When Brutus invokes the discourse of the "general good" (as when he tells Cassius that if what he has to say has anything to do with "the general good/ [then] Set honor in one eye and death in the other,/ And I will look on both indifferently" [1.2.87–89]), he refers to the very limited public of elite patricians that is (in its own eyes) fundamentally constituted by, and constitutive of, the state.

For the conspirators, the flip side of the elite, civic republican, virtue-maximizing "public" that defines the state is the life of the plebeians, which the conspirators conceive of as a state-regulated, economic formation that has no proper role in the public life of the state. The play begins with Murellus and Flavius, the tribunes of the people but ideological soulmates of the conspirators, complaining that the workers are swarming onto the streets to celebrate Caesar. Part of Murellus and Flavius's complaint is that the political allegiance of the people is fickle, since they once loved Pompey as they now love Caesar:

> Many a time and oft
> Have you climbed up to walls and battlements,
> To towers and windows, yea to chimney tops,
> Your infants in your arms, and there have sat
> The livelong day with patient expectation
> To see great Pompey pass the streets of Rome. (1.1.37–42)

Beyond accusing the people of fickleness, what Murellus and Flavius really object to is the workers' leaving behind their defined roles in the extra-political, economic realm and asserting for themselves a role in "public life":

> Hence, home, you idle creatures, get you home!
> Is this a holiday? What, know you not,
> Being mechanical, you ought not to walk
> Upon a laboring day without the sign
> Of your profession? Speak, what trade art thou? (1.1.1–5)

Once they exit the non-political, economic realm (marked by wearing the "sign/ Of your profession"), the plebeians can only appear to Murellus and Flavius as the amorphous "bare life" of people swarming over the architecture of Rome with "infants in your arms." Flavius promises to "drive away the vulgar from the streets" and tells Murellus: "So do you too where you perceive them thick" (1.1.69–71). From the perspective of the tribunes of the people, when the people swell out over the channels of their prescribed economic roles, they appear as a tide of raw, teeming life. For Flavius and Murellus, Rome is defined by a kind of quasi-racial class warfare; they and the conspirators see the state as a class property, one that is in fact constituted by their class, and with which the plebeians, conceived of as having a defined role only in the extra-political but state-regulated economic realm, have no business interfering. From the conspirators' perspective, when the plebeians exceed their prescribed economic roles, they appear not as a shaped "public" but as an unshaped mass of quivering "bare life" that must be "driven" away from the public streets.

From Caesar's perspective, of course, the people massed are anything but shapeless "bare life"; they are, instead, a politically potent rival "public" that Caesar has conjured into existence in order to check the power of his aristocrats. In place of the aristocratic vision of themselves as a state-constituting public surrounded by an institutionalized realm of extra-political economic life, Caesar constitutes the people as a "public" whose structural relation to the state is fundamentally different from the "public" of the conspirators. Caesar's quasi-tyrannical status is the inverse of his effort to level all other markers of social difference between persons in the population of Rome—Caesar inadequately acknowledges local elites (and this, of course, leads to the conspiracy), but he also fails to acknowledge the occupational differences that derive from the economic realm on which Flavius and Murellus insist. Like Queen Elizabeth, Caesar turns holidays and festivals (in the case of the play, the festival of the Lupercal) into state pageants, and Caesar's commitment to festivity converts what Flavius and Murellus intuitively see as a finely graded social and economic fabric that gives the people a state-regulated social and civic shape outside of politics, into a collection of more or less formally interchangeable persons who can assemble to constitute a new kind of mass public. We might call such interchangeable individuals endowed with a collective public life "citizens," though since these laborers are stripped of any real political content except formal equality, it might be better to call them proto-citizens. For Caesar, the basic unit of political discourse is not the face-to-face conversation between individuals, nor even a senate-sized debate governed by rules of procedure—modes of political discourse eminently suited to the conspirator's vision of a relatively small elite of virtue-maximizing aristocrats as constitutive of the state—but the mass rally, a gathering in which formally interchangeable proto-citizens are added together, one plus one plus one, and so on ad infinitum. While it is certainly true that Caesar is an expert crowd manipulator, these proto-citizen assemblies nevertheless have real political force that sometimes checks Caesar's own will—as when the crowd's cheers seem to force Caesar to decline the crown that Marc Antony offers him.

Casca reports this crown-offering rally in a highly tendentious form, but it is easy to extract from his words the real political logic of the event. Casca reports that Marc Antony raised the crown to Julius Caesar three times, and that Caesar refused it three times:

> And still as he refused it, the rabblement hooted, and clapped their chapped hands, and threw up their sweaty nightcaps, and uttered such a deal of stinking breath because Caesar refused the crown that it had almost choked Caesar; for he swooned and fell down at it. And for mine own part, I durst not laugh for fear of opening my lips and receiving the bad air. (1.2.243–250)

Casca's contempt for the "stinking breath" the "rabblement" emits is directly proportional to the political weight of this breath, for Casca believes that Caesar "would fain have had it [the crown]" (1.2.239–240), but was thwarted at this moment by the opposition of the people. Naturally, Casca hates the notion that Caesar should be a king, but what seems to provoke him even more at this moment is that Caesar has endowed the people—stripped of their economic markers and converted into proto-citizens assembled in the mass—with a real political force. Casca recognizes this political force, even as he tries to devalue it by comparing it to the approval and disapproval of a theater audience: "If the tagrag people did not clap him and hiss him, according as he pleased and displeased them, as they use to do the players in the theater, I am no true man" (1.2.258–261). If Casca means to say that Caesar's show was nothing but theater, as in some sense it was, the analogy to the theater nevertheless sketches a real institutional mechanism for measuring the will of the assembled proto-citizens by proposing political scenarios and then measuring the applause or hoots of the crowd. Casca's attack on the political validity of the crown-offering play is, paradoxically, a register of its real political force; Casca's attack acknowledges the political force of the crowd even as he tries to (politically) delegitimate it. In that sense, Casca's attack is a sign of Caesar's success in forcing the assembly of proto-citizens into the political field of the play as an effective power. However, what makes the analogy to the theater possible for Casca is the presumed vulgarity and rowdiness of a "tagrag" crowd at the theater; from Casca's standpoint, Caesar has converted the plebeians—who ought, by rights, to be confined to the economic realm and who have no proper role in the management of the state—into an unshaped mass, the very "bare life" that Flavius and Murellus encounter at the beginning of the play and that they try to drive from the streets. Where Caesar sees a "public" with a structurally different relationship to the state than the "public" of conspirators, Casca insists that he sees only swarming, bare life, which he instinctively reduces to its grossest physical manifestation, its "stinking breath."[5]

Here, the friction between rival visions of how the state organizes social life (Caesar's vision of a mass of proto-citizens who evaluate political proposals and Casca's vision of a public of virtue-maximizing elites who constitute the state surrounded by an institutionalized extra-political economic order of plebians) renders "bare life" visible in itself—as crowds swarming over Rome's architecture with their infants in hand, as the multitude with stinking breath that the conspirators fear. These ambivalent crowds are endowed with a strange, constitutive force even as they appear to exceed all available political forms, and it is precisely this ambivalent but now constitutive realm of bare life that asserts itself more and more radically after Caesar is killed.[6] Immediately after the assassination, Trebonius reports that "Men, wives, and children stare, cry out, and run,/ As it were doomsday" (3.1.98–99), a danger that Brutus recognizes when he asks Antony to "be patient till we have appeased/ The multitudes, beside themselves with fear" (3.1.180–181). Brutus tells Cassius "go you into the other street,/ And part the numbers" and proposes to the plebeians: "Those that will hear me speak, let 'em stay here;/ Those that will follow Cassius, go with him;/ And public reasons shall be rendered/ Of Caesar's death" (3.2.3–8). This image of an orderly exercise of "public" reasoning would surely warm the heart of Habermasians committed to the possibility of a universally human exercise of communicative rationality. Yet while one plebeian does propose to the others that they listen to both speeches and then "compare their reasons/ When severally we hear them rendered" (3.2.9–10), Brutus's clumsy effort to address the massed people as though they were an orderly debating club only highlights his inability to come to terms with what the people in fact represent, namely the reemergence of an ambivalent but constitutive realm of "bare life" triggered by the clash of rival versions of politically mediated "public life."

The brilliance of Marc Antony's funeral oration in contrast to Brutus's derives largely from his recognizing and exploiting this realm of "bare life" as a potent source of anti-political rage. Indeed, Antony's funeral oration draws on the profoundly marginal experience of "bare life" into which Antony himself is interpolated by the death of his friend. Immediately after Caesar's death, Brutus tells Marc Antony that he, too, loved Caesar, but that this personal tie had to take a back seat to public considerations; Antony, however, is drawn "beyond" the political logic that demands that what Cassius warily calls the "engrafted love" Marc Antony "bears to Caesar" (2.1.184) be sacrificed in the name of any supposed public goods, and this refusal triggers a rebellion against the notion of any state-mediated public life. Marc Antony refuses to see Caesar's assassination as a political act or a political problem, and his (irrational) commitment to loving Caesar produces a kind of crisis (or perhaps a breakthrough) in his experience of himself and others that is expressed in an anarchist wish for Sorelian violence.[7] Addressing Caesar's corpse, Antony promises that "a curse shall light upon the limbs of men":

> O pardon me, thou bleeding piece of earth,
> That I am meek with these butchers
> Thou art the ruins of the noblest man
> That ever livèd in the tide of man.
> Woe to the hand that shed this costly blood!
> Over thy wounds now I do prophesy—
> Which like dumb mouths do ope their ruby lips
> To beg the voice and utterance of my tongue—
> A curse shall light upon the limbs of men;
> Domestic fury and fierce civil strife
> Shall cumber all the parts of Italy;
> Blood and destruction shall be so in use,
> And dreadful objects so familiar,
> That mothers shall but smile when they behold
> Their infants quartered with the hands of war,
> All pity choked with custom of fell deeds;
> And Caesar's spirit, ranging for revenge,
> With Atë by his side come hot from hell,
> Shall in these confines with a monarch's voice
> Cry "havoc!" and let slip the dogs of war... (3.1.257–276)

Obviously, Antony outlines no pragmatic, political program here, but a program of violence for violence's sake, designed to register the validity of his personal love for Caesar. It is as if Antony feels that an irruption of politics has split a nuclear bond between himself and Caesar, a violation that must now release an enormous burst of transformative social energy that negates traditional social ties. Antony's cruel soliloquy has the merit of not concealing the naked reality of war beneath a lot of patriotic rhetoric, but in precisely its cruelest aspects Marc Antony's speech also points to the wish for a kind of radical transformation in the most basic patterns of social life emblematized in the structure of family allegiances; when Marc Antony looks forward to a time in which mothers will have become so hardened to violence that they will "but smile when they behold/ Their infants quartered," he is imagining a radical (if radically dystopian) transformation in social life that flows from his own, somewhat disorienting experience of the body of Caesar.

Indeed, Marc Antony himself seems captured by the unsettling gravity of the body whose "dumb mouths do ope their ruby lips/ To beg the voice and utterance of my tongue." Here, the opened body of Caesar calls to Marc Antony to enter it, to occupy it, to speak for it, to mingle with its fluids and especially its blood—a fantasy that had earlier led Marc Antony to wish he had "as many eyes as thou hast wounds,/ Weeping as fast as they stream forth thy blood" (3.1.201–202). In this fantasy, bodies recognize each other by means of a kind of fluid homeopathy that treats the body's humoral fluids as a mechanism for producing pre- or extra-social links. Almost the first wish that Marc Antony expresses after seeing the body of Caesar is the wish to be stabbed with the swords still covered in Caesar's blood:

> If I myself [am going to be killed], there is no hour so fit
> As Caesar's death's hour, nor no instrument
> Of half that worth as those your swords, made rich
> With the most noble blood of all this world. (3.1.154–157)

Brutus thinks Marc Antony is asking for death, and he tries to dissuade him—"O Antony, beg not your death of us!" (3.1.165)— but what Marc Antony is asking for is nothing so simple as death. What Caesar's death seems to provoke in Marc Antony is a kind of emotional derangement in which the violated, bleeding body of Caesar seems to call for some new interpersonal mode that relies on a radical experience of the body and its fluids, and that is figured here as being stabbed by a sword already "made rich" with "noble blood."

Marc Antony's fantasmatic experience of Caesar's body and the bodily fluids that provoke answering fluids from his own refolds a social connection (his friendship with Caesar) into an eccentric shape that defines a new intersubjectivity. And this form of intersubjectivity spreads throughout the social world of the play by folding functional social solidarity into a new intersubjectivity mediated, first and foremost, by the body and bodily humors. The vector of infection by which Marc Antony's eccentrically shaped experience of Caesar is introduced into

Rome is the funeral oration, which, to a surprising extent, simply trans-
fers Antony's own experience of Caesar's body onto the masses (with its
display of the alluring corpse and its wounds, with its call for tears to
answer blood). If the funeral oration is self-consciously theatrical and
even manipulative, then it is also a genuine expression of an eccentric
and potentially transformative psychic terrain that Marc Antony has
entered. Marc Antony shifts to a purely bodily level where social barriers
between people break down—but this also amounts to breaking down
the political register that tries to represent the social world through the
notion of a public of some kind. What is left after the political field has
been stripped of legitimacy is a radically bodily terrain in which fluids
and humors seem to leap from body to body, weaving them together
into new, radically extra-political networks.[8]

At one level, of course, the funeral oration triggers irrational rioting,
and Marc Antony celebrates the radical historical contingency he has
unleashed—"Now let it work. Mischief, thou art afoot./ Take thou what
course thou wilt" (3.2.252–253). But the rioting nevertheless has a kind
of interpersonal logic to it that picks up and extends the body-mediated
bonding that Marc Antony experiences in relation to Caesar. Here is the
beginning of the riot.

FIRST PLEBIAN:	Never, never! Come, away, away!
	We'll burn his body in the holy place,
	And with the brands fire the traitors' houses.
FOURTH PLEBIAN:	Go, fetch fire!
THIRD PLEBIAN:	Pluck down benches!
FIFTH PLEBIAN:	Pluck down forms, windows, anything! (3.2.245–251)

What begins as a perceptible political impulse—to cremate Caesar's body
in the "holy place" and then set fire to the houses of the conspirators—
quickly escalates into a kind of eschatological desire to transcend politics as such, for in attacking the benches and the windows (the benches
on which they have sat while listening to Brutus and Marc Antony's
competing accounts of the assassination, the windows through which
people gaze eagerly to catch a glimpse of public doings, not least Portia),
these plebeians are essentially stripping the material infrastructure of a
certain kind of public life into which they have been interpolated, by
Caesar as well as by the conspirators.[9] So seen, their rage is essentially
an anti-public rage, a rage against a certain version of political publicity.

Once liberated from any political framework, the riot reorients social
life and transforms the glue that ties persons together, something that

is especially evident in the cruelest and most irrational elements of the rebellion—as with the attack on Cinna the poet, who is initially mistaken for Cinna the conspirator, a mistake Cinna himself corrects, to little effect:

CINNA: I am Cinna the poet! I am Cinna the poet!
FOURTH PLEBIAN: Tear him for his bad verses, tear him for his bad verses.
CINNA: I am not Cinna the conspirator!
FOURTH PLEBIAN: It is no matter, his name's Cinna. Pluck but his name out of his heart, and turn him going.
THIRD PLEBIAN: Tear him, tear him!
They set upon Cinna. (3.3.29–36)

Though the plebeians begin with a nominally political desire—to kill conspirators—by the time they establish that this Cinna is not Cinna the conspirator, a kind of primal killing frenzy takes over. On the one hand, there is a social logic to this frenzy, for in rebelling against Cinna's very name the plebeians are expressing a kind of peasant resentment against those who have names as opposed to those who have none— the plebeians, after all, are merely assigned numbers. But on the other hand, if the plebeians are motivated by some class resentment, they are nevertheless not engaging in an act of compensatory status-building here; rather, they seek to reduce Cinna to their own level through a barrier-breaking emphasis on the body as the agent and the subject of physical violence. If this scene looks like mob violence, it also embodies a radical barrier-breaking impulse in which names, and the basic principle of social differentiation they represent, are reduced to bodies that can be physically assaulted ("Pluck but his name out of his heart"). It is unclear whether Cinna survives this assault (the stage directions give us only "Exeunt all the Plebeians, with Cinna" [after 3.3.39]), but if he survives and simply walks (or is dragged) off stage after his name has been plucked out of his heart, it may, from the audience's point of view, look very much as though Cinna has been interpolated by this group. What we can just see between the lines of irrational, non-pragmatic mob violence here is a desire to transform social life in a way that has to do with reducing names to bodies and then assaulting those bodies through collective (and binding) violence.

Some critics have argued that it is significant that it is a poet who is killed here. In a way, of course, that it is precisely wrong—it is a mere body that is attacked in this scene. Nevertheless, there is a kind of constitutive poetic or theatrical quality to the kind of anti-political vision that the play articulates. The transformation of mob violence into an emblem of an alternative sociability is possible only when violence is self-consciously theatrical, as it is throughout Shakespeare's play. The theater becomes a reservoir of what seem to be anti-social impulses that turn out to be the wellspring of an alternative sociability that early modern culture dreamt of even as it came to terms with the rising nation-state's effort to impose its hegemony on "bare life."

For it is only as theater—the theater that Marc Antony is said to love—that violence can be refunctioned into an emblem of an alternative mode of sociability that operates at the level of bodies. And when it is approached as a theatrical spectacle, the civil war that occupies the last two acts of the play comes to seem like Shakespeare's fullest exploration of a fundamentally perverse social formation that functions as a form of resistance to the emerging political modernity of the nation-state, to which both Caesar and the conspirators are fully committed. Among the disturbing features of Shakespeare's theater of war is the way pragmatic, self-preserving forms of relationship are infected by the marginal experiences of self and other that Marc Antony unleashes into Rome. This turn away from pragmatic self-preservation is especially evident in the rash of suicides that overtake the play, beginning with the report that Portia has died after she "swallowed fire" (4.2.208)—burning coals in Plutarch—and continuing with the suicides of Cassius, Titinius, and finally Brutus. Given the Roman cult of suicide, these suicides could seem a final triumph of personal autonomy over fate. In Shakespeare's telling, however, they seem to represent the colonization and replacement of the functional social and political ties on which the personal prestige of the Roman aristocrats depends by a perverse form of social bonding. When Cassius fails to find the courage to kill himself, he must beg his slave Pindarus for death:

> Come here, sirrah. In Parthia I did take thee prisoner,
> And then I swore thee, saving of thy life,
> That whatsoever I did bid thee do
> Thou shouldst attempt it. Come now, keep thine oath.
> Now be a freeman, and, with this good sword
> That ran through Caesar's bowels, search this bosom. (5.3.36–41)

On the one hand, Cassius frames his being stabbed with the very sword that stabbed Caesar as a kind of poetic justice that brings the political narrative of the conspiracy full circle (his dying words are "Caesar, thou art revenged,/ Even with the sword that killed thee" [5.3.44–45]).

But on the other hand, the fantasy of being penetrated by the sword that "ran through Caesar's bowels"—the very fantasy in which Antony indulges after the assassination—is a perverse way of reestablishing a relationship with Caesar at a level beneath political allegiance and class solidarity. Equally to the point, this perverse form of bonding depends on an inversion of a functionally hierarchical tie between master and slave on which Brutus insists when he mocks Cassius for losing his temper and sarcastically tells him to "go show your slaves how choleric you are,/ And make your bondmen tremble" (4.2.97–98). It is precisely to his bondman that Cassius finally turns himself over, presenting the spectacle of a Roman lord begging passionately for death at the hands of his slave, a spectacle repeated again with Brutus begging death at the hands of his servant Strato in 5.5. In both instances, the relationship between master and slave turns out to be the only truly reliable one, but by ejecting this tie from a legible social context where it has real status effects for master as well as slave, Shakespeare relocates the master–slave bond into a purely emotional space where the sublimated aggression of massive class disparity energizes a lurid interpersonal exchange that combines aggressive passion and passionate aggression.

For Cassius, this passionately suicidal inversion of a functional hierarchical relationship between master and slave is triggered by what turns out to be an incorrect report of the death of Cassius's "best friend" Titinius: "O coward that I am, to live so long/ To see my best friend ta'en before my face!" (5.3.34–35). Having violated the terms of friendship by failing to defend his friend in the moment he is "ta'en," Cassius seems to see suicide as a way of resurrecting that friendship as a corporeal connection in which the fate of the friend is registered by the fate of Cassius's own body. And if Cassius's suicide opens up a parallel social space in which bodies recognize other bodies by means of fluid homeopathy, then Titinius enters that parallel space, too, when he returns to find that Cassius has "misconstrued everything" (5.3.83) and promptly stabs himself with the sword with which Cassius has just been stabbed: "By your leave, gods, this is a Roman's part:/ Come Cassius' sword, and find Titinius' heart" (5.3.88–89). While Titinius comes closest to the canonical, stoical ideal of an honorable suicide ("this is a Roman's part"), he nevertheless joins Cassius and Marc Antony in affirming a form of bodily solidarity that transcends social status by stabbing himself with the sword still gory with Cassius's blood (and with Caesar's). The suicidal renunciation and corrosion of the functional social ties on which real-world status depends—the male–male friendship of aristocrats and the asymmetrical bond between master and slave, but also the glorified mastery over the self that Cassius and Brutus so spectacularly lack—opens up an alternative social grammar in which bleeding bodies are violated by already bloody swords.

It is important to read such moments—and indeed, the war as a whole—for what they open the door to philosophically—that is to say, theatrically. Pervaded as it is by anti-social desires—the desire to kill, the desire to be killed—this war is not so much the continuation of politics by other means (as Clausewitz's famous formula would have it) as it is the replacement of politics by other means. By bringing this fundamentally perverse and even anti-social war to the early modern stage, Shakespeare reveals a strangely inhuman social life—founded in "bare life" and mediated by bodies and their fluid humors—that rises beyond the iron clasp of state and state-mediated civil society. Read against the grain of the modern political imaginary that assumes the nation-state as the basic framework for social life, Shakespeare's play discloses a passionate life of bodies energized by—and then dissenting from—the political spectacle of the early modern state's penetration of "bare life."

II.   Varieties of Civic Republicanism

One of the key points I have tried to make in this chapter is that the version of civic republicanism Shakespeare uses to trigger the life of the flesh is quite different from a Habermasian public sphere rooted in a civil society that exists outside of political structures. As Shakespeare uses it, civic republicanism is essentially a theory of sovereignty that concerns itself with revealing and critiquing the effects of subjection to absolute sovereignty and attempts to constitute an alternative institutional form of collectivized power. Yet Shakespeare's distinctive understanding of early modern civic republicanism is not uncontroversial. In fact, many scholars argue that late sixteenth- and early seventeenth-century civic republicanism does indeed rely on an essentially Habermasian model in which a preexisting and predefined citizenry is simply mobilized to engage in political critique. Offering the economically founded version of this argument, Archer reminds us that in the Elizabethan and Jacobean context, the very word "citizen" contained an economic valence more than a political one. He writes that "citizenship primarily concerned the control of access to economic rights, the right to work for wages, to trade for materials, and to produce and sell one's own products" (9).[10] For Archer, this textured economic category provides the foundation for the communal element of early modern political life that he sees as the foundation for civic republicanism. Following in the tradition of Habermas, Archer posits an autonomous realm of economic exchange that gives people a position and status that can then be mobilized—*ex post facto*, as it were—to bear a political charge.

More typical in the historiography is an account of early modern civic republicanism that is rooted not in economic life but in the monarchical bureaucracy—the status, roles, and positions conferred on elites by the monarchical system itself. Hadfield identifies the "importance of offices and positions of responsibility held by ordinary citizens/ subjects, which can be seen to constitute a public realm developing alongside that of formal political representation in parliament."[11] This "public realm" is itself, of course, politically generated by the will of the monarch, but Hadfield and others argue that it could provide a standpoint for criticizing and even limiting the power of the monarch from the outside. This is the vision of civic republicanism that is posited by Collinson in his influential account of what he terms the Elizabethan "monarchical republic." Collinson looks at several examples of apparent self-government in early modern England, but his main focus is on the response by elites at court to the crisis presented by the fear that Queen Elizabeth might be assassinated and replaced by Mary, Queen of Scots. For Collinson, this crisis makes courtly elites conscious of themselves as potentially needing to effect a transition to a new king or queen on their own. On Collinson's account, these men do not understand or theorize themselves as the sovereign power in the realm; rather, they see themselves as non-sovereign actors who are nevertheless capable of temporarily shouldering power to effect a transition to a new monarch. Thus, on this account of civic republicanism, the monarchical system itself provides the foundation for a potentially active citizenry.

It should be obvious that, in the context of early modern English monarchy, a civic republicanism in which elites rooted in economic or political formations are activated to provide resistance to monarchical will could produce radical political effects.[12] The most extreme version of "resistance theory" is often associated with puritanism, though it also has its Catholic counterpart. The monarchomachs and resistance theorists who argued that it was within the rights of magistrates to depose a tyrant were obviously operating at the outer edges of the political culture in early modern England.

Nevertheless, insofar as such civic republicanism imagined the offices granted within the monarchical order as a starting point for resistance, it paradoxically relied on the sovereign power of the monarch even as it criticized it. As such, this version of civic republicanism avoids the hard question of whether it is possible to organize a politically active public in a way that is not dependent on a prior sovereign power.[13] Indeed, Sommerville criticizes the scholarship on pre-war civic republicanism precisely on the grounds that it identifies as republicanism something that by Sommerville's lights does not and should not count as republicanism at all, precisely because it does not concern itself with the question of emergency powers and, therefore, with the question of sovereignty, amounting only to a theory of advice and consultation. For Sommerville, a civic republicanism worthy of the name must be more than a theory of a pre-constituted public as a potential supplement to a sovereignty located elsewhere (that is, in the monarch). For Sommerville, a civic republicanism worthy of the name must contain a theory of the political community as the bearer of sovereignty; by that standard, Sommerville argues, there simply is no civic republicanism until the Civil War era forces the issue.[14]

For Skinner, the test of a civic republicanism worthy of the name is whether it contains what he terms a "neo-Roman" conception of liberty. On this theory, it is not actual tyranny that renders people unfree; it is any subjection to sovereign power. This theory gives rise to an indictment of any arbitrary sovereign power, and a concomitant quest for ways of structuring political communities that are not themselves premised on unaccountable sovereign power.[15] For if liberty on neo-Roman terms were to be achieved, then it would be necessary to find a form of sovereign power not external to the political community but internal to it. Though this is precisely what Schmitt sees as impossible, putting the problem this way does reveal the path by which civic republican thought could become more than an endorsement of the dubious principle of the real existence of an extra-political civil society.

Though a fully fledged civic republicanism fully engaged with the problem of sovereign power and the origin of the political community does not appear until the Civil War period, it has an active pre-life in the imaginative literature of the pre-war period. It is, in fact, critics of a literary bent who have been best at recovering the roots of a civic republicanism engaged with the problem of sovereignty in the pre–Civil War era. For Hadfield and Norbrook, pre–Civil War republicanism is not a political program so much as an actively imagined agenda.[16] Thus, Hadfield writes, "we need to remember that republicanism was as much a literary as a political phenomenon, originating principally in the historical and poetic works surviving from the Roman Republic—and Livy, Polybius, Ovid, Cicero, Lucan, and so on—studied by all boys at grammar school."[17] And *as* an actively imagined agenda, pre-war civic republicanism could indeed engage the problem of sovereignty.

My argument in this book is that in Shakespeare's plays, the radical *potential* inherent in pre–Civil War civic republican discourse is mobilized in the direction of an active, even deconstructive, engagement with absolutist power. As it appears in Shakespeare's plays, including in *Julius Caesar*, civic republicanism functions not as a reform movement, but as a rival (though always unsuccessful) claimant of sovereign power. As Shakespeare presents it in *Julius Caesar*, Brutus and the conspirators are not mere citizens or subjects within an already existing political order. Rather, they aim to shoulder state power in a way that would redefine state power itself. They are, in other words, participating in a radical form of civic republicanism in which they refuse to accept the sovereign power of the absolute monarch on the grounds that any subjection to arbitrary or discretionary power reduces them to slaves. In place of absolutist sovereignty, they seek to define a new structure of state in which sovereign power is in some vague way embodied in themselves.

Shakespeare is quite explicit in describing the aim of Brutus and the rebels as more than forcing the absolute sovereign (Caesar) to respond to complaints about abuses. Such a version of Brutus would be a much more limited character—essentially, a humanist adviser and reformer. Rather, Shakespeare suggests that Brutus encounters Julius Caesar as one sovereign will encounters another. By attempting (and ultimately failing) to constitute itself as a collectivized sovereign power, the radical civic republicanism of *Julius Caesar* delegitimizes absolutist government without, however, replacing it with a functioning alternative.[18] The effect of Brutus's rebellion is therefore to disclose the extent to which state power, by its very nature, contains a principle of arbitrary, sovereign power that answers to no one, and to open the door to a systematic exploration of the effects of exposure to such sovereign power.

III. Theories of Law

If Shakespeare works out his basic ideas about political sovereignty and the life of the flesh in the timeless fantasy space of ancient Rome and the abstract theories of sovereign power and citizenship it raises, then *Measure for Measure* (the subject of my next chapter) represents Shakespeare's effort to translate his ideas into the concrete reality of early modern English legal discourse in the 1600s. In closing, I want to look ahead to the next chapter and its concerns with legal theory, but I want to do so in a way that shows how arguments about law are rooted in the deep logic of arguments about where political community arises.

Early modern theorists of common law (notably Coke and Selden) saw common law as a codification and standardization of the moral practices of an imagined community with roots in the pre-Norman past. Pocock argues that at least some theorists of common law literally believed that common law had always existed, rooted in the practices and norms of a community that had always existed.[19] However, even if the origins of the common law are imagined as being inside a primordial community, Selden and Coke nevertheless emphasized that over time the common law had separated from everyday language and everyday moral practice and developed technical procedures that are quite specialized.[20] Thus, Coke famously argues that legal reasoning is "artificial" compared to the kind of moral reasoning in which people engage during the course of everyday life.[21] For common law theorists, no matter how technical the common law had become, it nevertheless remained historically and morally rooted in the (imagined) will of the community, something that is made manifest in the peculiar institution of the jury.

That imaginary communitarian foundation for common law defines the basic disagreement between common law theorists and positive law theorists aligned with the monarch.[22] For positive law theorists, law was, at its core, writ generated by duly constituted state authority, whether by the king alone or the king in parliament. By contrast, common law theorists defended their law as timeless, unwritten "custom" (as opposed to written, temporally delimited statutes).[23] For Schmitt, of course, the position of positive law theorists is unambiguously right; for him, all law is an expression of will backed by the arbitrary power of a sovereign, and the English common law fantasy of a law rooted in the norms and values of a political community whose origin could not itself be accounted for would seem to Schmitt to be profoundly naïve.

In fact, however, behind the fantasy of a timeless common law rooted in the norms of a timeless political community lies an important historical truth that is much closer to Schmitt's model. Historians of the law know quite well that despite the ideology of autochthonous and acephalous development, the common law has its actual origins in the royal will. In fact, the English kings of the twelfth century viewed the development of the common law as a way of unifying and centralizing the kingdom under one head, for a "common" law (and with it the ability to provide their subjects with a common "royal justice") was viewed as a way of breaking with the heterogeneity of narrow, local customs and practices for adjudicating disputes.[24] Only over the course of many centuries did the common law attain the technical and procedural perfection that made it seem genuinely independent of royal will—even an alternative to the unchecked prerogative power of the king. Nevertheless, the origin of the common law in the king's will and warrant remains visible in the rival system of justice that the king sponsors; namely, equity justice rooted in the right of the king to override common law decisions that produce manifestly unfair results, even if they are technically correct.

Legal historians emphasize that equity courts are the historical trace of the origin of the entire common law in the king's will.[25] The earliest common law court was literally the court of advisers around the king (the *curia regis*), with the king sometimes presiding literally and, in any case, always reserving the right of final decision according to his own conscience and judgment. Over time, this court spawned legally specialized sub-courts to which it delegated its power, and as these specialized law courts attained more procedural autonomy, they gradually separated from the royal court altogether, suppressing any appeal to the king's equitable judgment and conscience in favor of absolute loyalty to established common law procedure and custom. However, as an ideal, equity remained associated with the king as the seat of ultimate justice, and over time this ideal developed a technical machinery of its own, the machinery of the equity courts (a machinery that is famously simpler than the baroque complexity of common law procedure). As White writes, "the Court of Chancery, presided over by the Lord Chancellor, had since the fourteenth century stood as an alternative route to justice for plaintiffs. The Chancellor was 'the keeper of the King's conscience' and his discretion became ever wider, as Selden put it, under "the law of conscience, which is law executed in the court for default of remedy by Courts of the Common Law."[26] This alternative system of justice was understood to be rooted in the king's individual conscience, his ability to understand and embody Christian truth, but also in a natural law, in the name of which even community norms supposedly enshrined in common law could be overturned.[27]

On the one hand, the equity courts provided a kind of safety valve that allowed the common law to attain greater legitimacy by allowing it to be overturned when it produced manifestly unfair results. Yet, on the other hand, the equity courts also highlighted the historical origin of common law in the extra-legal power of the king, with the king continuing to function as the court of conscientious appeal. And this is what leads common law theorists to see the very idea of a court rooted in the king's conscience as a scandal because it threatened the central plank of common law's ideology—its autonomy from royal meddling, guaranteed by its imagined origin in the norms and practices of a supposedly timeless community. In fact, James and Charles used the equity courts to try to subordinate the increasingly independent common law courts to their will.[28]

In the next chapter, I will argue that this legal background provides the interpretive key for *Measure for Measure*. In that play, Shakespeare uses the presence, within the legal system itself, of the notion of equity justice rooted in the prerogative of the king as a deconstructive lever to unhinge the whole of the legal order by revealing its dependence on absolute sovereign will. In other words, Shakespeare uses the presence of equity justice as a deconstructive lever to undermine the whole common law ideology of a law that is rooted in a timeless community. For Shakespeare, in the realm of institutionalized politics (in *Julius Caesar*) as much as in the realm of institutionalized law (in *Measure for Measure*), arbitrary sovereign power comes first and is what makes any community life (and, therefore, any supposed community norms enshrined in the law) possible.

2
The Life of the Condemned: The Autonomous Legal System and the Community of the Flesh in *Measure for Measure*

In this chapter, I focus on one of the chief institutional organs of the nation-state, namely the legal system. In *Constitutional Theory*, Carl Schmitt argues that a legal system that appears to be an autonomous, extra-political set of juridical processes nevertheless always depends on the hidden will of a sovereign, who decides that the law will in fact be applied. Shakespeare's *Measure for Measure* makes precisely this point, revealing the dependence of the seemingly autonomous legal system on the arbitrary will of the sovereign. However, as in *Julius Caesar*, Shakespeare is not interested in theorizing the organs of state power for their own sake. Rather, Shakespeare's interest is in the transformative effects of encountering a legal system that has been stripped of its veneer of legitimacy and that therefore appears as a vehicle of raw sovereign power. As we reflect on what *Measure for Measure* teaches, we first come to see the raw sovereign will behind the law, and then we come to see the transformative consequences of exposure to such sovereign will for bodies living together with other bodies. *Measure for Measure* brings to the stage a form of life that is triggered when characters experience themselves as radically subjected to an arbitrary legal code, and then experience this subjection as a force that spins them out of the gravity of the legal and political order altogether.

I. Sovereignty and the Legal System

I want to begin by describing how Shakespeare represents the early modern legal system, and specifically how he represents the point of crisis in the legal system that energizes the life of the flesh. To approach this problem, I must first return to the two theories of sovereign power that Shakespeare explores in *Julius Caesar*; namely, divine right absolutism and civic republicanism.

It is a critical commonplace that the duke represents the absolute sovereignty that James understood himself to possess. And yet, the critical pressure of the civic republican tradition can nevertheless be felt in the character of the duke, insofar as he resigns his absolute power and rallies a public of virtuous men (and one woman) in opposition to what he identifies as a predatory state apparatus. Civic republican values also appear in the duke and Isabella's obsessive concern with their own virtue, and their reputation for virtue, and with their reliance on "persuasion" (a word whose cognates appear seven times in the play) in place of unquestioning obedience to state-sanctioned authority figures. Throughout the play, the duke and his confederates try to make people virtuous as a way of making them free of what looks like tyrannical power. Moreover, the play seems to end with something like a civic republican "coup," when the duke reenters the city with a group of "friends" with Roman-sounding names whom he assembles at the city gates.[1]

Nevertheless, unlike Brutus in *Julius Caesar*, the duke does not really aim to organize a functioning civic republican form of political power. In fact, the duke begins and ends as an absolute monarch ("like power divine" [5.1.367], as a shocked Angelo puts it at the end of the play), and in that sense the duke only organizes his civic republican counter-power on a round trip from absolute power back to absolute power.[2] We can therefore think of the play as staging a divine right and absolutist framework that spawns a temporary, internal, civic republican critique that is then digested back into absolutist government.

The point of the play's gambit of staging an internal civic republican critique of absolute power is to lay bare the deep structure of the early modern state, and in particular the central role of arbitrary power within the legal system.[3] The legal system is one of the best-developed bureaucracies of the early modern state, designed to transmit the power of the sovereign monarch down to the level of individual subjects. *Measure for Measure* adverts to an absolute monarch's tendency to dissolve himself in a legal bureaucracy in the duke's own professed shyness about revealing himself to his people ("I love the people,/ But do not like to stage me to their eyes./ Though it do well, I do not relish well/ Their loud applause and aves vehement [1.1.67–70]). Though this is certainly also a reference to James's aversion to processing into the city of London, there is also a sense in which the sovereign withdraws himself behind a growing, semi-autonomous administrative bureaucracy that carries his will, ideally without his needing to appear at all. Even a devoted absolutist like James, the play suggests, abdicates in small ways every day in favor of the administrative organs of the state. Indeed, the play demonstrates an interest in managing and improving various arms of the legal bureaucracy, including the police system; Escalus wants to improve the functioning of the police arm of the legal bureaucracy when he encounters the incompetent constable Elbow and asks him to "bring me in the names of some six or seven, the most sufficient in your parish" (2.1.259) so that he can find a more capable police functionary.

On the one hand, therefore, the play suggests that politics is the power of the sovereign over the life and death of his subjects, but on the other hand, it suggests that one should not expect to see this power show itself very often, because the prerogative power of the monarch is increasingly veiled behind a growing and increasingly autonomous bureaucracy, notably including the legal bureacracy.[4] In early modern England, the legal bureaucracy embodies the will of the sovereign prince, but it also veils (we could almost say "cooks") his raw power by vectoring it through a set of technical legal procedures. King James said that his will was law, but the early modern English legal system was quite capable of imagining that it could function independently of the king, and perhaps even indict absolutist claims of pure personal will in the name of legal procedures that were "above" the monarch.

Indeed, at least at the outset, the play highlights the autonomy and professionalism of the legal apparatus, and its seeming independence from sovereign will. *Measure for Measure* is thought to have been first performed for law students, and to flatter their nascent sense of professional expertise. Formally, the play bears a resemblance to the elaborate "moot cases" by which Jacobean law students would practice legal reasoning and argument, by attempting to apply the law to highly contrived and highly convoluted legal scenarios.[5] The play foregrounds various technical legal questions that would be of interest to aspiring lawyers. By pointing to the technical rhetoric of the law, including the technical conflicts the law encompasses, the play outlines an increasingly autonomous field of law. Indeed, from its very first lines, the play highlights the existence of a technical administrative elite that has exclusive access to the technical legal language of the state. The play begins with the duke declining to give Escalus any technical instruction in the institutional forms of "common justice," since he knows this "science" already:

> Of government the properties to unfold,
> Would seem in me t' affect speech and discourse;
> Since I am put to know that your own science

Exceeds, in that, the lists of all advice
My strength can give you. Then no more remains
But that, to your sufficiency, as your worth is able,
And let them work. The nature of our people,
Our city's institutions, and the terms
For common justice, you're as pregnant in
As art and practice hath enrichèd any
That we remember. (1.1.3–13)

The existence of a highly specialized and technical field of law is again suggested by the comic exchange between constable Elbow and Escalus in 2.1. Elbow is doing the actual work of enforcing the anti-prostitution law that Angelo has reactivated after the duke's disappearance, but Elbow's legal malapropisms (he confuses the legal terms "malefactor," "slander," and "battery," to supposedly great comic effect) suggests that in his very language, Elbow is barred membership of the specialized realm where legal reasoning is undertaken and legal decisions are made.

Yet, *Measure for Measure* teaches that no matter how autonomous the law seems to be, it is always, in fact, an instrument of the sovereign power embodied in the absolute monarch. The duke places Angelo in the position of absolute power over Vienna ("Mortality and mercy in Vienna/ Live in thy tongue") *because* he wants the laws on the books to be enforced (1.1.44–45) when the duke himself has not enforced them over the past 14 years: the duke tells the friar, "We have strict statutes and most biting laws,/... Which for this fourteen years we have let slip" (1.3.19, 21).

The theatrical device of appointing Angelo as acting sovereign in order to activate the dormant laws foregrounds the fact that, as Carl Schmitt argues in *Constitutional Theory*, the legal system that appears to be autonomous nevertheless depends on a sovereign who decides to apply the law. By resigning and giving Angelo an absolute power that Angelo then uses to enforce the "letter of the law," the duke foregrounds the role that the personal will of the ruler plays within what appears as an autonomous legal apparatus.[6] One of the central effects of *Measure for Measure* is to make the technical process of the law seem inseparable from the personal and even arbitrary authority of an acting sovereign who is above the law. Indeed, just after he resigns, the duke tells the friar that part of the point of turning power over to Angelo is to force him to reveal his character in a true light:

More reasons for this action
At our more leisure shall I render you;

Only this one: Lord Angelo is precise,
Stands at a guard with envy, scarce confesses
That his blood flows, or that his appetite
Is more to bread than stone. Hence shall we see,
If power change purpose, what our seemers be. (1.3.48–54)

The duke's lack of confidence in the "precise" nature of Angelo's character would seem to be at odds with the duke's other stated goal of using Angelo to bring his subjects into conformity with the law. However, the duke's experiment (really: Shakespeare's experiment) is meant to reveal the *coincidence* of law and the pure will of the sovereign (and thus the coincidence of the law and Angelo's true character, whether good or bad). The duke makes it clear, in other words, that what he is in fact doing is turning the state and its legal apparatus over to Angelo's raw will as acting sovereign, and he expects the nature of Angelo's will to become evident *through* the way he administers the law.[7]

In a sense, therefore, the duke abdicates, appoints Angelo as his replacement, and then generates a civic republican counterpower to oppose Angelo's will, all in the name of endorsing the central lesson of early modern civic republican critiques of absolutism; namely, that the will of even a good king is arbitrary and above all institutions, even the law. The play does not teach this in order to propose a real civic republican alternative. Rather, it does so in order to force characters to encounter raw, sovereign power and take stock of the consequences.

To accomplish this, the play links the Schmittian point about the dependence of all positive law on raw sovereign power with the central discursive conflict *inside* the early modern English legal system itself, the debate between two institutionalized forms of justice: the common law deference to precedent on the one hand; and the flexible, prerogative justice that is associated with the equity courts on the other. I have reviewed the historical relationship between common law courts and equity courts in my previous chapter. Here, it suffices to say that if common law courts were said to embody the will of the community, then prerogative courts were said to embody the conscience of the king, and they therefore allowed for setting aside settled common law in order to achieve "morally" correct (rather than merely technically correct) judgments. Some commentators have investigated the play's interest in "mercy" in a moral register, by applying Aquinas's discussion of the role of immoral actions in achieving moral ends in the context of reforming or saving souls.[8] Nevertheless, most commentators have recognized that the play roots its interest in "mercy" in the technical infrastructure of the early modern legal system, in which juried common law courts stand in an uneasy relation with the equity courts, which theoretically represent the king's conscience and which offer to "correct" common law judgments that are legally correct but morally wrong.[9]

Though the internal conflict between common law courts and equity courts could strain the legal system, the conflict could nevertheless also strengthen the legal system's institutional autonomy, insofar as the legal system was itself called on to devise arcane, technical solutions to this internal conflict.[10] Indeed, grasping the institutional and historical relationship between these two different forms of justice would itself be part of the institutional training for aspiring lawyers.

Yet Shakespeare is not interested in running through the technical debates for the sake of edifying aspiring lawyers. Rather, he radicalizes the conflict, showing how the presence of equity courts inside the legal system can be used to unhinge the claims of the entire legal system (including the common law courts) to be free of arbitrary sovereign will. And here, the internal legal debate between common law courts and equity courts links up with the background conflict between civic republican and absolutist theories of the state. In *Measure for Measure*, the civic republican opposition that still appears as a political formation in *Julius Caesar* is dissolved into the legal field, where it appears as a radical intensification of the role the internal legal principle of equity plays within the seemingly autonomous legal system. Somewhat surprisingly, however, it is not the absolute ruler who is associated with equity; Angelo embodies the principles of common law deference to settled law. By contrast, it is the temporary civic republican counterpower centered on the duke that represents the claims of equity. This is surprising, of course, in view of the association of equity courts with the absolute monarch; civic republicanism would more "naturally" be aligned with the common law perspective, and yet here Shakespeare reverses the equation in the name of his ultimate goal of staging a critique of the seeming autonomy of the entire legal order. By intensifying the role of prerogative justice—associated with the criterion of mercy—inside the legal system through its association with a civic republican counterpower headed by the temporarily deposed duke, *Measure for Measure* is able to stage a devastating, deconstructive critique of the entire institutionalized legal framework that claims to be autonomous of the arbitrary will of the sovereign. The play reveals, in other words, that no matter how autonomous the legal system appears to be, the legal system as a whole is in fact an expression of absolute sovereign power. To put it bluntly, the lesson of the play is that when push comes to shove, the word of the monarch is law, just as James claimed. Teaching this lesson lines up with civic republican goals, since civic republican critique operates by ferreting out traces of arbitrary sovereign will where there do not appear to be any, and would be especially concerned to find such traces of sovereign will inside the legal system.

II. Two Forms of Justice

As I have just suggested, the central technical legal question the play explores is the relationship between common law courts and equity courts. Louise Halper sees Angelo as representing the common law perspective, and his rejection of "mercy" as a rejection of the countervailing legal principle of equity. According to Halper, Angelo views settled legal procedure, custom, and precedent as a system that cannot be overridden by the personal prerogative of a king or a prerogative court that claims to represent the conscience of the king. When Angelo reactivates a long-dormant law against premarital sex and condemns Claudio to death for getting his betrothed pregnant, he is repeatedly invited to correct the technical letter of the law by considering extenuating circumstances, the very essence of the work of equity courts. Escalus, for example, asks Angelo to look within and consider whether, if the circumstances had been different, he might not have done the same as Claudio:

ANGELO: We must not make a scarecrow of the law,
        Setting it up to fear the birds of prey,
        And let it keep one shape, till custom make it
        Their perch and not their terror.
ESCALUS: Ay, but yet
        Let us be keen and rather cut a little,
        Than fall and bruise to death. Alas, this gentleman
        Whom I would save had a most noble father!
        Let but your honor know,
        Whom I believe to be most strait in virtue,
        That, in the working of your own affections,
        Had time cohered with place or place with wishing,
        Or that the resolute acting of your blood
        Could have attained th' effect of your own purpose,
        Whether you had not sometime in your life
        Erred in this point which now you censure him,
        And pulled the law upon you. (2.1.1–16)

Angelo replies to Escalus's plea for a justice of mercy by denying that his own personal dispositions are relevant; for him, the law is endowed with absolute authority and he imagines that he is simply enforcing it: "You may not so extenuate his offense/ For I have had such faults, but rather tell me,/ When I that censure him do so offend,/ Let mine own judgment pattern out my death/ And nothing come in partial. Sir, he must die" (2.1.27–31). To Escalus's claim that Angelo's decision to condemn Claudio is a personal one, Angelo replies with a positivist conception of judgment. For him, judgment is not a matter of applying reason and common sense in a discretionary way to adjudicate on an abstract law's application to a complex human situation. Operating very much within a common law framework, Angelo sees judgment as a more or less automatic process in which a human person in a specific situation is placed under the relevant legal heading and the consequences read off (what Coke would term "artificial reasoning").[11] Angelo sees his own judgment as an abstract pattern that applies universally and indiscriminately, and if he were to commit the same offense as Claudio, then he would expect the law to come down on him and "nothing come in partial."

The irrelevance of intention to common law legal procedure is one of the clearest points of contrast between common law courts and the equity courts, which are *designed* to take intentions into account in order to correct the letter of the law when it seems to produce morally unfair results.[12] For Angelo, intention is simply irrelevant to the work of justice. "'Tis one thing to be tempted," he tells Escalus, "Another thing to fall.../ ...What's open made to justice,/ That justice seizes; .../ 'Tis very pregnant/ The jewel that we find, we stoop and take't/ Because we see it; but what we do not see/ We tread upon, and never think of it" (2.1.17–26). On the one hand, these lines hint that Angelo would in fact like to prosecute even desires, impulses, and intentions, except for the technical fact that he cannot access them; they are hidden, like a buried jewel that "we tread upon, and never think of it." But on the other hand, the point of the exchange is ultimately to put thoughts— intentions and temptations—beyond the scope of the legal process. In contrast to equity courts, common law courts bypass the murky work of establishing intention and instead apply law to visible actions (whatever the intentions of the actors involved) in the almost mechanical way that Angelo describes. And of course, the whole metaphor of the jury that Angelo uses foregrounds the institutional hallmark of the common law courts as against the equity courts (presided over by a judge only).

However, against Halper, I would argue that the point of the staged debate between two different visions of legal justice—one founded on precedent, the other on prerogative—is not simply to identify Angelo as a proponent of common law courts (compared to Escalus, Isabella, and the ever-merciful disguised duke as avatars of equity dispensed by prerogative courts), but rather to point to the fact that the conflict between common law justice and prerogative justice is a technical debate inside the field of law itself. The autonomous domain of the law, in other words, is characterized, in part, by an arcane technical debate between two very different ways of understanding legal adjudication. And no matter how heated this technical debate becomes, the power and prestige of the autonomous field of law are surely strengthened by the debate, which non-lawyers may not even fully understand. Indeed, as I have already suggested, from the perspective of the law students in the audience, understanding this technical debate is itself part of the training to become a lawyer, a member of the legal bureaucracy.[13]

Yet the Duke's resignation and the civic republican counterpower he organizes have their effects precisely here, for his rebellion transforms a technical internal debate into an existential crisis that places the autonomy and legitimacy of the entire legal system—the legal arm of state power—in question. Because Angelo offers such an absolute affirmation of the common law principle of automatic deference to precedent, he ejects the countervailing principle of equity from the legal system altogether; it is picked up by the extra-legal, quasi-civic republican characters of the duke and Isabella, in whose hands the internal legal principle of justice becomes a deconstructive lever that pries open the entire, seemingly autonomous order of the law on which Angelo insists. The duke's resignation and his effort to subvert what he sees as bad legal process in the name of a seemingly extra-legal "mercy" intensifies and radicalizes the internal legal criterion of equity justice rooted in the prerogative of the judge or sovereign, to the point where it reveals the dependency of the whole, seemingly autonomous legal system on arbitrary, sovereign will. This is most evident in the disguised duke's interactions with the prison provost, that representative of state power, whom the duke pushes, in good civic republican form, to substitute his own moral judgment about Claudio's guilt or innocence and his belief in the integrity of the disguised duke for slavish obedience to positive legal process. The duke's persistent emphasis on mercy, and his willingness to engage in subterfuge and even illegal activity in the name of mercy, has the effect of intensifying the technical legal position of equity justice into a deconstructive lever that unsettles the whole of the legal order, and therefore reveals that the whole system (comprised of both common law courts and prerogative courts) is radically dependent on arbitrary sovereign will.

To some extent, of course, this is going to be news to Angelo, who really does believe in the autonomy of the legal system, and that his job as magistrate is to defer to settled law. It falls to Isabella, the duke's ally in civic republican subterfuge, to force Angelo to recognize that no matter how much he wants to hide behind the claim of deferring to settled positive law, in fact there is no normative basis for his legal judgments other than his own will. When Isabella appeals to Angelo for clemency for her brother Claudio, Angelo responds by reciting the basic tenets of common law justice, in which the role of the magistrate is simply to apply the law (rather than making an independent moral judgment about the wrongness of the actions in context):

ISABELLA: I have a brother is condemned to die.
          I do beseech you, let it be his fault,
          And not my brother.
PROVOST: Heaven give thee moving graces.
ANGELO: Condemn the fault, and not the actor of it?
          Why, every fault's condemned ere it be done.
          Mine were the very cipher of a function,
          To fine the faults whose fine stands in record,
          And let go by the actor.
ISABELLA: O just, but severe law!
          I had a brother then. Heaven keep your honor. (2.2.34–42)

Nevertheless, after some goading from Lucio, Isabella goes on to articulate the countervailing principle of equity justice as forcefully as Escalus does earlier. Isabella argues that equity justice—and the willingness to show mercy even when the letter of the law has been violated—is the very essence of the role of the judge, more essential than the mere robes a judge wears:

ISABELLA: No ceremony that to great ones 'longs,
          Not the king's crown, nor the deputed sword,
          The marshal's truncheon, nor the judge's robe,
          Become them with one half so good a grace

> As mercy does.
> If he had been as you, and you as he,
> You would have slipped like him; but he, like you,
> Would not have been so stern.

ANGELO: Pray you, be gone.

ISABELLA: I would to heaven I had your potency,
            And you were Isabel; should it then be thus?
            No, I would tell what 'twere to be a judge,
            And what a prisoner. (2.2.59–71)

Echoing Escalus's argument from earlier in the play, Isabella claims that the very essence of secular legal power ("what 'twere to be a judge") is to exercise the prerogative of equity, and the procedure that the true judge should follow is precisely to identify with the offender in order to consider his or her intentions. Angelo replies by reasserting the technical letter of the law ("Your brother is a forfeit of the law,/ And you but waste your words"), but Isabella does finally succeed in prying an unsettling admission from Angelo, namely that the law does not enforce itself, that the law has no independent autonomous force, that the law is ultimately only Angelo's own will:

ISABELLA: Yes, I do think that you might pardon him,
            And neither heaven nor man grieve at the mercy.

ANGELO: I will not do't.

ISABELLA: But can you if you would?

ANGELO: Look what I will not, that I cannot do. (2.2.49–52)

Angelo's claim to serve the law notwithstanding, when push comes to shove the only foundation Angelo can offer for the exercise of the law is his will: "I will not do't" and "what I will not, that I cannot do."

However, the point of the play is not merely to reveal the presence of arbitrary power behind the seemingly autonomous legal order as a way of critiquing that order. Rather, the point is to demonstrate that once law has shown its wolf's face, it has the power to transform those subject to it into that special, transformative category of being, the life of the flesh.

III.   The Life of the Flesh

The way in which law stripped bare of its pretensions to being free of arbitrary power energizes a transformative life of the flesh is precisely what is illustrated by the fate of Claudio. In Act 1 scene 2, the provost seizes Claudio in the name of the anti-fornication law that Angelo has chosen to reactivate and publicly parades Claudio off to jail to await execution. Insofar as he is condemned and made an example of, Claudio functions as a scapegoat, but one who stays in the midst of the community and generates around himself a kind of community of scapegoats, insofar as everyone in Vienna is able to see in the condemned Claudio a version of him- or herself.

When he is first seized, Claudio expresses skeptical bafflement at the new rigor of the authorities:

> Thus can the demigod Authority
> Make us pay down for our offense by weight.
> The words of heaven: on whom it will, it will;
> On whom it will not, so. Yet still 'tis just. (1.2.119–122)

Claudio cites the language of divine right absolutism and admits his helplessness before the "demigod Authority" that is inscrutable in its decisions "on whom it will" seize. He argues that it is only "for a name" that Angelo seizes him; that is, to secure a reputation for himself as the new ruler. Casting himself as a latter-day Job, Claudio makes the law seem as alien as the decisions of an incomprehensible God. Claudio's final claim that "yet 'tis just" notwithstanding, his speech suggests the fundamental inscrutability of the law rather than its justice. By enforcing the technical letter of the law, Angelo plunges Vienna into a Kafkaesque state of affairs in which citizens encounter a law whose origin and meaning they cannot understand, though they must accept its validity even when it condemns them and sends them to their deaths, as it has Claudio.[14]

Yet what is most distinctive about Shakespeare's dramatic imagination is that this Kafkaesque law triggers an intensified experience of being flesh and being connected to others as flesh. Under the pressure of the newly activated law, the outlawed sex for which Claudio is condemned is intensified into a potentially transformative experience of the flesh; at the level of metaphor, this intensified experience is captured through the images of cannibalism that, in fact, run through the entire play. Under the weight of condemnation, Claudio now imagines sex with Juliet as having drunken too much (human) juice:

> Our natures do pursue,
> Like rats that ravin down their proper bane,
> A thirsty evil, and when we drink we die. (1.2.127–129)

Other characters catch the cannibalism metaphors. Two scenes later, Lucio's account of Juliet's pregnancy combines the notion that Juliet has eaten Claudio and gotten fat (that is, pregnant) with the idea that the fetus will itself be food for human consumption, like an agricultural crop:

> As those that feed grow full, as blossoming time
> That from the seedness the bare fallow brings
> To teeming foison, even so her plenteous womb
> Expresseth his full tilth and husbandry. (1.4.41–44)

The notion that Claudio and Juliet's sleeping together has something to do with the production and consumption of human flesh for food is also picked up by Isabella when she pleads with Angelo to spare Claudio's life. She paints a gruesome picture of Angelo as a butcher, slaughtering Claudio and then serving his flesh to the heavens:

> Even for our kitchens
> We kill the fowl of season; shall we serve heaven
> With less respect than we do minister
> To our gross selves? (2.2.84–87)

Isabella literally says that if Angelo executes (or butchers) Claudio now, the heavens will have to eat his flesh out of season, but her metaphor's vehicle (the fowls that we kill in order to "minister/ To our gross selves") is so vivid that it spills into the tenor of the dialogue and invites us to imagine Angelo feeding on Claudio as he might on his lunch; that gruesome image might be part of Isabella's shaming point here. And indeed, Angelo experiences his own desire for Isabella (which I will discuss later) as a desire to tear into forbidden human flesh. When he is first touched with desire for her, he expresses the wish to "feast upon her eyes" (2.2.178), a desire that he identifies as perverse. In this context, Angelo's indecent proposal that Isabella give up her own body for Claudio's would amount to substituting one meal of human flesh for another.

Such cannibalism metaphors invite us to imagine a whole subterranean network of bodies groping toward each other on blind, bodily volition, nibbling on one another, figuratively digesting one another's flesh into themselves. From the perspective of the humoral self, of course, the membrane of the self is never sealed off from the other; the self is always physically, corporeally open to the other, always taking in corporeal bits of the other—its humors, its passions, its fluids, its words.

The humoral self must recognize that it has, in some sense, ingested the other already and been ingested in turn. These hungry, humoral bodies register another society beyond the norms and legal codes that differentiate and distinguish persons and regulate their connections within conventional social life.

Central to my argument in this book is that Shakespeare's fantasy of a humoral self and its open relations with other humoral selves is first triggered, inside the play, by the radical exposure to sovereign will, a radical exposure that sets aside conventional, socially defined, bounded personhood. The transformative experience of fleshly life begins with the legally condemned Claudio and then spills into the whole social world of Vienna. And the vector by which Vienna comes to be transformed into condemned but radically alive flesh is the illegal practice of prostitution that Angelo repeatedly tries to stamp out.

Prostitution is at once alien to the official, legally mediated collective life of Vienna and utterly irrepressible. And like cannibalism, prostitution (and the syphilis that dogs it) comes to symbolize the collective fleshly life of the community writ large. Prostitution stands symbolically for the fleshly life that is the flip side of the collective life of political subjects consolidated by firmly institutionalized state power. When Angelo decides to enforce an anti-prostitution ordinance and has all the brothels outside the city plucked down, they nevertheless remain inside the city limits:

POMPEY:	You have not heard of the proclamation, have you?
MISTRESS OVERDONE:	What proclamation, man?
POMPEY:	All houses [of prostitution] in the suburbs of Vienna must be plucked down.
MISTRESS OVERDONE:	And what shall become of those in the city?
POMPEY:	They shall stand for seed. They had gone down too, but that a wise burgher put in for them. (1.2.92–99)

The more prostitution is attacked, the more it seems to become universal, and therefore to figure an alternative form of life. And indeed, prostitution is itself shot through with the cannibalism metaphors that, I have argued, represent Shakespeare's effort to make legible a life of the flesh that is triggered by the touch of absolute law.

As the object of legal condemnation, prostitution opens the door to the alternative experience of self and other that Shakespeare merges with his humorally inflected cannibalism metaphors. When constable Elbow first brings the pimp Pompey before Angelo and Escalus, he calls Pompey a "wicked Hannibal," his malapropism for "cannibal" (2.1.166–167). The duke, too, equates Pompey's trade—selling human bodies for sex—with eating (and maybe even skinning) human bodies when he tells Pompey to "think/ What 'tis to cram a maw or clothe a back/ From such a filthy vice" (3.2.19–21). Standing before Angelo and Escalus, Pompey tries to extricate himself from the charge of being a pimp by claiming that Froth came to Pompey's brothel not for sex but to eat, that he was looking for the "stewed prunes" that were kept in bawdy houses because they were popularly thought to be a prophylactic against syphilis, but that were also a pun for testicles and that Froth paid for "very honestly" (2.1.96–99).[15] Pompey claims that Mistress Elbow, too, came in looking for stewed prunes: "Sir, she came in great with child, and longing—saving your honor's reverence—for stewed prunes" (2.1.86–87). The appetite for the kind of food that is sold at brothels traces secret convergences between characters who would have no contact with one another according to normal procedures of social life—between the dumb but rich gentleman Froth and the smart but low-class pimp Pompey, but also between Pompey and constable Elbow's pregnant wife and thus between Pompey and constable Elbow himself, that ineffective representative of state power.

When flesh becomes aware of itself in the face of an angry law, it is energized and clings ever more tenaciously to life. Pompey, for one, responds to being seized by the law with pride in his status as a pimp and pride in the collective life of the flesh that he manages. The conflict between him and Escalus represents the conflict between the law that seems simply arbitrary and the fleshly life of the body, thrown into a world inhabited by other bodies, tied together through lines of desire and passion, the lines of desire and passion that Pompey sees himself as operating on and with.

ESCALUS: What's your name, master tapster?
POMPEY: Pompey.
ESCALUS: What else?
POMPEY: Bum, sir.
ESCALUS: Troth, and your bum is the greatest thing about you, so that, in the beastliest sense, you are Pompey the Great. Pompey, you are partly a bawd, Pompey, howsoever you color it in being a tapster, are you not? Come, tell me true; it shall be the better for you.
POMPEY: Truly, sir, I am a poor fellow that would live.
ESCALUS: How would you live, Pompey? By being a bawd? What do you think of the trade, Pompey? Is it a lawful trade?

POMPEY: If the law would allow it, sir.

ESCALUS: But the law will not allow it, Pompey, nor it shall not be allowed in Vienna.

POMPEY: Does your worship mean to geld and splay all the youth of the city? (2.1.202–220)

In Escalus's eyes, Pompey is beastly, more akin to an animal than a human being, and his physicality is confirmed by his last name of "Bum" and the large bum to which his last name points. Pompey also sees himself primarily as a body; his vision of the self-as-body, his vision of the self-as-flesh, is confirmed by his reduction of his self to its most basic fleshly needs ("I am a poor fellow that would live") and by his commitment to the flesh that he serves (the sexual desires of the "drabs," the youth of the city who "will to't"). Pompey tells Escalus that the only way to stamp out fleshly desires is to "geld and splay all the youth of the city" (as though they were horses and dogs and not men) and that Escalus's (really Angelo's) anti-sex crusade amounts to a desire to depopulate the city (which, he says, would cause a real estate crash). Pompey ends the conversation by thanking Escalus for his advice to stop being a bawd, but then tells the audience, in an aside, "I shall follow it [i.e., Escalus's advice] as the flesh and fortune shall better determine" (2.1.241–242). Pompey does not respect social and legal gravity (the gravitas embodied in Escalus) but the gravity of the flesh, a gravity to which Froth also points when he tells Escalus, "I never come into any room in a taphouse but I am drawn in" (2.1.198–200). Vienna is shot through with a gravity of the body that "draws" people like Froth and Pompey together to meet at places like Mistress Overton's brothel. Prostitution traces a gravitational field of the body that operates beneath (or at some tangent to) the official, technical-legal discourses of collective life, drawing together clusters of characters in ways not governed by the legal-political norms of Shakespeare's Vienna.

IV. The Sexuality of the Sovereign

In the Introduction to this book, I have suggested that sexuality is one privileged place where the interpersonal geometries of the flesh appear in a concrete way. We see that already in the strange, disoriented way in which Claudio and other characters start to experience sexuality as a kind of cannibalism. These characters are all on the losing side of arbitrary, sovereign power, but one notable feature of *Measure for Measure* (as well as of *Othello*) is that the figure who embodies sovereign power himself experiences a transformative sexuality rooted in the life of the flesh. In the Act 2 scene in which Isabella tries to convince Angelo to exercise the sovereign prerogative of mercy, it is certainly true that in the very moment Angelo recognizes himself as arbitrary sovereign power (rather than servant of the law), he experiences himself as the subject of an alien sexual desire. The first consequence of Angelo's horrifying recognition of himself as the embodiment of sovereign power is to see all bodies, notably including Claudio's and Isabella's, as radically subject to this power. Suddenly, he sees neither Claudio nor Isabella as persons subject to his legal authority; rather, he comes to see them as flesh radically subject to his personal will. And at the same time, Angelo finds himself consumed with a desire for that abjectly exposed flesh, even when this desire threatens to unmake him. In a sense, once Angelo grasps himself as arbitrary sovereign power, he feels a masochistic desire to identify with the objects of that arbitrary power. Contemplating Isabella's body as flesh that is utterly at his mercy, Angelo seems to experience a masochistic desire to undermine his own legally codified self as magistrate, to make himself legally forfeit just as Claudio and Isabella are. This is, paradoxically, the effect of Isabella's plea that Angelo identify with Claudio by seeing himself as condemned in the eyes of heaven.[16]

> Go to your bosom;
> Knock there, and ask your heart what it doth know
> That's like my brother's fault: if it confess
> A natural guiltiness such as is his,
> Let it not sound a thought upon your tongue
> Against my brother's life. (2.2.136–141)

Much to Angelo's bafflement, his own body now feels the touch of Isabella's words: "She speaks, and 'tis/ Such sense that my sense breeds with it" (2.2.141–142). It is precisely this touch of the abject body that Angelo explores in lines that move quickly from the (thrilling) recognition that Isabella is as much utterly and corporeally at his mercy as she has shown him that Claudio is, to the rebounding (and equally thrilling) recognition that this status (of bodily subjection, of "natural guiltiness") rubs off on Angelo himself, nominal absolute monarch but now able to see a reflection of himself in the flesh that is radically at his mercy.[17] Angelo responds to this plea to recognize a universality of condemnation by feeling a desire to join Isabella on the very (condemned) terrain she has brought to light—the beating heart, the bleeding body, the flesh:

> Having waste ground enough,
> Shall we desire to raze the sanctuary
> And pitch our evils there? O fie, fie, fie!
> What dost thou, or what art thou, Angelo?
> Dost thou desire her foully for those things
> That make her good? (2.2.169–174)

For Angelo, the desire to desecrate the other is a desecration of self ("what dost thou, or what art thou, Angelo?" he asks himself disgustedly), for his recognition of himself as desiring coexists uneasily with his public reputation for virtue and self-restraint, which Angelo says he will use against Isabella if she goes public with his behavior: "Who will believe thee, Isabel?/ My unsoiled name, th'austereness of my life,/.../ Will so your accusation overweigh/ That you shall stifle in your own report/ And smell of calumny" (2.4.153–158).

If Angelo imagines using his public reputation as a way of covering up his secret desire, then he nevertheless must also know (and take pleasure in) the danger of the game he is playing, a game that ultimately imperils his public identity and reputation.[18] Indeed, Angelo's (secret) aggression toward his public self is still evident in the last scene of the play, when the duke returns and Angelo eagerly participates in his own punishment: "let my trial be mine own confession./ Immediate sentence, then, and sequent death/ Is all the grace I beg" (5.1.370–372).[19]

Having understood that law is only another name for his own arbitrary will, Angelo experiences himself and Isabella translated into a realm of flesh where interpersonal connections are mediated by humoral forces emanating from the body, like the blood that clogs his heart:

> O heavens,
> Why does my blood thus muster to my heart,
> Making both it unable for itself,
> And dispossessing all my other parts
> Of necessary fitness? (2.4.19–23)

In these lines Angelo is all blood, the humor that incites lust and has now made the socially recognized person Angelo into a mere puppet for its whims; Angelo ends his second soliloquy by casting himself as nothing but blood: "thou art blood!" (2.4.15). It is to the impulses of this humor that Angelo finally turns over his autonomous, language-afflicted self when he hisses, "I have begun,/ And now I give my sensual race the reign" (2.4.158–159).

Moreover, at the level of the blood, Angelo's claim on Isabella elicits an answering pulse of her blood and body, too. For while Isabella rejects his blackmail attempt—her body for Claudio's life—it is hard to miss the erotic response she highlights with her answer to Angelo:

> [W]ere I under the terms of death,
> Th' impression of keen whips I'd wear as rubies,
> And strip myself to death as to a bed
> That longing have been sick for, ere I'd yield
> My body up to shame. (2.4.99–103)

Though her social self rejects Angelo's advances (as a social person, Isabella fears the social stigma of shame), the body undeniably responds to them and does so by offering its own blood in the form of "rubies" that would be raised by "th'impression of keen whips." In a cascading fantasy of erotic martyrdom, blood answers blood, and body answers body.[20] This experience of the flesh arises out of a (perverse) use of arbitrary authority, one that we have already glimpsed in Isabella the first time we see her in the midst of a discussion with one of the nuns at the convent that she is about to enter about the scope of the rules to which the nuns must submit themselves:

ISABELLA: And have you nuns no farther privileges?
NUN: Are not these large enough?
ISABELLA: Yes, truly. I speak not as desiring more,
But rather wishing a more strict restraint
Upon the sisterhood, the votarists of Saint Claire. (1.4.1–5)

In the scene with Angelo, at the level of narrative and social norms, there is no doubt that Angelo attempts a sexual assault of Isabella, whose "no" really does mean no.[21] But at the level of the bodies themselves and the speech of their humors and their gestures on the stage, a very different interpersonal grammar becomes visible, one that connects the flesh of Angelo and Isabella when no social connection between them as state-sanctioned persons is possible at all. At the risk of anachronism, we might say that Isabella's response frames Angelo's advances (grounded as they are in an explosion of raw sovereign power) as a kind of sadomasochistic scene in which the power of the sovereign is reduced to mere will, a will that is then transformed into a self-conscious performance designed to produce a sexual charge. As Isabella frames it, her exchange with Angelo is one in which the social person's value and legibility are performatively erased and in which "no" really means "yes," a vision that seems to offer a solution to Angelo's inability to integrate an explosion of desire into his understanding of his social identity. The scene certainly invites itself to be read "out of context" in this way, and allows audience members to attach themselves fantasmatically at the level of the physical actions of the actors and their gestures.[22]

It is easy to dismiss Angelo's advances on Isabella as sexual assault. Still, to dismiss Angelo's actions in this way is to miss their philosophical and theatrical import, for Angelo's aggressive (and at the same time masochistic) advances on Isabella are just one more constellation in a whole parallel cosmos of bodies relating to other bodies in the shadow of a radically arbitrary and therefore groundless law. Angelo uses the newly arbitrary law, and Isabella's radical exposure to it, to set aside the law and enter into a domain of the flesh that exists at a tangent to the official life that is sanctioned and recognized by the political and legal system. Thus, the scene enacts a basic pattern in the play: the touch of the law-as-pure-will crystallizes flesh, and flesh has its own ways of interacting that are not illegal so much as they are extra-legal.

V. The Return of the Duke

The structural premise of the genre of the "disguised prince" play is that the prince is always the prince, no matter what disguises he has put on, and that he returns at the end to reveal himself and reimpose order. When the duke is finally unhooded at the end of *Measure for Measure*, he does complain that he has seen "corruption boil and bubble/ Till it o'errun the stew" (5.1.317–318). And yet, the way the duke returns to power maintains the life of the flesh as much as it cleans it up. This is especially evident in the path to and from the prison that the duke defines at the end of the play.

In Vienna, all roads lead to the prison, a place where the experience of legal condemnation opens the door to a countervailing experience of collective life or even community. Under the pressure of the angry law, Mistress Overdone and Pompey both find themselves seized by the provost and taken to the same prison where Claudio already resides. On his arrival at the prison, Pompey finds a whole parallel society that is in fact the same society he knew outside, since he says that all of Mistress Overdone's former clients are behind bars:

> I am as well acquainted here as I was in our house of profession. One would think it were mistress Overdone's own house, for here be many of her old customers. First, here's young Master Rash [and so on, in a long, vivid tableau of his former clients]. (4.3.1–4)[23]

The fact that Pompey finds his old customers behind bars blurs the line between life outside the prison and life inside. Indeed, we have seen that under Angelo's rule, life outside the prison is conditioned by the state of being legally condemned, the same state that applies to the bodies of the prisoners. And as on the streets of Venice, in the prison, subjection to the law fails to make bodies compliant, but instead makes them aware of their corporeality, and of the solidarities of the flesh.

That there is an intensity of fleshly life to be found in the prison's state of bodily condemnation is vividly suggested by the character of Barnardine, the prisoner who has been long condemned but whose fleshly life seems to block the ability of sovereign power to operate. The provost complains that he cannot intimidate Barnardine, since he is "a man that apprehends death no more dreadfully but as a drunken sleep: careless, reckless, and fearless of what's past, present, or to come; insensible of mortality, and desperately mortal" (4.2.140–143). The state of being "desperately mortal" is as good an emblem as any of the life of the flesh that the prison brings to light. Robert Zaller argues that Barnardine is natural man who deprives sovereignty of its power by declining to feel fear.[24] However, if Barnardine is "natural man," then his naturalness is produced only by legal condemnation. For Barnardine, the life he leads in jail is inseparable from the (permanent) state of condemnation to which he is subjected, so much so that even when given an opportunity to escape he declines to: "He hath evermore had the liberty of the prison; give him leave to escape hence, he would not. Drunk many times a day, if not many days entirely drunk. We have very oft awakened him, as if to carry him to execution, and showed him a seeming warrant for it; it hath not moved him at all" (4.2.145–150).

Within the plot of the play, of course, Barnardine's function is to be a body who might be killed and whose head could be sent to Angelo in place of Claudio's. When the duke asks the provost to disobey the order to execute Claudio, the provost notes that he will need to produce a head:

PROVOST: Alack, how may I do it, having the hour limited, and an express command, under penalty, to deliver his head in the view of Angelo? I may make my case as Claudio's to cross this in the smallest.

DUKE: By the vow of mine order I warrant you. If my instructions may be your guide, let this Barnardine be this morning executed, and his head born to Angelo.

PROVOST: Angelo hath seen them both, and will discover the favor.

DUKE: O, death's a great disguiser, and you may add to it. Shave the head, and tie the beard, and say it was the desire of the penitent to be so bared before his death; you know the course is common. (4.2.162–174)

Part of the function of the prison is to foreground the substitutability of (legally condemned) persons insofar as they are mere flesh. Though "Angelo hath seen them both, and will discover the favor [i.e., face]," subjected to the ultimate expression of legal condemnation, identity is unhinged, and one body will do for another.[25]

When the duke returns at the end of the play, this substitutability should, presumably, end as the duke restores the legal codes that enforce individuated personhood. In fact, however, the return of the duke seems to maintain and even expand the indeterminate state of the decomissioned characters of the prison.[26] Indeed, the true character of the duke is itself somewhat unhinged by the end of the play, a process initiated by Lucio's allegations that the duke has been known to roam the streets seeking out beggar women who reek of garlic for sex. Lucio's slander threatens to pull the duke into the counter-public of blindly volitional, condemned bodies groping toward one another, digesting each other into their own substance. Lucio suggests, in other words, that beneath the duke's official role as duke lies a fleshly life that connects him to the teeming, fleshly life that runs through the streets of Vienna.[27] The questionable status of the disguised duke is punctuated by the fact that he comes within a hair of being seized and paraded off to be tortured to death: "Such a fellow is not to be talked withal. Away with him to prison! Where is the provost? Away with him to prison! Lay bolts enough upon him: let him speak no more" (5.1.342–345).

However, even once the duke has succeeded in reasserting himself ("O power divine," says Angelo), he seems to *maintain* the life of the flesh that the play has put on the stage. The best emblem of this is the puzzling way in which he orchestrates the return of Claudio, whom he had saved from execution and deposited in a lightless hold in the prison. The duke does not simply produce Claudio; rather, he first (falsely) affirms that Claudio has indeed been killed (to Isabella's dismay), only to produce his body while claiming that it is not really his body at all, merely that of someone who looks just the same:

PROVOST: This is another prisoner that I saved,
           Who should have died when Claudio lost his head,
           As like almost to Claudio as himself.
DUKE: If he be like your [Isabella's] brother, for his sake
           Is he pardoned, and for your lovely sake. (5.1.485–489)

The duke seems to want to affirm that he is not merely preserving Claudio's life but actively granting it, *giving* the gift of life, *making* Claudio a state-sanctioned person through a sovereign gift of grace. Yet even as the duke seeks to stamp his own secular sovereign power on the person of Claudio, there is a strange animated force in that body that exceeds the duke's grasp.

In his monumental study of incest in *Measure for Measure*, Marc Shell argues that on his return, Claudio is the emblem of the setting aside of the incest taboo. "Claudio is," he writes, "as it were, the creature to which Isabella has given birth, as the result of her incestuous union with her brother; as such Claudio's return marks the possibility that 'incest' no longer begets shrinking terror and reactive curse but allows us to entertain the spiritual, yet humanizing scandal of 'universal siblinghood,' an implicit acknowledgment of the limits and potential dangers of our culture's frenetic attempts to enforce rules of legitimacy in love, reproduction, or commerce" (100). However, while I agree that the play is interested in pushing to a point beyond "rules of legitimacy," I think it frames this not in terms of a supposedly universal incest taboo (in Shakespeare's pre-psychoanalytic imaginary, this supposedly universal taboo is not in place), but rather in terms of the legal power of the state to affirm or deny personhood. And in this regard, it is certainly noteworthy that the touch of legal condemnation persists in Claudio, who is not pardoned so much as rendered permanently condemned: he is, says the duke, someone who "should have died when Claudio lost his head,/ As like almost to Claudio as himself." He is, in other words, pardoned to a life beyond the life of the legally sanctioned person (call it "Claudio") that he once was.

The strangeness of the duke's return to sovereign power, his desire to contain the life of the flesh and to maintain it, is also evident in the forced marriages at the end of the play. In the strange justice the duke then dispenses, he tries to bring the corporeal geometries traced by the life of the flesh in Vienna into alignment with the artificial social life of legal fictions (including the legal fiction of marriage). Indeed, forced marriages are the order of the day, beginning with that of Angelo and Mariana on the grounds that Angelo has inadvertently slept with Mariana and thus sealed his earlier betrothal with her. Taken in by the Duke's bed trick, Angelo's body has done something that Angelo the legal person has not consciously willed, a point Mariana makes during the trial scene in a suitably paradoxical form; Angelo, she says, "thinks he knows that he ne'er knew my body,/ But knows, he thinks, that he knows Isabel's" (5.1.202–203). Mariana refers to bodies interacting with other bodies at a level beneath the willed actions of legally sanctioned persons; Angelo's body "knows" Mariana's body although "he" (the socially legible person) does not, and that is because "he" (the socially legible person) knows Isabella though his body does not. Now in the trial, Angelo is forced to legally acknowledge the wife his body already knows, just as Lucio is forced to marry his former whore and to recognize the illegitimate child his body has generated. Isabella's ultimate fate—to marry the duke—fits the same pattern since, in one last bed trick, the duke essentially substitutes his own body for that of Angelo, for whom Isabella's blood has already answered. Just as Angelo does not know that he knows Mariana, so too Isabella does not know that she knows the duke, even as her body moves inexorably (and wordlessly) across the stage toward a marriage (a legal joining of socio-symbolically validated life) that she cannot, and indeed need not, consent to.

This silent theatrical movement takes its place in the entire choreography of kneeling and standing and veiling and unveiling and bodily substitution that marks the end of the play. These movements amount to an invitation to a gestural theater in which the audience responds to the movements of bodies on the stage rather than the imagined situation of persons in the imagined world of the play, and as such it connects back to the gestural theater in the scene in which Angelo makes his indecent proposal to Isabella. The abiding force of this gestural theater marks the futility of the play's closing efforts to seal up the life of the flesh within legally defined forms of relationship. The notably unsatisfying sense of its conclusion is testimony to the failure of this rearguard action.[28] For the flesh that the play discloses (in Isabella, in prison, in Angelo, on the streets of Vienna) is *actively generated* by the touch of a law that has lost its institutional legitimacy, that has been stripped, as it were, of the veil of right and appears instead as arbitrary will. In that sense, the flesh the play puts on the stage does not escape from the orbit of the law, since it needs the touch of the law for its starting point; however, neither does it "serve" the law (and thus "deify" power, as Milton's Satan puts it in *Paradise Lost*). The life of the flesh is, in fact, animated anew by every new effort to impose law on it, as the duke does at the end of the play. In the prison, in the brothel, even within the sacred confines of marriage, *Measure for Measure* homes in on a form of life in which the touch of the law crystallizes a shared life of the flesh that bypasses the collectivizing institutions of the sovereign nation-state.

VI. Conclusion

The only theoretical language I have used in my discussion of *Measure for Measure* is the theoretical language implicit in the early modern jurisprudential debate between the common law perspective, on the one hand, and theories of equity justice rooted in an absolutist conception of sovereignty, on the other. I have attempted to show how Shakespeare maneuvers the internally fractured discourse of law into a kind of impasse that makes all law seem like an arbitrary force. And I have tried to show that once law seems like an arbitrary force, the fact of being subject to the law transforms selves into flesh. The reduction of the self to flesh is an almost universal experience in the play, and this fleshly selfhood provides the ground for an experience of communal life that is very different from a community of political subjects.

However, it should be obvious that the stakes of this argument go beyond simply describing the complexities and conflicts of early modern legal thought. In fact, the legal system is one of the primary mechanisms through which the rising early modern state projects its will onto its subjects. For many people living in early modern England, the law would have represented one of the primary ways in which they experienced the touch of state power. And for many people living in early modern England, acknowledging the law of England would have been one of the primary markers of national identity. By writing a play that deconstructs the legal system, transforming it from a mechanism of political community-building to a mechanism of political community-unbuilding, Shakespeare offers a vision that is legible today in terms of theoretical debates about the nature and extent of state power, and about the possibilities for resistance to state power. Though Agamben's political theory terminology has been largely absent from this chapter, it should be obvious that I take Shakespeare to offer a correction to his pessimistic vision of political communities. For Agamben, political communities are, by their very nature, structured around an arbitrary power that defines the community by excluding someone or something from political legitimacy. His analysis has the salutary effect of undermining naïve communitarian fantasies of the spontaneous nature of communities. For Agamben, behind any community, no matter how spontaneous it appears to be, lies the institutional expression of sovereign power. And in this analysis, Agamben is surely right. He is also surely right in his further claim that every inaugural act of political community formation draws a line between life that will be acknowledged and life that is excluded, and that this inaugural act leaves a mark even on those inside the political community. In Agamben's universe, to be a political subject is to suffer from a dependence on arbitrary sovereign power, and to know (sometimes consciously and sometimes not) that this sovereign power can always be directed against you and turn you into the life that is excluded from political legitimacy. The knowledge that the state, by its very nature, has already seized the political subject in the very sinews of life, as it were, is the price paid for political subjecthood, as Agamben sees it. Largely because of its resolute anti-communitarianism, this theory has become near orthodoxy in critical theory circles today. Yet it is precisely here that *Measure for Measure* offers a corrective. In good Agambenesque form, the play does not suggest that it is possible simply to bypass political power to enter into communities that are free of the pressures of politics. But the play does suggest that it is possible to use political power—including its legal expression—against itself, so to speak, to engineer forms of community that flourish in the shadow of sovereignty.

3
Unsettling the Civic Republican Order: The Face of Sovereign Power and the Fate of the Citizen in *Othello*

Whereas in Chapters 1 and 2 I analyzed the way raw sovereign power unsettles the "public sphere" and the legal sphere, respectively, in Chapter 3 I focus on how raw sovereign power unsettles the nominally civic republican political order represented in *Othello*. As a political ideal, civic republicanism exercised a deep fascination for many early modern English intellectuals because it seemed to offer a basis for political order other than the arbitrary will of the sovereign. In the plays I have examined thus far, civic republicanism acts as a kind of acid that unsettles an absolutist order and by doing so opens the door to a life of the flesh. In *Othello*, by contrast, Shakespeare imagines a nominally civic republican order only to show that it is subtended by a suppressed version of the same absolutist power that the absolutist order explicitly celebrates. As Shakespeare depicts Venice, the civic republican order assumes political subjects ("citizens") with stable socio-symbolic identities who are capable of carrying out their duty to the state. However, the play reveals the reliance of these civic republican subjects on an exceptional person, namely, Othello, who embodies raw sovereignty and answers to no one. The play explores how an encounter with raw sovereign power generates fleshly bodies that can be reassembled into new configurations, creating clusters of bodies that are theatrically separated from state-imposed social norms of interpersonal bonding. As such, the play offers a distinctive, theatrical exploration of forms of life that flourish in the shadow, as it were, of the civic republican order.

The character who disrupts the normal functioning of the civic republican order of Venice is obviously Iago. That Iago has a somewhat detached relation to social space is widely agreed on. Iago's status in the military hierarchy is unhinged, since he has a position that he considers unworthy of himself and he therefore looks in on his own social position with something of an outsider's perspective. This skewed perspective opens the door to a distinctive kind of sociological analysis. For Magnusson, Iago applies a Bourdieuvian analysis of the Venetian symbolic economy, in which rank and status are an effect of the interaction between a pre-structured social position and a market for words or symbolic acts. She argues that Iago knows that what words are worth is defined by specific markets of reception and that Iago is good at conjuring up or staging the markets in which his words will work best.[1]

There is certainly something right about Magnusson's vision of Iago as a cultural sociologist, but also something wrong about it. He is not a scientist but a participant, and from a participant's perspective, the premise of Bourdieuvian analysis is normally the desire to win in the game of social competition (though part of the strength of Bourdieu's analysis is that what counts as winning for you is itself an effect of your position; winning means winning in the social space that you consider legitimate). Magnusson, in fact, assumes that Iago does want to win and that he has a smart analysis of how people win in the game of social life. In this, Magnusson is taking Iago at his word, since he occasionally says that he aims to get ahead through deceiving Othello or undermining Cassio. Yet at the same time it seems obvious enough that Iago is not playing to win anything so limited as a better position in the army or more favor from Othello.[2]

I want to suggest that Iago does indeed have a kind of analysis of social space, but that it goes well beyond the ultimately comforting assumptions of Bourdieuvian sociology. Iago may well see how the symbolic economy works and how symbolic properties are distributed in social space, though his desire is not merely to win in a game of social positioning, but rather to push out of this structured social space altogether. As with Marc Anthony in *Julius Caesar*, Iago's motivation is a kind of anti-political rage, a rage against the notion that a functioning political order should define identities and regulate the ways in which selves can connect to other selves.[3] Iago does not so much look at the surface of social life and chart its sociological patterns and economic rules as look through or past structured social and symbolic life, and in that sense his desiring analysis of social space is "trans-social."

The best tool for analyzing this trans-social vision is the Schmittian theory of sovereignty and its Agambenesque application to all of social and relational life.[4] For Iago, the symbolic economy (the orderly distribution of symbolic properties in social space, which assigns social characteristics to persons and on which the civic republican order depends) is rooted in a prior political decision that establishes the parameters of sociological life, a political decision that is not grounded in any norms but is radically groundless, rooted in sovereign will and the threat of violence. As Iago imagines Venice, it is the character of Othello who represents the sovereign power that secretly anchors the civic republican order. Iago forces this hidden or veiled fact into the open, thereby revealing that when push comes to shove, even proudly civic republican subjects (with well-defined identities within the civic republican symbolic economy) are radically subject to a sovereign power that is embodied in Othello.[5]

Iago's goal is to use Othello (the hidden principle of sovereign power) to unsettle the settled civic republican order. When I suggest that Iago will use Othello to "unsettle" the functional socio-political order, what I mean by "unsettle" is something very particular: Iago will make Othello unsettling only by making him more obviously what he already is, namely, the bearer of sovereign power. Much *Othello* criticism is premised on the notion that Iago dismantles or unmakes Othello, but I want to suggest that in a strange way Iago is actually building up and clarifying Othello, forcing him to reveal himself as the core of raw sovereign will that anchors Venetian life. And in particular, this requires Iago to "protect" Othello from the threat that Desdemona represents; that is, the threat of being domesticated, of being interpolated into the Venetian order rather than remaining the exception outside of that order.[6]

In *Othello*, as in other plays I have examined, the effect of directly encountering sovereign power is radically unsettling. For once characters in the play are exposed to the (normally veiled) power that is the precondition for the orderly symbolic universe of the play in which their characters are legible as persons, these characters are "unmade," reduced to flesh. And once characters are reduced to flesh in this way, they become capable of theatrically enacting a new experience of self and other and of the connection between self and other; it is this terrain—what I call the life of the flesh—that becomes the real focus of Shakespeare's play. As Shakespeare stages it, the appearance of raw power within the heart of normally quiet state power deranges the fantasy that makes people functional subjects and citizens, instead making them susceptible to a new experience of being flesh and of clustering together with other flesh in predictable morphological patterns. As in the two preceding chapters, my argument here will be that the appearance of raw sovereign power opens the door to an erotics of bodies that have been violently extruded from the symbolic systems that assign them recognizable social value.

I. Civic Republicanism in Shakespeare's Venice

In early modern England, Venice is the very emblem of a civic republican order. In imagining the social and political order of Venice, Shakespeare draws on Contarini's celebratory account of its civic republican institutions and values.[7] For Contarini, the political community of Venice is defined not by a divinely appointed ruler, but by the aristocrats born into the Venetian order who themselves constitute and embody the state. Contarini highlights the byzantine committee system of the Venetian state, which is designed to preserve public-spiritedness among Venetian aristocrats. And for Contarini, the doge who represents the community as a whole is nevertheless not its originator or its guarantor. In fact, as Contarini represents his role, the doge is almost the prisoner of the Venetians' collective will as expressed through the committee system. The Venetian collective identity is not guaranteed by a miraculous, divinely appointed ruler; rather, the collective body of the citizens is itself empowered to define and defend its own way of life through the decisions it makes within what J.G.A. Pocock calls "secular time."[8]

Yet in Contarini's account there are persistent hints that the Venetian republic fails to define a basis for a political community that truly does avoid appealing to the arbitrary will of a sovereign separate from the community over which he presides. Ultimately, Contarini must assume what he ought to explain; namely, the existence of a political community of virtuous men that is the precondition for the exercise of collective reasoning and decision-making that is supposed to define the political community in the first place. Contarini defines the civic republican community of Venice as having a culture of public-mindedness, but he also argues that in and of themselves, Venetians are neither more nor less virtuous than people elsewhere; instead, they live in the institutional framework of an "artificial angel," the elaborate system of rotating state offices that checks and balances any tendency toward individual interest or "corruption." In that sense, the public-minded virtue that is the precondition for civic republican public life is also the product of inherited state structures, so that the political community is imagined to exist before the exercise of state power, yet is also imagined to be a product of state power. In fact, Contarini's account is marked by a logical regress to some hypothetical ancestors who laid the foundations of the republican order and thus "founded" the political community that, in turn, founds the state.

In *Othello*, Shakespeare suggests that if civic republican political theory fails to account for the foundation of civic republican political life, then the foundation for a civic republican political culture must lie outside of itself in some arbitrary act of sovereign will. Unlike Contarini, Shakespeare's goal in *Othello* is not to celebrate a functioning, institutionalized civic republican political order. Rather, Shakespeare homes in on the dependence of Venice's civic republican order on what seems its very opposite—namely, arbitrary absolute power that turns out to be seated in Othello—and Shakespeare uses the fact of the civic republican order's foundation in arbitrary sovereign power as a deconstructive lever to undermine the functional claim of the civic republican order on its citizens and subjects.[9]

The battle with the Turks reveals that the Venetian political order is essentially founded on a core of extra-republican sovereign power that can unhinge settled political life as readily as it can guarantee it. Under the pressure of the state of emergency triggered by the Turkish attack, the dependence of the Venetian order on a form of pure force that is outside the civic republican political order becomes evident. When faced by the existential threat of a Turkish invasion, the senate meets in emergency session. However, like the guardians of Kafka's castle, the Venetian senators project the illusion of mysterious power but are, in fact, utterly impotent, for they depend on Othello and the army of mercenaries he leads to guarantee their survival and project their power in the world.[10]

Othello is black and exotic and perhaps Muslim, but what he really represents in the play is the raw political will and violence that the civic republican order needs and yet disavows. Othello represents the military force that is at once inside and outside the venerable constitutional order of Venice. That is precisely how Iago introduces the figure of Othello to the audience (before Othello appears on the stage himself). Speaking to Roderigo in 1.1, Iago says that the state cannot hold Othello to the same laws to which it holds everybody else, because Othello is in some sense the precondition for any law, the state's very survival depending on him. Speaking of Othello's covert marriage to Desdemona, Iago tells Roderigo that the senators cannot punish Othello because they depend on him for their very existence:

> For I do know the state,
> However this may gall him with some check,
> Cannot with safety cast him; for he's embarked
> With such loud reason to the Cyprus wars,
> Which even now stands in act, that for their souls
> Another of his fathom they have none
> To lead their business. (1.1.145–151)

Even the senators who are supposed to *be* the state cannot cast Othello out with safety, for their very souls are in Othello's hands. From Iago's perspective, Othello is all that keeps death, biological and symbolic, out of the Venetian symbolic order. Losing Othello would amount to an existential crisis in which Venetian identity itself would be shattered.

Othello shares Iago's view of himself as exceptional, as outside the Venetian republican structure that he nevertheless anchors. When Brabantio demands that Othello be sent "To prison, till fit time/ Of law and course of direct session/ Call thee to answer," Othello points to his own exceptional status in the constitutional order:

> What if I do obey?
> How may the Duke be therewith satisfied,
> Whose messengers are here about my side
> Upon some present business of the state
> To bring me to him? (1.2.87–91)

Othello obviously feels excluded from the state; he is deferential to the duke and the senators and he casts himself as their servant. Yet at the same time, Othello feels like a king, he believes he descends from kings—"I fetch my life and being/ From men of royal siege" (1.2.21–22)— and he sees his color and his past as making him exceptional and placing him outside the reach of the law. Implicitly, if not explicitly, Othello believes that he is what Iago thinks he is—namely, the veiled sovereign power that roots the symbolic-social order—and he feels himself invested with the power of life and death.

II. Sexuality

The question of Othello's status within the political order of Venice is central to his relationship with Desdemona. I am going to argue that Othello's marriage with Desdemona threatens to take away his exceptional status by domesticating him, by implanting him too firmly within the constitutional-political-symbolic order. And it is precisely from this threat of domestication that Iago "protects" Othello, making him, by the end of the play, what he was all along: the "pure" threat of violence that founds the political and symbolic order, even as it is also antithetical to that order. Under Iago's tutelage Othello finally recovers his sense of exceptionalism, and his belief at the end of the play that he can kill Desdemona without any consequences to himself expresses his view that he is sovereign, that he can kill at will, that he has the power of life and death over the subjects of Venice.

That "protecting" Othello's special role requires him to turn against the specific form of sexual intimacy that joins him to Desdemona highlights the fact that sexuality itself is a central part of Venice's civic republican order. One of the ways in which the civic republican political order tries to provide a foundation for its political culture is the famous Venetian "golden book." As Contarini describes it, the golden book represents a finite list of the Venetian families empowered to attend the great council from which all officers of the state are drawn through a combination of balloting and chance. Shakespeare does not mention the golden book directly, but it does leave a detectable signature in the play in the Venetian concern with inbreeding, the responsibility to make sure that women marry inside the political and social order in order to maintain a finite number of politically authorized bloodlines. This foundation of endogamy is suggested in the play when Brabantio remembers parading the "wealthy curlèd darlings of our nation" (1.2.68) in front of Desdemona, and it is this endogamous norm that Othello's marriage with Desdemona threatens.[11]

Indeed, from the perspective of Brabantio and the other senators, the main problem with the Othello–Desdemona marriage is not that it breaks any supposed color line, but that it threatens the political imaginary of Venice, because it raises the question of what will become of children who will be neither inside nor outside the civic republican constitutional order. As Brabantio puts it, "if such actions may have passage free,/ Bondslaves and pagans shall our statesmen be" (1.2.98–99). That may be part of what Othello is talking about when he hints (in a set of famously convoluted lines) that he is impotent. Speaking of his request that Desdemona accompany him to Cyprus, Othello assures the senators that,

> I therefore beg it not
> To please the palate of my appetite,
> Nor to comply with heat – the young affects
> In me defunct – and proper satisfaction. (1.3.261–264)

No children would mean no vitiation of the golden book fantasy of a perfectly closed circle of Venetian aristocrats. Venetian republicanism rests squarely on the patriarchal control of women and reproduction, and to make the civic republican order work, to make this state form last through time, it is necessary to dominate women completely. As Shakespeare represents it, Venice is essentially a political-sex commune that holds women in common to guarantee the continuity of the bloodlines of the governing class. And at first glance, the Othello–Desdemona marriage threatens this social imaginary, since it breaks one very eligible woman out of the closed circle (and it is certainly true that Desdemona experiences her love of Othello as a kind of escape). Equally to the point, the Othello–Desdemona marriage also threatens to put one "new" man, namely Othello, on the inside, thus casting doubt on the ability of the golden book to provide what the civic republican order so desperately needs: a membership list that exists before the exercise of any political decision-making.

This way of understanding the political culture of Venice and the role of endogamous sexuality within it may make it seem surprising that the senate ultimately endorses Othello and Desdemona's elopement. Listening to Othello's explanation of his wooing (by describing his military exploits to Desdemona), the duke says, "I think this tale would win my daughter too" (1.3.171). However, the opening council scene in which the marriage of Othello and Desdemona is put on public trial and receives an explicit state sanction illustrates one of the basic premises of the civic republican form, which is that there can be no private life separate from the public life of the republic, since any private life might trigger factions that would threaten the culture of public-mindedness. In *Julius Caesar*, Marc Antony objects to precisely this hostility to extra-public affections in Brutus's civic republicanism. In *Othello*, the point of the trial scene is to insist on the right of the civic republican state to affirm (or, by implication, to block) sexuality as it sees fit. By overriding Brabantio's veto power, the civic republican state even appropriates the traditional rights of fathers. The state-sanctioned intimacy of Othello and Desdemona therefore becomes an emblem of Venetian civic republican state power and its ability to bring all aspects of life under its aegis.[12] Affirmation by the state converts the Othello–Desdemona relationship from a threat to the continuity of the state into an emblem of the state, an emblem of the subordination of personal life to public life that is characteristic of the civic republican order.

The problem, of course, is that this validation threatens to take away some of the alienness that Othello needs in order to play his constitutional role as guarantor of the constitution. Othello experiences his relation to Desdemona precisely in terms of its ability to give him a house, but at the same time he knows that this sense of fixity and insiderness represents a threat to his special status within the state. As he puts it to Iago:

> For know, Iago,
> But that I love the gentle Desdemona,

> I would not my unhousèd free condition
> Put into circumscription and confine
> For the sea's worth. (1.2.24–28)

Under the pressure of a normalizing, state-sanctioned, essentially "public" sexuality with Desdemona, Othello is in danger of losing the outsider status that is central to his sense of self, and also central to the role he plays within Venice's constitutional order.[13]

It is here that Iago does his work, attacking Othello in the very place where his desire to be a self (a Venetian gentleman, of sorts, an honorary "brother of the state," a householder like Brabantio) and his desire not to be a self (to be unhousèd and free and therefore capable of anchoring the civic republican order from the outside) come together. Over the course of the play, Iago disrupts the normalizing intimacy that Othello and Desdemona share, and he does so in order to force (or allow) Othello to assert his role as raw power at the very heart of the civic republican order.[14] And Othello's ultimate embrace of his special identity (as against the normalized identity that Desdemona offers) is confirmed by his asserting of the power of life and death over Desdemona herself in the final scene of the play.[15] In place of a partner within a socially affirming, domesticating envelope of state-sanctioned intimacy, Iago forces Othello to reveal himself as a (sovereign) monster, as raw power that eats all symbolic identities, ultimately including Desdemona's. However, as I shall show, this sovereign power also energizes an alternative experience of sexuality that is fundamentally not identity affirming, neither for Othello nor for Desdemona. Thus, Othello's relationship with Desdemona is both the means through which Iago attacks Othello and the place where the effects of this disruption (namely, the revelation of Othello as raw power) are most vividly displayed.

III.   The First Riot

The coincidence of forcing Othello to reveal the raw power that he embodies and disrupting Othello's experience of a socially reaffirming and integrating intimacy with Desdemona is marked by the first riot that Iago engineers in Cyprus, which forces Othello to emerge from his bedroom to restore order. Othello's role as the exception at the center of the socio-symbolic system is highly veiled in Venice, but becomes more explicit once the action shifts to Cyprus, a liminal space at the edge of empire, at the existential border with the Turk, where Othello is all that can "give renewed fire to our extincted spirits," as Cassio puts it while awaiting Othello's ship (2.1.81).[16] Having arrived in Cyprus and seen the attacking Turkish fleet sink in bad weather, Othello, as military governor, declares a feast that is a celebration and affirmation of Venetian/Cypriot/Christian identity as against Turkish identity. It is, in other words, a celebration of socio-symbolic identity successfully sutured onto persons by the collectivizing power of the state. At the same time, the feast is "a celebration of [Othello's] nuptial," as the herald puts it (2.2.7). The functioning intimacy of Othello and Desdemona is itself an emblem of the victory of the Venetian/Christian state against the Turks.

Othello withdraws from the party to consummate his marriage with Desdemona: "Come, my dear love./ The purchase made, the fruits are to ensue;/ That profit's yet to come 'tween me and you" (2.3.8–10). Just before Othello leaves the stage, he makes a point of affirming state power, both through the general proclamation and by reviewing the terms of the military hierarchy at whose head he stands. He takes particular care to delegate power formally to Cassio with the advice, "Good Michael, look you to the guard tonight./ Let's teach ourselves that honorable stop/ Not to outsport discretion" (2.3.1–3). However, while Othello is offstage—in the bedroom, presumably being cemented into the Venetian order through the sexuality of person-affirming intimacy with Desdemona—Iago engineers a riot. On the one hand, this riot looks like the breakdown of functional political order anchored by a sovereign, and at its end Othello is forced to emerge from the bedroom to restore order via threats of sovereign violence. Yet, on the other hand, looked at as a manifestation of the life of the flesh I have been exploring throughout this book, the riot itself looks like a systematic theatrical exploration of a form of life founded on the recognition of exposure to the raw power that Othello represents and that he reaffirms before he leaves the stage.

In fact, Iago uses Othello's hierarchical social order against itself, as it were, to reverse engineer the fantasy work that uses functioning sovereign power to suture socio-symbolic identity onto flesh. The raw material with which Iago works to trigger the riot is a couple of Cypriots who are overly sensitive about their identity as Cypriot aristocrats in the face of obvious Venetian military control over the island ("Three else of Cyprus—noble swelling spirits,/ That hold their honors in a wary distance,/ The very elements of this warlike isle") and, of course, Cassio, whose sense of identity is profoundly involved with his rank, the military system of identity that is explicitly anchored by Othello (2.3.51–53). (Cassio's sense of self depends utterly on Othello's good will, so much so that after he gets fired he begs Iago to intercede for him in order that, as he puts it, "by your virtuous means I may again/ *Exist*, and be a member of his love" [3.4.110–111, emphasis added].) Cassio reveals his passionate overinvestment in rank with his drunken religious prattle, in which he expresses the hope that "the lieutenant is to be saved before the ancient" (2.3.103–104). And it is precisely this fantasmatic cathexis of his rank within the military hierarchy (centered on Othello) that leads Cassio to take offense at whatever it is that Roderigo says to him offstage: "A knave teach me my duty?" says Cassio, "I'll beat the knave into a twiggen bottle" (2.3.139–140). Suddenly stripped of his normal psycho-social bearings, Cassio becomes an enraged and dangerous swordsman and cudgeler, and after beating Roderigo black and blue he stabs Montano, who in turn stabs Cassio.

Just before the riot, Cassio and Montano had been "in terms like bride and groom/ Devesting them for bed" (2.3.169–170), as Iago later puts it. Yet the riot does not split them up so much as put them together in a new way, through a transformative, theatrical violence that links them at the level of the flesh and its passions, even as it also links them to the theatrically bloodied Roderigo. Read at a tangent to the story of the play, read as a visual spectacle, the theatrical violence of the scene defines a new interpersonal geometry. To put it artfully, Iago assembles these three characters into a large molecule bound together not by stable social identities, but by a theatrical, performative violence that strips the person of the conventional socio-symbolic identities that Othello, as the power that anchors the symbolic economy, attempts to affirm before he leaves the stage. In other words, Iago uses the psychic tendencies to glue the self to a state-mediated socio-symbolic identity like military rank, and to overinvest in or even fall in love with such a socio-symbolic identity, to energize an interpersonal practice that dissolves rank and opens the door to clusters of bodies bound together by theatrical, performative violence. In Cassio's encounter with Roderigo, Cassio's fantasmatic overinvestment in rank energizes a theatrical interpersonal practice that undoes rank by reducing self and other to an ambiguous fleshly state that is both strong and vulnerable at the same time.

The riot forces Othello to leave his bedroom and to reassert his status as the exceptional power that anchors the political order. However, the raw power that Othello threatens to unleash to end the first riot casts a retrospective light over the riot, making it resemble not the absence of order but an exploration of the very force that also brings order. Though Othello does bring order, this process is anything but orderly, since when Othello reappears on the stage he is in an emotionally unhinged state, saying that his anger could discharge itself in any direction, on any person:

> Now, by heaven,
> My blood begins my safer guides to rule,
> And passion, having my best judgment collied,
> Assays to lead the way. Zounds, if I stir
> Or do but lift this arm, the best of you
> Shall sink in my rebuke. (2.3.193–198)

The reimposition of sovereign order is imagined as an act of rage that equalizes everyone by making everyone potentially subject to killing ("the best of you/ Shall sink in my rebuke"). In a sense, therefore, the order that Othello manages to impose at the end of the riot looks like a continuation of the riot in another key. Othello's threatening speech suggests that raw power is all that can impose stable categorical differences, like the difference between Turk and Christian. And yet, at the same time, Othello's violence also threatens to undermine those stable symbolic differences:

> Why, how now, ho? From whence ariseth this?
> Are we turned Turks, and to ourselves do that
> Which heaven hath forbid the Ottomites?
> For Christian shame put by this barbarous brawl!
> He that stirs next to carve for his own rage
> Holds his soul light; he dies upon his motion.
> Silence that dreadful bell! It frights the isle
> From her propriety. (2.3.158–165)

Here, Othello identifies the brawl as a resurgence of the existential enemy within (are we turned Turks?). Yet his speech imposes a categorical difference between Turk and Christian only to vitiate it, since Othello threatens to reimpose order in a way that will kill souls; he hints that he will send people to hell, as he will explicitly wish to do later in the play, too, as though he were an agent of the devil inside the Christian order. The violence that will reimpose Christian identity is itself un-Christian; the violence that will reimpose normalcy is itself un-normal.

Moreover, despite Othello's nominal efforts to end the riot, the scene ends with a lingering sense that these characters have touched a life beyond the sovereign order of stable socio-symbolic identity. Roderigo is the best emblem of the life beyond socio-symbolic identity that Iago has opened. Roderigo is foolish, but he is nonetheless also a Venetian gentleman, though one who allows himself to be beaten black and blue (or rather, in Cassio's artful threat, he is a body that will have an intricate wicker pattern beaten onto it: "I'll beat the knave into a twiggen bottle"), and he ends by saying, "I have been tonight exceedingly well cudgeled; and I think the issue will be... [that I,] with no money at all, and a little more wit, return again to Venice" (2.3.353–356). Iago advises him to take pleasure in his beating: "Cassio hath beaten thee,/ And thou by that small hurt hast cashiered Cassio./ Though other things grow fair against the sun,/ Yet fruits that blossom first will first be ripe" (2.3.361–364).[17] Though Iago means that early fruits also spoil early, he does not actually say that Roderigo's fruit will eventually ripen at all, only that he should understand his project outside of the conventional economy in which it is ripe fruits that bring pleasure. Iago hints that the theatrical unmaking of identities—for Roderigo this means a beating—is an end in itself, even a source of pleasure.

It is certainly true that Iago derives pleasure from the scene; he is surprised at how quickly the night has passed: "By the mass, 'tis morning!/ Pleasure and action make the hours seem short" (2.3.365–366). Part of Iago's pleasure may be his sense of mastery over other characters. However, such a pleasure is inseparable from a kind of fantasmatic identification with his victims and the way they theatrically undermine their own rank and symbolic identity and cluster together as raw flesh. After all, Iago is himself psychotically overinvested in his rank, which he thinks insufficient, and such hyper-investment might well be eased by watching higher-ranking characters theatrically strip themselves of their socio-symbolic status. Moreover, the riot allows Iago to detach himself from his own socio-symbolic identity as the loyal army ensign, "honest, honest Iago" (5.2.155), by showing himself (to himself, but also to the audience) as an anti-social agent of violence. More than all of that, there is a sense that Iago's pleasure derives from being himself physically swept up in what he terms here the "action" of the night; it is the action of the body in which Iago is interested and his body is at the center of the physical action of the scene; is indeed, from an audience perspective, the hyper-energized molecule at the very center of the cluster of bloodied, black-and-blue bodies that the scene puts together. For Iago, the riot is not so much the means to an end (whatever end we take Iago to have) as an end in itself, because it allows him to explore transformative forms of bonding mediated by the flesh rather than by the socially recognized person.

Insofar as the riot begins and ends with Othello heading off to the bedroom, the scene seems to posit a zero-sum economy in which intimacy with Desdemona is disrupted to the precise extent that Othello is forced to show his hand as the raw power that guarantees public identity and public order. Nevertheless, at the end of the first riot, some of the performative, theatrical violence of the riot infects the state-sanctioned intimacy of the Othello–Desdemona relationship and begins to transform it into a new, very different species of sexuality. Montano, the ruler of Cyprus before Othello's arrival who is described to the Duke as "your trusty and most valiant servitor" (1.3.40), ends the scene reduced to a quivering mess of blood ("Zounds, I bleed still. I am hurt to th' death") and by his own account unable to explain what happened: "Iago, can inform you,/ While I spare speech, which something now offends me,/ Of all that I do know" (2.3.152, 187–189). While Othello reimposes order, Desdemona appears on stage (pointing to her, Othello says, "Look if my gentle love be not raised up") and when Othello and Desdemona retire to the bedroom they take the bleeding Montano to bed with them (Othello says he will be Montano's surgeon [2.3.239]). In short, even as the riot pulls Othello out of Desdemona's normalizing embrace, it also discharges its perverse energies back into the bedroom; the scene ends by conjuring up an image of Othello with two kinds of blood on his hands, Desdemona's and Montano's.

IV. The Second Riot

Iago's work in the scenes that follow this first riot is to further infect Othello and Desdemona's mutually admiring, publicly intimate relationship with the disorienting corporeal energies revealed in the riot. His strategy is well known: he encourages Desdemona to champion the cashiered Cassio's cause and then "I'll pour this pestilence into his ear," he says, "That she repeals him for her body's lust" (2.3.344–345). The emphasis on the ear as the point of attack, and therefore on the power of ideas to unsettle the emotional life, is noteworthy and it is something to which I will return in the final section of this chapter. The point I want to underscore here is that throughout the play, as in the first riot, Iago undermines Othello's intimacy with Desdemona as a means of restoring to Othello his radically exceptional nature as the raw power that anchors functional social life and yet also unhinges conventional social life. Far from being unmade by Iago's deceptions, when Othello presides over the riot (and afterward, over the murder of Desdemona), he becomes what he truly is, willing, finally, to take responsibility for anchoring social life in raw force.[18] In the final scene in which Othello kills Desdemona, he appears as what Carl Schmitt says all sovereign power is—a monster with the power of life and death in its hands.

The run-up to Desdemona's murder is a second riot in Act 5 that is, in some sense, authorized by Othello's sovereign power. The ultimate sign of Othello's apotheosis as sovereign is his willingness, now, to authorize (and even to engage in) extra-judicial killing, as when he tells Iago, "Within these three days let me hear thee say/ That Cassio's not alive" [3.3.472–473]). These words loom over the second riot, making it seem like an expression of the sovereign's right to kill. Yet, as in the first riot, the explosion of sovereign power can *feel* like the absence of order. After he is stabbed, Cassio cries out in surprise that Cyprus seems to be without a police watch and therefore without the ability to guarantee the life of its citizens:

CASSIO: What, ho! No watch? No passage? Murder! murder!
GRATIANO: 'Tis some mischance. The voice is very direful.
CASSIO: O, help!
LODOVICO: Hark!
RODERIGO: O wretched villain!
LODOVICO: Two or three groan. 'Tis heavy night.
                  These may be counterfeits. Let's think't unsafe
                  To come into the cry without more help.
RODERIGO: Nobody come? Then shall I bleed to death.
LODOVICO: Hark! (5.1.37–46)

Lodovico and Gratiano cannot distinguish the persons involved in the riot, or even number them correctly: "two or three groan" is all they know, and moreover they may be "counterfeits"—presumably they mean a set-up for a robbery, but the question of who could possibly count as a "genuine" person under this state of emergency is also in play. Once Iago comes with "light and weapons," he makes a point of theatrically under-recognizing the two authority figures from Venice:

IAGO: What may you be? Are you of good or evil?
LODOVICO: As you shall prove us, praise us.
IAGO: Signor Lodovico?
LODOVICO: He, sir.
IAGO: I cry you mercy. (5.1.65–69)

Gratiano himself is panicky at discovering that Roderigo, his fellow Venetian nobleman, has become involved in the strange grammar of the body that the riot seems to represent:

IAGO:	Know we this face or no?
	Alas, my friend and my dear countryman
	Roderigo? No. – Yes, sure. – O heaven, Roderigo!
GRATIANO:	What, of Venice?
IAGO:	Even he, sir. Did you know him?
GRATIANO:	Know him? Ay.
IAGO:	Signior Gratiano? I cry you gentle pardon.
	These bloody accidents must excuse my manners
	That so neglected you.
GRATIANO:	I am glad to see you. (5.1.89–96)

The shock seems to come in recognizing that Roderigo, a Venetian, a member of the club of Kafkaesque castellans, has been swept up in an unsettling, corporeal experience that threatens to touch Lodovico and Gratiano, too, since Iago again goes out of his way to highlight that they are not what they seem any more than Iago is: "Signior Gratiano? I cry you gentle pardon," says Iago, citing "these bloody accidents" as his warrant for setting conventional social identities (and thus conventional social deference) aside. For Gratiano and Lodovico, beneath the narrative fear of ambush lies a more profoundly philosophical fear of losing the distinct identity they have as Venetian noblemen. Individuals are reduced to bodies that drip blood and words into one another in ways that make the psychic and corporeal borders between them permeable.

As with the first riot, what we see here is an alternative interpersonal grammar that is energized by the emergence of raw sovereign power. As with the first riot, at the heart of the second riot is a triangle of bodies bound together through thrusts of swords and spurts of blood: Roderigo stabs Cassio, Cassio stabs Roderigo, Iago stabs Cassio. However, these bodies that are stuck together with blood, as it were, seem to generate an intense corporeal gravity that captures all the other characters of the play. During the second riot all the characters of the play appear on stage except for Desdemona: Iago, Roderigo, Cassio, Lodovico and Gratiano, Bianca, Emilia, and finally Othello himself. They are characters the audience has gotten to know and—sociologically speaking—to classify; they are also characters who, within the imagined world of the play, know each other quite well. Yet, as with the first riot in Cyprus, in this scene, on this night, all these characters' socio-symbolic identity is unhinged, they are reduced to bodies, to the flesh, and reassembled in new configurations. (In that sense, the space of the second riot is analogous to the prison in *Measure for Measure*.) And, again as with the first riot, Iago is the supercharged particle at the center of the action—he seems to be everywhere at once, stabbing, seizing, tripping, accusing, bandaging bodies, and carrying them away like a demonic master of ceremonies. The violence is obviously "staged" or theatrical in the sense that the audience knows that no one is actually hurt (because it is enacted by actors on a stage). It is, in other words, a luminously fantasmatic violence that Shakespeare brings to the stage here; as with the first riot, once we are in possession of the key, we can see it as an articulation of a new form of life that has passed beyond the political power that affirms selfhood by suturing it into a collective symbolic order.

Standing behind all of this is the long shadow cast by Othello, now transfigured into the emblem of monstrous power that transforms the other characters of the play into flesh engaged in a spectacle of performative, transformative violence. When he shows up at the scene of the riot, Othello hears the cries of the wounded and, like Gratiano and Lodovico, he fails to distinguish their identities by confusing Roderigo and Cassio:

CASSIO: I am maimed forever. Help, ho! Murder! murder!
    [Falls.]
    Enter Othello.
OTHELLO: The voice of Cassio. Iago keeps his word.
RODERIGO: O, villain that I am!
OTHELLO: It is even so.
CASSIO: O, help, ho! light! a surgeon!
OTHELLO: 'Tis he. O brave Iago, honest and just,
    That hast such noble sense of thy friend's wrong!
    Thou teachest me. Minion, your dear lies dead,
    And your unblessed fate hies. Strumpet, I come.
    Forth of my heart those charms, thine eyes, are blotted.
    Thy bed, lust-stained, shall with lust's blood be spotted.
    (5.1.27–36)

Othello fails to respond to individual characters as individual characters anymore; screaming bodies are all interchangeable to him. And indeed, he leaves the riot only in order to make the body of Desdemona interchangeable with the bleeding bodies of the men he has found on the streets: "Thy bed, lust-stained, shall with lust's blood be spotted." Othello does not restore calm as he had after that earlier riot during the victory feast; this time he relishes the smell of blood in the water, as it were, and then disappears to let the scene unfold according to its own logic (in that sense, he is like Marc Antony in the "let slip the dogs of war" speech I discuss in Chapter 1).

V. In the Bedroom: To Kill Only to Kill Again

By moving from the streets to the bedroom, Othello imposes on the bedroom the same condition of transformative exposure to sovereign power that he imposes on the streets of Cyprus. And Othello's apotheosis as pure sovereign power leads to the invention of a new form of sexuality with Desdemona, one that bypasses the intimacy that affirms person-hood. In the murder scene, Othello has given up the intimate connection that makes Desdemona his equal; instead, he seems now again to possess the sovereign power of life and death to which Desdemona is abjectly exposed. Othello seems to believe that murdering Desdemona is within his authority as military governor; when Desdemona asks to be banished but not killed, she seems to be addressing him not as a husband but as the bearer of sovereign power. However, as much as on the streets of Cyprus, in the bedroom the abject exposure to the raw sovereign power that Othello represents makes Desdemona into something other than a sanctioned person, and this new status stands at the heart of a new experience of non-intimate sexuality that appears (paradoxically) at the moment she is killed.

When Othello returns from the riot, Desdemona notices that some-thing has changed: "Alas, why gnaw you so your nether lip?/ Some bloody passion shakes your very frame" (5.2.43–44). Othello's embodiment of raw force has begun to "show through" the socio-symbolic character she has come to know. Othello makes Desdemona afraid with his "talk of killing," as she puts it. In the imagined world of the play, what Othello does to Desdemona counts as murder. The scene between Othello and Desdemona nevertheless takes on the charge of an eroticized theatrical practice, where conventional social identities are used (or perhaps we should say abused) to energize a drive down to the flesh as what subtends these identities. Transformed into flesh, Desdemona is perversely animated in a way that makes it possible for Othello to kill her again and again. In a sense, these characters are engaged in a scene in which they "play" with death, with imposing their wills on others, with fantasmatically having their wills defeated at the level of the flesh—just as characters do in the two riots.

In Othello and Desdemona's bedroom, the desire to perform murder signifies the central desire of the play as a whole; namely, to kill the socially sanctioned person in favor of a new form of social connection built on a recognition of subordination to sovereign power. Othello had earlier said farewell to Desdemona, to the socially sanctioned lady with all her virtues:

OTHELLO: No, my heart is turned to stone; I strike it, and it hurts my hand. O, the world hath not a sweeter creature! She might lie by an emperor's side and command him tasks.

...

IAGO: She's the worse for all this.

OTHELLO: O, a thousand, a thousand times! ... But yet the pity of it, Iago! O Iago, the pity of it, Iago! (4.1.179–193)

Othello still registers the force of Desdemona's social identity ("She might lie by an emperor's side and command him tasks"), but now this identity only energizes his determination to violate it (4.1.181–182). On her bed, Othello progressively deprives Desdemona of any signification within the symbolic structures of state power (in which she is white, Christian, the daughter of a Venetian senator, a trophy wife); instead, he aims to approach her only as flesh, utterly subject to him.

Moreover, as Othello reduces Desdemona to this perversely animated fleshly life, it has a kind of rebound effect on him as well, as it seems to make him, too, into flesh, rendering visible the soft core within or beneath the role of the sovereign that he plays. (This pattern repeats the encounter of Isabella and Angelo in *Measure for Measure* that I discuss in Chapter 2.) In the bedroom, at the climax of the play, the sovereign power that Othello embodies is revealed as the condition of an eroticized experience of flesh meeting flesh in ways that pass beyond functional subordination to a social and political order. It is true, after all, that by stripping Desdemona of her socio-symbolic status, Othello also strips her of her ability to function as a prop for his own socio-symbolic status (he now stains his own wedding sheets). In place of the fantasy of identity-affirming intimacy, the operative fantasy for Othello here is that as flesh, Desdemona can die and yet live, that he can kill her and yet conserve her, a fantasy that binds Othello to Desdemona most intensively at the very moment when he kills her:

> I'll smell thee on the tree.
> O balmy breath, that dost almost persuade
> Justice to break her sword! One more, one more!

> Be thus when thou art dead, and I will kill thee,
> And love thee after. One more, and that's the last!
> So sweet was ne'er so fatal. I must weep,
> But they are cruel tears. This sorrow's heavenly;
> It strikes where it doth love. (5.2.15–22)

Othello's desire to kill off the socio-symbolic person is the precondition for a love beyond death, as it were—"I will kill thee,/ And love thee after." What Othello enters into is a fleshly connection, mediated by the body, the body that feels pain but also pleasure, the body that feels anger but also pity, the body that is full of gases like the breath that leaves Desdemona's body and enters Othello's, and full of running fluids like the tears that Othello sheds at the thought of what he himself is about to do and that fall on Desdemona's "alabaster" skin—his sorrow "strikes where it doth love." The sovereign power of life and death has not been abrogated; instead, it has exploded into a transformative, theatrical practice that provides a potentially universal set of terms for the distinctive life of the flesh.

Once this new form of life (conditioned by a new way of experiencing sovereign power) has taken root in Othello's relation to Desdemona it spreads, refolding other social relationships around itself. The deranged interpersonal fantasy that has caught Othello projects a grid into which other characters can be inserted and on which connections between bodies can be graphed. Predictably enough, Cassio appears on this grid. Just before killing Desdemona, Othello has Cassio very much on his mind, saying that he wishes Cassio, too, could be killed and killed again: "Had all his hairs been lives, my great revenge/ Had stomach for them all" (5.2.74–75). Othello had earlier expressed the same wish, the same fantasy, to Iago:

> O, that the slave had forty thousand lives!
> One is too poor, too weak for my revenge. (3.3.442–443)

Othello wishes that Cassio were functionally incapable of death so that Othello could give his lust to torture free rein without fear of accidentally ending the game prematurely, so that he could kill in order to kill again, in which case killing would become an emblem of an abiding connection rather than the abrogation of a connection, as killing becomes an emblem for abiding connection in Othello's relation to Desdemona.

Emilia, too, appears on the grid of the interpersonal practice that takes the death of the person as its precondition rather than its end, that transforms death into a kind of playing with death. After

Desdemona's (apparent) death, Emilia imagines herself as a victim who will be killed only to be killed again. Emilia says that she would speak the truth though it killed her twenty times over: "I care not for thy sword; I'll make thee known,/ Though I lost twenty lives" (5.2.166–167). Moreover, Emilia says that she has a greater capacity for pain, a greater ability to digest pain, than Othello has power to inflict: "Thou hast not half that power to do me harm/ As I have to be hurt" (5.2.163–164).

In fact, both Desdemona and Emilia are operatically killed and live to talk about it: Desdemona to indict and then clear Othello of murder; Emilia to say that she dies in bliss. These women end up in bed, in each other's (performatively dead) arms, together with the (performatively dead) body of Othello. Lodovico famously tells Iago to "Look on the tragic loading of this bed" (5.2.363). The bed loaded with theatrically violated bodies is a perfect emblem of the life of the flesh that has transcended the realm of socio-symbolic identities.

In the 1995 film of the play directed by Oliver Parker, Iago ends up on that tragically loaded bed, too, on top of the bodies of Othello and Emilia and Desdemona, leering at the camera.[19] That, I think, is exactly the direction the play wants to move. As with Desdemona and Emilia, Iago ends the scene in a state of undeadness; Othello stabs him but Iago rises again, chipperly announcing: "I bleed, sir, but not killed" (5.2.288). Moreover, Lodovico's lurid promises to torture Iago past the limit of death, to torture him in a way that will keep him alive, makes him join the same fantasy space that Othello, Desdemona, and Emilia (and for that matter the undead Cassio and Roderigo[20]) have all entered:

> For this slave,
> If there be any cunning cruelty
> That can torment him much and hold him long,
> It shall be his. You shall close prisoner rest,
> Till that the nature of your fault be known
> To the Venetian state. Come, bring him away. (5.2.332–337)

The whole statement is undertaken inside a legal frame, but if this is the act by which state authority is put back together, then state authority again seems founded on an act of raw will exercised on a body, notably the body of Iago, whose torture the audience is left to contemplate at the very end of the play: "To you, lord governor," says Lodovico, "Remains the censure of this hellish villain,/ The time, the place, the torture. O, enforce it!/ Myself will straight aboard, and to the state/ This heavy act with heavy heart relate" (5.2.367–371).

My premise here is that Iago gets what he wants, and that what he wants is to force more and more people to recognize themselves as abjectly and inescapably subject to sovereign power, and thereby to force them to interact with each other and then also with Iago himself at the level of the flesh and its perverse vulnerabilities when exposed to raw state power. Iago seeks, and ultimately finds, an expression of self that is a genuine alternative to the constraining, limiting experience of self-as-responsible-before-the-law against which he is rebelling, and it is expressed in his willful silence in the face of a legal inquiry and in his willingness and even eagerness to be tortured. There is a perverse pleasure, an ecstasy, for Iago in becoming what he has made others into; namely, bare life, flesh finally stripped of its socio-symbolic coordinates, and stripped of those coordinates by acts of state terror in the darkness of the torture chambers.

Throughout the play, under Iago's tutelage, characters cease to respect and celebrate the bounded ego that is affirmed by a sovereign political order and come to interact with each other at the level of flesh theatrically stripped of socio-symbolic personhood, as Iago's socio-symbolic personhood will now be stripped from him by a spectacle of torture. And, as with the violence of the riot, as with the violence of the bedroom, the violence of the torture will be rendered performative, theatrical, fantasy more than reality. For the torture of Iago is not, of course, real at all; it is only playing with the limits of life rather than really violating those limits.

And if Iago has finally found a liberating experience of selfhood, then so has Othello when he is stripped at long last, when at long last he strips himself, of his socio-symbolic identity, and therefore of the responsibility to anchor socio-symbolic identities. Once captured, Othello is disarmed of his sword but threatens to kill even in nakedness: "naked as I am, I will assault thee" (5.2.259). That is not a bad emblem for what the play as a whole explores, a form of interpersonal practice that combines socio-symbolic nakedness, even death, with a transformational theatrical violence. Othello is disarmed twice before he brings out a third dagger to stab himself. These weapons are no longer signs of his socio-symbolic potency and his power as the sovereign linchpin of the republican order; they have become comically detached from Othello's body and they signify weakness or perhaps a yearning for the kind of bodily relationships outlined by the theatrical swordplay of the riot scenes. As Othello puts it, "I am not valiant neither;/ But every puny whipster gets my sword./ But why should honor outlive honesty?/ Let it go all" (5.2.244–247). Moreover, Othello's final detachable sword also mediates a fantasmatic union with "the turbaned Turk," the "circumcisèd dog," whom Othello once "took by th' throat.../ And smote him—thus" (5.2.353–356). Here, Othello is both the stabber and the stabee, both the Venetian Christian and the Turkish traducer of the state, and in that sense this final act of transformative, theatrical violence allows Othello to transcend the very symbolic difference that Othello has meant to anchor in this play. Othello's suicide is an explicit act of theatricalization, since he is playing (or replaying) a role from his earlier life, and this act of violence is therefore endowed with the luminous, playful quality that most violence in the play acquires. We half expect Othello to rise from the dead, as of course he does a few lines later, once the story has run its course. As with the riots and stabbings and the final, lurid promise of torture, no one dies, no one is even hurt. That is the founding convention of the theater: they are only playing parts, enacting fantasies, which only means that everyone who is killed can be killed again (every time the play begins anew). It is also the founding convention of a fleshly experience of others that is not about affirming identity and personhood, but is essentially about an escape from the responsibility to invest in, to fall in love with, the socio-symbolic attributes of personhood, an escape into a kind of freedom that comes from passing through sovereign power and into the multiplying, clustering geometries of the flesh.

VI. Humors

I want to explore now the way in which the play theorizes the life of the flesh it displays. Famously, Iago works by implanting new ideas, or what he calls "conceits," into the minds of those he manipulates (from Roderigo to Cassio to Othello). It is, of course, somewhat paradoxical that the body-mediated forms of interaction I have been describing are triggered by cognitive ideas. I will argue that the play sees the life of the flesh as a result of substituting a cognitive theory of the emotions (associated with Iago) for a humoral theory that the play associates with a kind of baseline social and psychological health. From an early modern standpoint, it is not only the specific ideas that Iago implants that are perverse, but any cognitively triggered emotional life, any emotional life triggered by and defined by ideas.

One of the most exciting developments in Renaissance studies over the past decade has been the exploration of the humoral experience of emotions. Gail Kern Paster and Mary Floyd-Wilson have been key figures in this regard, and it is noteworthy that both of these critics have written important accounts of *Othello*.[21] One of the key questions that the humoral perspective raises is how emotional experience is valued or what kind of information it is thought to carry. Following in the wake of critics like Paster and Floyd-Wilson, others treat the humoral perspective on emotional life as if it suggested that emotions were brute facts that had no meaning or significance for the subjects experiencing them—as if they were "brute facts" about the state the body is in or, perhaps, as if they were like "hormones." However, both Paster and Floyd-Wilson make clear that from the humoral perspective emotions are not brute facts that make no reference to the self or a self-conception; rather, they place the self within a larger horizon of meaning, though the ways humors do so differs somewhat for Paster and Floyd-Wilson.[22]

From Paster's perspective, for example, the emotions give the self various kinds of information about itself in registers that are no longer available to us. Paster argues that early modern humoral experiences could be understood within the context of a cosmological reality in which the self is embedded. It is the patterns of the stars or the weather that penetrate the self and give it an emotional experience that registers the self's location in space and time. Even humoral character types (and the mechanical proneness to feeling certain emotions that they bring) are aligned with a cosmic perspective insofar as they are defined by the time of year of conception, a view that Edmund ridicules in his famous speech in *King Lear* making fun of his father's astrological superstitions. Paster also makes clear that this cosmic hierarchy is at the same time aligned with a social hierarchy, and that certain humoral patterns of experience are characteristically associated with certain class (and gender) positions. Moreover, from a religious perspective, the humors could be felt to point to the self's position on a cosmic stage, where an epochal battle is fought out in which sin is pitted against grace, and where what happens within the "soul" is inseparable from what happens in the world.[23] Finally, Paster argues that passions could also be intelligible as individual etiological narratives—as in her revealing account of the greensickness as a context for understanding Desdemona's trajectory in the play.[24] In all of these instances, humoral emotions are characterized by their intelligibility, by their orientation to the world.

The same can be said, of course, even more obviously for Floyd-Wilson's geo-humoralism; it, too, greatly expands rather than contracts the ways in which emotions express and reflect what we would term social and symbolic identity. In her account of *Othello*, for example, Othello is essentially defined by being a southerner, by having a southern disposition; as Desdemona says, when confronted by evidence of Othello's jealousy, "I think the sun where he was born/ Drew all such humors from him" (3.4.30–31). From a humoral perspective, in short, emotions give the self (and observers) information about the self's make-up and about its coordinates in space and time.

It is against this background assumption that Iago does his work. He stages a movement in the other direction in which characters are pushed away from being legible and visible in a socio-humoral, cosmo-humoral, geo-humoral, or etiological framework. And oddly, Iago accomplishes this derangement by means of something that is essential to the way emotions are made meaningful in our modern context; namely, a cognitive framework. In the default modern cognitive framework, emotions represent judgments by a person about who or what he or she is and what is important to him or her. From this modern perspective, therefore, emotions give you information about yourself, they tell you who you are and what you care about. In a modern perspective, cognitive emotions affirm your innermost sense of selfhood.

Yet in the early modern period, against the default backdrop of the humoral framework, a vision of emotions as triggered by something as ephemeral as a cognitive judgment is downright perverse. It is a perversion that Iago eagerly champions, nevertheless. He sees emotions as judgments by the self regarding what the self cares about and where it is attached to the world, therefore he sees emotions as being at least potentially under the control of the individual. Iago famously compares the management of the emotional life to gardening. In advising Roderigo to adjust his suicidal disappointment that Desdemona has married Othello, Iago advises him to adjust his feelings:

> Our bodies are gardens, to the which our wills are gardeners; so that if we will plant nettles or sow lettuce, set hyssop and weed up thyme, supply it with one gender of herbs or distract it with many – either to have it sterile with idleness or manured with industry – why, the power and corrigible authority of this lies in our wills. If the beam of our lives had not one scale of reason to poise another of sensuality, the blood and baseness of our natures would conduct us to most prepost'rous conclusions. But we have reason to cool our raging motions, our carnal stings or unbitted lusts; whereof I take this that you call love to be a sect or scion. (1.3.320–332)

Though Iago does speak of an innate, bodily component to love and lust ("the blood and baseness of our natures"), his point is that Roderigo should manage his passionate life by rearranging his conscious expectations and judgments about the world.

In modern psychological theory, the cognitive approach functions as a norm: the emotional life is understood as judgments by the self about the world and what matters to the self. From this modern perspective, emotions therefore affirm a certain socio-symbolic theory of personhood. However, in this play, in Iago's hands, in the context of a basically humoral culture of the emotions, the cognitive approach to the emotions is deviant or dysfunctional. Iago's cognitive theory of the emotions is central to his project of exploding the geo-social coordinates that are conventionally carried by emotional experience. Iago rewires basic humoral dispositions by implanting judgments or ideas. Yet from an early modern perspective, the problem is not merely that the specific judgments Iago implants in Othello are wrong, but that any emotion-as-idea is deviant.

When Iago first starts deranging Othello, it is the very notion that there is an idea that has the power to generate emotional experience that horrifies Othello:

IAGO: Did Michael Cassio, when you wooed my lady,
          Know of your love?
OTHELLO: He did, from first to last. Why dost thou ask?
IAGO: But for a satisfaction of my thought;
          No further harm.
OTHELLO: Why of thy thought, Iago?
IAGO: I did not think he had been acquainted with her.
OTHELLO: O, yes, and went between us very oft.
IAGO: Indeed?
OTHELLO: Indeed? Ay, indeed! Discern'st thou aught in that?
          Is he not honest?
IAGO: Honest, my lord?
OTHELLO: Honest. Ay, honest.
IAGO: My lord, for aught I know.
OTHELLO: What dost thou think?
IAGO: Think, my lord?
OTHELLO: Think my lord?
          By heaven, thou echo'st me
          As if there were some monster in thy thought
          Too hideous to be shown. Thou dost mean something:

> …
> [Thou] didst contract and purse thy brow together,
> As if thou then hadst shut up in thy brain
> Some horrible conceit. If thou dost love me,
> Show me thy thought. (3.3.94–116)

Iago does not (yet) spell out the idea, he only suggests that there *is* an idea—"a horrible conceit," as a horrified Othello puts it—that has the power to change everything about Othello's emotional make-up. Part of the point of the play is that a character as thoroughly submerged in a humoral framework as is Othello is unusually vulnerable to any cognitive manipulation. Only a few lines later, Othello has completely given himself over to this new fantasy of the emotional life, of the self as essentially defined and determined by something as weak as words:

> Nay, yet there's more in this.
> I prithee speak to me as to thy thinkings,
> As thou dost ruminate, and give thy worst of thoughts
> The worst of words. (3.3.130–133)

When Iago goes on to claim that what he has installed in Othello is a "dangerous conceit" (3.3.326), there is no humoral component to his understanding of what he is doing to Othello at all.

From the early modern perspective, cosmological humoral emotions are "real" or stable; the cognitively triggered emotion is the false, inauthentic, theatrical emotion, by contrast. As Brabantio says during the opening council scene, "But words are words. I never yet did hear/ That the bruised heart was pierced through the ear" (1.3.218–219). In the absence of even a rudimentary cognitive structure of self, Iago is surprised at how easy it is to unhinge basically humoral character types by injecting ideas into their inner life.

> Trifles light as air
> Are to the jealous confirmations strong
> As proofs of holy writ. This may do something.
> The Moor already changes with my poison:
> Dangerous conceits are in their natures poisons,
> Which at the first are scarce found to distaste,
> But with a little act upon the blood
> Burn like the mines of sulphur. I did say so.
> Look where he comes! (3.3.322–330)

Part of the reason mere "conceits" are so powerful in deranging Othello's emotional life is that they are so different from the early modern humoral norm. In this context, a character like Othello can be imagined to have very little experience of thinking of himself and his emotional life as a distinctive and irreducibly individual expression of his personal preferences and judgments about the world. He is used to thinking of his self as having a geo-humoral stability; it is precisely this normative stability that is radically disrupted by Iago's "conceit." If Othello were defined as a character who—like modern readers, for instance—thought of his entire emotional life as being the result of a bundle of cognitive judgments about the world, then he would not be so vulnerable to the power of a single conceit, a single thought, to radically unsettle him. However, absent a fully developed and hegemonized personality framework for explaining emotional life, Othello is an easy mark for Iago's conceits. Whereas modern subjects consider that they are most fully themselves when they feel cognitively structured emotions, Othello feels as though the powerful emotions Iago's conceit conjures up are an alien force that will take away the old self he values.

If Iago holds a view of emotions as basically driven by conceits—or judgments by the self about the world—he certainly does not view emotions as an expression of core personality, but rather as an expression of theatrical self or body management. For what ensues from Iago's cognitive derangement of the self's humoral investment in the world is the (theatrical) spectacle of bodies that are perversely animated. In other words, by implanting "conceits," Iago unsettles the standard humoral networks by which the self is inserted into a world, leaving behind emotionally inflamed bodies that are moving and interacting at a tangent to legible social patterns.

In the play, what replaces the stable social identity secured by a stable socio-humoral fabric is an intensified emotional experience, but one in which emotions are deprived of any legible social significance. Whereas in a humoral framework the passions can be "read" for the information about the self that they convey, within the emotional space generated by the play, emotions come to seem a primary, corporeal reality that undermines any notion of a legible socio-symbolic self, an experience that Othello describes as his name becoming blackened:

> By the world,
> I think my wife be honest, and think she is not;
> I think that thou art just, and think thou art not.
> I'll have some proof. My name, that was as fresh

> As Dian's visage, is now begrimed and black
> As mine own face. (3.3.383–388)

And as Iago's conceits shred Othello's old sense of self, he substitutes for it a performative hatred that does not offer a compensatory experience of selfhood:

> Arise, black vengeance, from thy hollow hell!
> Yield up, O love, thy crown and hearted throne
> To tyrannous hate! Swell, bosom, with thy fraught,
> For 'tis of aspics' tongues! (3.3.447–450)

When Emilia asks Desdemona whether Othello has become jealous, Desdemona answers, "I think the sun where he was born/ Drew all such humors from him" (3.4.30–31). In other words, Desdemona reasserts Othello's geo-humoral identity, but the point of the play is surely that, unbeknownst to her, this humoral legibility has been eroded and replaced by a radically unmoored and therefore theatricalized emotional life driven by conceits.

In that sense, the difficulty with Floyd-Wilson's account is that she sees (quite rightly) that there is such a thing as geo-humoralism operating in the play, but fails to see that the play is about a disruption of this perspective. While the emotions that arise once this humoral frame has been disrupted by Iago's cognitive attacks have no significance for Othello, they nevertheless drive him more and more; specifically, they drive him into an increasingly physical, body-mediated relationship with both Iago and Desdemona. Iago's conceits trigger an emotional storm, and the emotional life that ensues has an existence of its own, quite unhinged from the conventionally social self. The non-humoral emotions that Iago triggers with conceits take on a kind of operatic grandeur, which is to say they pass beyond the essential smallness of the ego, the self with a functioning personality that structures emotional life, and into a transformative life of the flesh.

The kernel of the idea that Shakespeare explores here is connected to his experience of the theater. For if Iago uses cognitive ideas to unhinge a self from its "normal" connections to a humoral nexus, then Shakespeare's script does precisely the same thing, first to the actors and then to audience members. Shakespeare's words act as a perversely animating force: they represent a set of judgments and ideas that animate the actors' bodies by stripping them out of their humoral world. Moreover, as a medium, the theater is essentially defined by implanting conceits in audience members who "know" that the conceit is untrue, but are nevertheless emotionally affected (even unhinged) by the conceit. It is to the essential role of the theater in representing the life of the flesh, and even in transferring that life of the flesh to spectators via the emotional experience the theater generates, that I turn next in considering Shakespeare's cruelest play, *King Lear*.

4
Life Outside the Law: Torture and the Flesh in *King Lear*

Like *Measure for Measure*, *King Lear* is a clear-eyed investigation of the nature of sovereign power. And like that other play, it discloses the transcendental potential of the life of the flesh that is woven into the very fabric of sovereign power. After Lear resigns, power is reconstituted in the hands of Goneril and Regan, but insofar as Lear keeps for himself the "name, and all th' addition to a king," their power is devoid of the legitimating veil of tradition and ritual (1.1.137).[1] Their dark reign reveals the truth that sovereign power makes bodies into subjects only by making them utterly and even abjectly subject to arbitrary will.[2] Indeed, the play suggests that the purest emblem of the institution of sovereign power is torture, the torture to which Gloucester is explicitly subjected and to which Lear and the others who are cast off into the wilderness are implicitly subjected. However, like the other plays I have examined, *King Lear* uncovers a path through abject exposure to sovereign power into an alternative form of life, founded on the transformative recognition that the self's utter dependence on sovereign power for an identity also unhinges that identity. This recognition brings to light the substrate of the flesh on which any socio-symbolic identity is mounted. In characters who recognize that they are mercilessly exposed to sovereign power, the play brings to light a luminescent fleshliness that is capable of entering into new forms of connection with other flesh.

In this chapter I will make two interconnected arguments. First, insofar as the play connects a crisis in sovereignty to a crisis in the socio-symbolic identities of characters inside it, the play reconfigures the same philosophical question investigated by Eric L. Santner in his *On the Psycho-Theology of Everyday Life*.[3] Santner argues that there is always a disconnect in psychic life between the experience of self and the symbolic identities conferred on selves by social life. Shakespeare's basic

gambit in *King Lear*—and the core of the play's unsettling radicalism—
is to force together an investigation of how individuals within the
social order experience their own relation to the symbolic identities their society assigns them with an analytical recognition of the
essentially arbitrary nature of sovereignty. Thus, Lear's resignation and
the consequent destructuring of sovereign power appear inside Lear
and other characters as a derangement of the way the self inhabits
its socially given roles and a shift to a compensatory experience of
collectivity founded on the flesh.

I will also make a second argument. More than the other plays I have
examined, *King Lear* makes clear that the collective life of the flesh is
brought to the stage primarily through a self-conscious use (or perhaps
abuse) of the theatricality of the medium. Inside the imagined world
of the play, characters are exposed to represented forms of sovereign
power, and through this exposure they are gradually deprived of their
socio-symbolic legibility within the symbolic universe of the play.
In other words, exposed to sovereign power inside the framework
of the play, characters are separated out of their defined roles within
the drama, but without being quite reduced to actors (or the bodies
of actors). In being incompletely separated from their socio-symbolic
identity, actor-characters come to inhabit that luminous, liminal
category of the flesh. And as flesh, they engage in gestural interactions
(often with a subtext of ritual violence) with other characters on the
stage who are also incompletely separated from their identities. Again
and again in *King Lear*, characters are stripped of their roles within the
imagined socio-symbolic order of the play and come to rely instead on
histrionic, gestural interactions to connect to one another in ways that
bypass functional integration into a functioning socio-symbolic order.
Following the work of Shell in *The End of Kinship*, I will wind up arguing
that one emblem of the transformed life of the flesh enacted by this
gestural theater is a lateral evasion of the incest taboo that depends
on the existence of stable social identities. As staged by the play, flesh
stripped bare of its socio-symbolic coordinates is capable of experiences
of love that transcend the love mediated by stable socio-symbolic
identities that Cordelia, at the beginning of the play, calls love "according to my bond" (1.1.93).

I. Sovereignty and Social Identity

Lear initiates the process of laying bare the unsettling nature of
sovereignty, and he does so by divesting himself of power only to then

undergo (for the first time, as it were) the phenomenological experience of exposure to sovereign power. Having lost sovereign power, Lear is forced to recognize the utter dependence of his own socio-symbolic identity on the good will of his (now de facto sovereign) daughters. Confronting this experience, Lear develops a general theory of the paradoxical link between exposure to sovereign power and the ability to inhabit a social identity. He articulates this theory in the two most important set speeches of the play, the "reason not the need" speech that he delivers before he enters the wilderness, and the "poor naked wretches" speech he delivers when he meets Edgar masquerading as Poor Tom.

Trying to defend his wish to maintain a retinue of knights, the last outward mark of his old identity, and confronted with Goneril's question of why he "needs" these knights, Lear argues that persons are defined as persons by being allowed more than they need. And he will go on to argue that the "extra" that endows anyone with human personhood is, in fact, a grant of sovereign power:

GONERIL: Hear me, my lord:
        What need you five-and-twenty, ten, or five [of your own
        knights]
        To follow in a house where twice so many
        Have a command to tend you?
REGAN: What needs one?
LEAR: O reason not the need! Our basest beggars
        Are in the poorest thing superfluous.
        Allow not nature more than nature needs,
        Man's life is cheap as beasts'. Thou art a lady;
        If only to go warm were gorgeous,
        Why, nature needs not what thou gorgeous wearest,
        Which scarcely keeps thee warm. (2.4.260–270)

In this speech, Lear argues that human beings are differentiated from animals only by being treated as though they were entitled to a symbolic surplus, something more than the bare minimum they need for physical survival. Lear argues that if the standard of necessity alone is applied to human beings, then they in fact cease to be human beings and become indistinguishable from animals: "Allow not nature more than nature needs,/ Man's life is cheap as beasts'." What Lear homes in on is the essential and irreducible disconnect between the life of a person as defined by society and the mere fact of biological/corporeal life that subtends that social investiture. According to Lear, the bare life of man is in fact as cheap as a beast's, except for the superficial uniforms that society (embodied in the sovereign) puts on that life—a retinue of knights in the case of Lear, a fancy gown in the case of Goneril and Regan. Persons are made by the social roles they inhabit and carry out; the social role alone confers dignity and status as a person and there is nothing underneath—in the soul, as it were—that would justify or anchor that symbolic status; what is underneath is a mere animal.

Later on, when Lear meets Edgar masquerading as a madman, he believes he is encountering the animal core of humans:

Is man no more than this? Consider him well. Thou owest the worm no silk, the beast no hide, the sheep no wool, the cat no perfume. Ha! here's three on's [i.e., "of us," referring to Lear, Kent, and Gloucester] are sophisticated. Thou art the thing itself; unaccommodated man is no more but such a poor, bare, forked animal as thou art." (3.4.103–108)

Stripped of all the layers of beautiful clothing and perfume that normally envelop persons, Lear finds in Edgar only "a poor, bare, forked animal." Yet Edgar is merely masquerading as a mad beggar and at the end of the play his conventional social identity as an aristocrat is restored to him; what Lear identifies as the unaccommodated man, the thing itself, is, in fact, a disguised aristocrat. But, paradoxically, this is precisely Lear's point in the "reason not the need" speech: to be (essentially) human is to be (contingently) protected from having the naked and thoroughly animal core itself appear, as Edgar (ironically) protects himself from having his core identity show by assuming the disguise of Mad Tom.[4]

The important point for my understanding of *King Lear* is that the process by which the extra bit that makes humans human and not animal is attached to the fleshly underpinning is an essentially political process. Lear's initial insight comes as he stands before daughters who are now functionally his sovereigns; as the play unfolds, Lear becomes more and more committed to defining the state (or the sovereign) as having the responsibility to stamp human beings with the symbolic surplus that defines a person (as against a mere animal). Lear theorizes the essentially *political* force of his insight about "human" identity in a second speech—the "poor naked wretches" speech—that he delivers once he is cast out from the social world that is structured by the sovereign power of his daughters. When Lear first meets Edgar disguised as Mad Tom, he says that he now recognizes this apparent madman as a failure of state power. Lear imagines that universal personhood can only be an achievement of state power, and that bringing about such universal personhood was a political function that he neglected when he was king himself:

> Poor naked wretches, wheresoe'er you are,
> That bide the pelting of this pitiless storm,
> How shall your houseless heads and unfed sides,
> Your looped and windowed raggedness defend you
> From seasons such as these? O, I have ta'en
> Too little care of this. Take physic, pomp,
> Expose thyself to feel what wretches feel,
> That thou mayst shake the superflux to them
> And show the heavens more just. (3.4.30–38)

By invoking the essentially political virtue of "justice," even if transplanted from the court to the heavens, Lear frames his own experience of poverty as medicinal ("Take physic, pomp,/ Expose thyself to feel what wretches feel"), correcting a sovereign structure that had failed to equally distribute the extra bit that makes human animals into persons. As with the "reason not the need" speech, Lear does not imagine any kind of really existing core identity in human beings that should simply be respected or acknowledged by the state—Lear is no proto-liberal "natural rights" theorist. Instead, he imagines that it is the ideal responsibility of the state voluntaristically to invest bodies with personhood on a universal scale. The ideal that Lear posits here is a state that guarantees to all the "superflux" needed to grant them human dignity, and it is as if he imagines that if he were to return to being king himself, he would act by universalizing this sovereign investiture of identity. Lear invokes a redistributive vision of justice and indulges in the fantasy that human society might be regenerated in a more just way around a more universalized notion of personhood, if only a more benign representative of sovereign power than his daughters could be instituted.[5]

Yet comforting as Lear's vision of a beneficent state that bestows on everyone the sacred excess of personhood may be, the agenda of the play is to recognize something much darker, but also something potentially more liberating. The fact that persons are utterly at the mercy of sovereign power for the superflux that alone makes them persons is itself disabling, as it is for Lear when he must beg to be allowed to hang on to his soldiers. However, I will argue that for Lear and the other characters in the play, when the sacred surplus of personhood is withheld through a disabling encounter with raw sovereign power, what becomes visible is not "animal life" but the ambivalent, generative substrate of all human life. Human beings are always born into an order of sovereign power and are only secondarily excluded; the fact that humans *qua* humans always presumptively inhabit some socio-symbolic role or other within social life means that when characters like Lear and Edgar, Gloucester and even Kent shear off their social role in the imagined world of the play, they do not become "mere" animals whose existential identity is unproblematic. I will argue that by being stripped of identity by a sovereign power that is itself the precondition for any identity, characters are transformed into that special, luminous category of the flesh that I have explored throughout this book. It is this category and its possibilities for social interaction that Shakespeare investigates in *King Lear*.[6]

II. The Wilderness: The Deformation of Social Identity

Immediately after confronting the discursive knot of sovereignty and identity in the "reason not the need" speech, Lear feels his own socio-symbolic identity cracking open and an alien life of the flesh arise within him. As he senses his old identity as king being taken away from him, he does not feel like a "mere" animal or like a "nothing," to use one of the play's operative words that always turns out to be a red herring; instead, he feels like flesh: "O me, my heart! My rising heart! But down!" (2.4.112). The heart here ceases to be an organ that merely enables symbolic life, the life of the person; instead of being subordinated to socio-symbolic personhood, the heart takes on a life of its own, pointing to a beating, pulsating thing within Lear that lies beneath all social identities and yet is not identical to any social identity. In the play, the "heart" is often used as an emblem of an alien life of the flesh, as are tears, like the tears that Lear produces (or that are produced through Lear) at this eruptive moment:

> Life and death! I am asham'd
> That thou hast power to shake my manhood thus,
> That these hot tears which break from me perforce
> Should make thee worth them. Blasts and fogs upon thee!
> Th' untented woundings of a father's curse
> Pierce every sense about thee! Old fond eyes,
> Beweep this cause again I'll pluck ye out

And cast you with the waters that you loose
To temper clay. (1.4.293–300)

These tears are not an expression of a true, emotional core self. Rather, Lear experiences them as an animated, alien life that has seized the surfaces of his body to produce non-self fluids, and he threatens to pluck his eyes out to stop this process, which feels like it is undermining his personhood from below or from within. At this early moment, Lear still resists the process, but soon enough he will give himself over to the life of the flesh. And as he comes to see himself as essentially a living, breathing, pulsating lump of flesh that has been forcibly divorced from any socio-symbolic identity, he comes to think of his former socio-symbolic identity as a lie: as he puts it near the end of the wilderness sequence, "They told me I was everything. 'Tis a lie—I am not ague-proof."[7] Similarly, later, when Lear and Gloucester are reunited, Gloucester offers to kiss Lear's hand, to which Lear replies, "Let me wipe it first; it smells of mortality."

The animated, fleshly life that Lear encounters within himself becomes the focus of the play's most sustained investigative energies, and what the play turns out to be especially interested in are the possibilities for a kind of collective life founded on this fleshly life. Lear's resignation initiates a process that discloses the flesh in himself and in everyone and anyone who touches him. It will be no surprise that I see the wilderness as the theatrical space in which this question is most insistently explored. What is characteristic of the wilderness is a form of gravity that connects "characters" who have been de-characterized in just the way that Lear has been de-characterized.

While the space of the wilderness may appear to be outside of sovereign power, it is in fact not outside sovereign power at all but is a creation of sovereign power. The wilderness is shot through with agents of state authority—Goneril and Regan's agents including Oswald, and later Cordelia's soldiers, and, moreover, everyone who is cast out into the wilderness is there by virtue of exposure to sovereign power—Lear, obviously, but also Edgar, Gloucester, Kent, and the fool. And yet, the wilderness does allow a different way of living with sovereign power, using exposure to sovereign power to animate a fleshly life that provides an alternative foundation for interpersonal (or better: intercorporeal) connections. In the wilderness, the insistent focus is on the morphologies of connection between characters who have all been stripped of their conventional socio-symbolic identity, as Lear has been stripped of his, and who have all felt the flesh arise within themselves, as Lear has.

By situating the life of the flesh within the structurally complex space of the wilderness, *King Lear* illustrates, perhaps better than the other plays I have examined in this book, that the category of the flesh is not pre-political, but rather is fully political, because it arises only in the moment that the self experiences its necessary and inescapable exposure to sovereign power. To return to the terms I used to describe *Julius Caesar*, it is almost as if the wilderness is an inverted version of liberal fantasies of a civil society, but divorced of any sense of the foundational status of the individual person that liberal theory silently assumes as a gift of the gods rather than a contingent achievement of sovereign power, the sovereign grant of a symbolic garment, as Lear now understands human dignity. In the experience of exposure to the sovereign power that grants stable socio-symbolic identities, the play discovers a door to an undiscovered country of collective life that lies beyond the bourn of the human, that contingent, state-created form of life. And if a collective life in humans who have been stripped down to the point where they lose their humanness—as Lear and Edgar and the fool and even Kent and Gloucester seem to do—seems dystopian, then it is nevertheless also liberating, in allowing us to imagine a network of social connections that rise beyond the contingent, and often abusive, dictates of a state-imposed collective identity.

All of the major relationships that Lear has with other characters are reconfigured in the wilderness. The transformation is most obvious in Lear's concern for the fool, and most especially his concern for the fool's flesh:

> Come on, my boy, How dost, my boy? Art cold?
> I am cold myself. Where is this straw, my fellow?
> ...
> Poor fool and knave, I have one part in my heart
> That's sorry yet for thee. (3.2.69–74)

Similarly, the wilderness relationship between Lear and Edgar comes to seem mediated by the care of the flesh. Exposed as he is to a sovereign power that hunts him throughout the kingdom, Edgar attempts to preserve himself by tactically assuming the identity of a madman and beggar, while claiming that the "true" Edgar always remains beneath this costume. Indeed, Edgar's design in taking on the role of Mad Tom is to "preserve myself" (2.3.6), and within the conventions of the theater an actor is always presumptively a character, so that when an actor strips off his or her costume it is only to be his or her character at a deeper level. On the face of it, this is exactly what happens to Edgar, who gives up his socio-symbolic identity only in order to hang on to it all the more tenaciously. However, in the wilderness, what begins as a merely tactical stripping away of his costume does become a real stripping of his identity, one that discloses a core of animated flesh that is the same as the core of flesh that Lear has discovered beating and crying within himself. For Edgar, as with Lear, the first sign of the emergence of an alien life of the flesh are tears, the tears that Edgar begins to shed when he sees Lear. In an aside to the audience Edgar says, "My tears begin to take his part so much/ They mar my counterfeiting" (3.6.59–60). At one level, he seems to say that his true identity surfaces here. But at another level, Edgar experiences his tears as something that is forced on him, the result of a larger phenomenological sizing up of the situation to which the ego must catch up, as it were.[8] At the moment his tears mar his counterfeiting, Edgar is not a self who encounters an object and thinks about what it means to him; rather, as a psychological subject, he merely recognizes a situation he is already inside of, he catches up to the fact that he is already inside Lear and Lear's state of affairs rather than remaining protectedly apart from him, and he catches up to this by taking note of the fluids his body is emitting toward Lear. By means of his tears, Edgar here has a transformed experience of the self and of the self's ineluctable connection to others. Suddenly, the connection between self and other is not mediated by the social role onto which Edgar has hung so tenaciously; rather, the connection between self and other is mediated by a shared experience of the flesh, and of the fluids that the flesh emits. It is as if the social disguise (not merely the disguise of Mad Tom, but the disguise of "Edgar" himself) is penetrated to reveal a naked body, naked flesh subject to the radically unsettling phenomenon of corporeal passion that ties him overwhelmingly to Lear, despite his best efforts to maintain his distance.

One of the most important mechanisms by which flesh connects to other flesh in the wilderness is through a self-conscious theatricality. Once Edgar feels the tears that connect him to Lear welling up within him, he enters into the theatrical fantasy world that Lear has constructed. Lear imagines that he sees his daughter's little lap dogs before him and Edgar now pretends to yell at them:

LEAR: The little dogs and all,
         Trey, Blanch, and Sweetheart, see, they bark at me.
EDGAR: Tom will throw his head at them. Avaunt, you curs! (3.6.61–63)

The constitutive theatricality of the wilderness is one of its most distinctive features. It is almost as if, once reduced to flesh, characters become raw material that must be reassembled by means of the fantasized role-playing that Lear constantly sponsors.[9] In a sense, the role-playing exercises over which Lear presides in the wilderness are ways of taking bodies that have ceased to be characters in the story of the play called *King Lear* and setting them into motion with one another. In such moments, theater comes to seem a way of working with the life of the flesh, managing it, building it, structuring it into a new form of sociability.

The purest emblem of this way of using the theater is the trial scene that exists only in the Q version. (In general, I would say that the Q version of the play explores most fully the radical possibility of a life of the flesh that goes beyond a functional subjection to sovereign power.) In setting up the trial, Lear does not imagine getting rid of sovereign power. Rather, he imagines exposing his daughters to the same desiccating power to which he has been exposed, and thus to bring them, also, into the alternative community he has founded in the wilderness. Lear does not imagine simple personal revenge but a form of revenge that parallels his own fate, in which the daughters are imagined to encounter a legally constructed form of sovereign power. Lear invites Edgar, the fool, and Kent to act as judges: "Thou robèd man of justice, take thy place;/ And thou, his yokefellow of equity,/ Bench by his side. You are o' th' commission" (Q 3.6.32–34).[10] By referring to the fool as Edgar's "yokefellow of equity," Lear invokes the prerogative power ("equity") of the king to amend and ameliorate legal judgments that are technically correct but morally wrong. And because the trial-play puts characters who have ceased to be characters in the play called *King Lear* into motion with one another, it is a scaffold for the life of the flesh. The play-within-the-play is imagination-work that puts the body of Lear into active, moving relation with the bodies of Edgar and the fool and Kent, even as the trial-play also puts Lear into an active relationship with the (imagined) bodies of his daughters.

Lear can imagine a relationship with his daughters only by imagining them as inhabiting the same state of utter condemnation that Lear himself now inhabits. Drawing again on the legal framework that Shakespeare uses in *Measure for Measure*, Shakespeare has Lear imagine Chancery Court proceedings that are an extension of the prerogative power of the monarch to correct the common law when needed. When Lear imagines himself appearing as a witness, he imagines taking an oath that derives from the seemingly independent authority of the court, rather than his own (now defunct) authority as king: "I here take my oath before this honorable assembly she kicked the poor king her father" (Q 3.6.42–44). Yet Lear's fantasy does not seem to be about restoring his own authority or dignity, nor about being compensated for the morally wrong way he has been treated—on the road Lear is traveling, there is no way home. Rather, Lear's legal fantasy seems to be about exposing Goneril and Regan to the same "raw" sovereign power that Lear himself has encountered, therefore reducing them to the same condemned status as mere flesh to which he has been reduced, and then reconnecting with them on that terrain. As condemned flesh, Lear fantasizes about fantasmatically entering into them, something that is suggested by the (horrifying) curses that Lear casts at their imagined bodies and Lear's fantasy of "anatomizing" Regan. Lear imagines Regan escaping as a result of having paid off one of the officers of the court (a "false justicer"), and vivisection is the response he proposes: "Then let them anatomize Regan, see what breeds about her heart. Is there any cause in nature that makes this hardness?" (Q 3.6.71–73). The word "anatomize" invokes the practice of anatomical dissection after death, a way of revealing the body's hidden secrets, but also a spectacular way of violating the body; in Lear's mind "anatomize" verges on vivisection, since he imagines it as a (quasi-judicial) response to Regan's (imagined) escape from legal custody a few lines earlier: "And here's another [i.e., Regan], whose warped looks proclaim/ What store her heart is made on. Stop her there!/ Arms, arms, sword, fire! Corruption in the place!/ False justicer, why hast thou let her scape?" (Q 3.6.48–51). In place of a "family reunion" in which Lear and Regan would relate as father and daughter, Lear imagines a much more unsettling, profoundly corporeal union between them built on recognizing and spectacularly destroying the body beneath the role.

This transformative, theatricalized life of the flesh carries a potent if disturbing sexual charge. Almost from the first instant he is exposed to the unsettling force of sovereignty in Goneril's house, Lear responds to the experience of having his identity unhinged with a heightened interest in the sexuality of his daughters, a sexuality that he specifically seeks to deprive of its so-called natural reproductive function, as when he curses Goneril:

> Hear, Nature, hear, dear goddess, hear:
> Suspend thy purpose if thou didst intend
> To make this creature fruitful.
> Into her womb convey sterility. (1.4.271–274)

Obviously Lear is condemning Goneril, but the vividness with which he imagines nature penetrating her womb to convey sterility into it suggests the operative force of sexuality. The desire to penetrate the hidden depths of the daughter's body that Lear's curse reveals reappears in the fantasy of "anatomizing" Regan while she is yet alive, and both suggest a *wish* for a form of connection between Lear and his daughter, a forbidden touch of the flesh that violates not only the narrative logic of the play (Lear and his non-Cordelia daughters will have no reunion), but also the incest taboo.[11] It makes sense that the wilderness is marked by the possibility of a suspension of the incest taboo, since it is a space created by power for those it has abandoned, and already in his first moments in the wilderness Lear imagines that what the wilderness contains is precisely incest:

> Hide thee, thou bloody hand,
> Thou perjured and thou simular of virtue
> That art incestuous. (3.2.53–55)

There is a certain logic to the notion that the universalized experience of being flesh that is characteristic of the wilderness as a dramatic space—a space in which all characters find themselves seized by legal sovereignty that refuses to grant stable socio-symbolic identity—is associated with a loosening or even an evasion of the incest taboo. The anthropological vision is that the prohibition on incest is what founds the civilized/natural divide, but what *King Lear* suggests is that the taboo itself is secondary to a prior sovereign decision on identity, which defines socio-symbolic identities and therefore is a precondition for the distinction between licit love (love according to a bond, as Cordelia puts it in the love game that begins the play) and illicit love.

III. The Theater of Cruelty

The ritualized, gestural theater we glimpse in the wilderness is a way of defining and structuring the life of the flesh. The most central emblem of the "use" of the theater to put the life of the flesh on the stage comes in the Gloucester/Edmund sub-plot, with its staged scene of torture and the histrionic, gestural interactions between a father and child who have ceased to function as father and child. I see the Gloucester sub-plot as the key that unlocks the play, since it foregrounds the way the rawest form of sovereign power, namely torture, can trigger an experience of fleshly life that yearns to connect to others as fleshly life.

I want to prepare to look at these sequences by engaging in some theoretical reflections on the theater as a medium, and on how it can be used to reveal the life of the flesh. One set of theoretical terms for what happens in the Edgar/Glloucester sub-plot is Antonin Artaud's influential notion of a "theater of cruelty." Artaud famously argues against the representational focus of modern theater, its attempt to reflect "real life," and its development of characters and plot lines that have an entertainment function. He writes, "for four hundred years, that is since the Renaissance, we have become accustomed to purely descriptive theater, narrative theater, narrating psychology. ... Shakespeare himself is responsible for this aberration and decline, this isolationist concept of theater, holding that a stage performance ought not to affect the public, or that a projected image should not cause a shock to the anatomy, leaving an indelible impression on it" (Artaud, *The Theater and Its Double* 58).[12] Artaud complains about the promotion of speech and language into the heart of the theater at the expense of what he views as more essentially theatrical elements, including the physical gestures enacted by the bodies on the stage, as well as potentially disorienting visual and sonic experiences.[13] In place of a "Western" representational theater, Artaud celebrates non-Western theater, including the Balinese theater and indigenous Mexican theater (both of which he treats in an ethnographically naïve way). He sees these theater traditions as focusing on gesture and on the ritual movements of bodies in relation to other bodies, in ways that do not merely enact stories or describe characters but connect to the bodies of the spectators in a direct way.

Artaud views theatrical gestures as having a significance that cannot be spelled out in spoken language. In essence, Artaud treats the movements of the body as a language like sign language or hieroglyphics; part of the interest of his work is his effort to imagine a new category of "universal" experience by emphasizing the elements of theater that are legible across different culture and language communities. In a brilliant discussion, Kunin writes that in Artaud's "description of Balinese theater actors themselves, by performing gestures that are difficult or uncomfortable, and by wearing costumes that give their bodies non-humanoid shapes, take on the character of 'animated hieroglyphs.' The deformed shapes make visible a history of cruelty on the bodies of the actors. Unlike ordinary writing, the shapes are not arbitrary, and, precisely because of the violence of their production, they communicate across cultures to any audience without the need for translation" (Kunin, "Decoration, Modernism, Cruelty" 90). As Artaud writes, "No, these spiritual signs have a precise meaning which strikes us only intuitively but with enough violence to make useless any translation into logical discursive language" (Artaud, "On the Balinese Theater" 54). In Derrida's influential essay on Artaud, he analyzes this fantasy of a language that is not arbitrarily related to meaning but rather directly embodies it, a language in which the signifiers (the body and its movements) are non-arbitrarily related to what they say. This fantasy plays a role not only in Artaud's theory of theater but also in his often powerful poetry, in which he included such non-arbitrary gestures as cigarette burns on the paper that conveys the poem. For Derrida, of course, the fantasy of a non-arbitrary language is very deeply inscribed in Western metaphysics.

However, the nature of the "universality" that Artaud's hieroglyphic gestures attain is somewhat ambiguous. In order to account for what he sees as the inherent meaningfulness of gestures, Artaud sometimes writes as if gestures could have a universal positive meaning, and as if it would be possible to construct a periodic table of gestures that constitute the basic hardware of human life. Thus, he writes that "theater, inasmuch as it remains confined within its own language and in correlation with it, must make a break with topicality. It is not aimed at social or psychological conflicts, to serve as a battlefield for moral passions, but to express objectively secret truths, to bring out in active gestures those elements of truth hidden under forms in their encounter with Becoming" (52). When he writes this way, Artaud seems to believe that modern Western culture and therefore modern Western theater have lost touch with the basic structuring principles of any human culture, and that only a wrenching experience of theatrical "cruelty" can drag the Western mind back into contact with such basic fountains of culture.

Yet at other times Artaud suggests that *any* settled cultural and any communicative linguistic system loses contact with the primeval sources of occult power. Even in his celebratory account of the masked, dancing theater of Bali, for example, there is attention to the way the deep, potentially shattering power of the non-representational dance is shadowed, "doubled" to use Artaud's technical term, by a more tamed, more traditionally representational and narrative level that he sees as offering refuge to audience members too disturbed by the occult power of the dance. And indeed, its very emphasis on violence and cruelty suggests that Artaud's aesthetics is built on a *negation* of some existing cultural system (within whose terms conventional representation is possible).[14]

In my description of *King Lear*, I am essentially translating Artaud's neg-ative vision of the theater of cruelty into a historically specific context. I describe a set of historically specific conditions that energize and animate a theater of gesture that approximates the theater Artaud imagined. Rather than positing gestural theater as a negation of a general Western debase-ment of theater that privileges representation (and representational or communicative language functions), I see Shakespeare's gestural theater as a negation of a (historically specific version of) sovereign political order, capable of imposing stable socio-symbolic identities (on "real" people, but more immediately on "characters" inside the imagined world of the play). Shakespeare uses a historically specific contradiction in his society's thinking about political power to generate a plot and characters, but the ultimate aim of the plot and the characters is to set the bodies (of the actors) in motion in ways that have an immediate, visceral impact on each other and on the bodies of the spectators. Rather than enacting some timeless cosmic dance, I see the gestures that appear in Shakespeare's plays as placing on the stage the historically specific repressed—the life of the flesh defined by a contingent configuration of sovereign power, and endowed, on the stage, with the power to chart an alternative geometry of corporeal interpersonal ties. If Shakespeare offers something like a gestural theater of cruelty, then he nevertheless always begins by charting the (discursive) conditions of possibility for such theater; and for him these conditions of possibility lie in the specific ways in which early modern state power seizes bodies and thereby, inad-vertently, energizes those bodies to break out of functional subjection to state power.

The purest and most shocking instance of a theater of cruelty rooted in the discourse of sovereignty is the staged torture of Gloucester. In a useful discussion of the historical context for the torture scene, Rocklin notes that the common law tradition does not allow torture, and that torture is therefore always seen as an expression of the prerogative power of the king. Rocklin cites the great theorist of the common law tradition Sir Edward Coke, as well as Sir Thomas Smith, who argues, in his *De Republica Anglorum* (written in 1565 and published in 1583), that the common law does not allow torture because no one could go on to serve the commonwealth as a free man after his body had been so humiliated and mistreated. Torture always had to be authorized by royal writ, and the royal writ ordering someone to torture conferred immunity on the torturers. If the torturers were not subject to common law prosecution for their actions, any information they gained through torture was nevertheless inadmissible in common law proceedings, and because confessions extracted under torture were not admissible in legal proceedings, royally authorized torture usually aimed to achieve extra-legal goals such as finding the names of accomplices or demoralizing an oppositional party. At its origin and in its aims, therefore, torture is the expression of the exceptional power of the sovereign.

When Cornwall proposes to torture Gloucester, he seems to go out of his way to identify torture as outside the normal channels of legal power:

> Go, seek the traitor Gloucester.
> Pinion him like a thief; bring him before us.
> Though well we may not pass upon his life
> Without the form of justice, yet our power
> Shall do a curtsy to our wrath, which men
> May blame but not control. (3.7.22–27)

Here, Cornwall homes in on the conflicted legal status of torture, at once explicitly disallowed by the law (at a minimum he says he cannot kill Gloucester: "Though well we may not pass upon his life/ Without the form of justice") and yet a prerogative of the acting sovereign ("yet our power/ Shall do a curtsy to our wrath").[15] Yet even in making this second claim, Cornwall does not quite say that torture is his prerogative as acting sovereign, since he frames it as something like an angry outburst "which men/ May blame but not control." He seems at one and the same time to advert to the raw fact of his "power" and also to frame torture as a crime of passion. Cornwall's wariness about asserting a royal right to torture may refer obliquely to the fact that his wife, Regan, is the nominal sovereign and he merely the consort. But the lines also have the effect of foregrounding what Shakespeare seems always to foreground; namely, the fact that pure assertions of sovereignty are rooted in nothing but will or passion, so that at its purest level, sovereign power *is* a "wrath, which men/ May blame but not control."[16] Since Gloucester has gone out into the wilderness to save his old king rather than obeying his new lords, he is now identified as a "traitor" to the legal and political order that Cornwall and Regan represent and anchor. Gloucester's utter physical subjection to Cornwall's power is initially marked by being bound "like a thief," and of course the whole point of the torture scene that follows is to highlight how abjectly Gloucester is exposed to the power of Cornwall.

It is possible to imagine that the body of Gloucester subjected to torture is the object of "pity" for spectators, who see it as a violation of universal human rights.[17] Gloucester himself cries out to the gods just before Cornwall puts out his first eye with the heel of his boot:

CORNWALL: Fellows, hold the chair.
                 Upon these eyes of thine I'll set my foot.
GLOUCESTER: He that will think to live till he be old
                 Give me some help. O, cruel! O you gods! (3.7.68–71)

Gloucester appeals to both the gods and to something like human solidarity ("He that will think to live till he be old/ Give me some help. O, cruel! O you gods!"). However, the point of the scene is surely to make such appeals to divine justice or universal human rights seem naïve. Indeed, the point of the scene seems to be to shred any social norms from which standpoint torture would be "wrong" by making it seem that there are no norms that exist outside of a specific structure of sovereignty. The servant who rebels against Cornwall invokes the important Renaissance social norm of the reciprocal duties and rights of masters and servants: "Hold your hand, my lord," says the servant as he draws his sword, "I have served you ever since I was a child,/ But better service have I never done you/ Than now to bid you hold" (3.7.74–76).[18] Of course, this servant's rebellion leads to Cornwall's death, but it does not save Gloucester, and the servant himself is killed and thrown on a dung heap at the end of the scene, together with the blinded Gloucester. This last-ditch invocation of the "norms" of service echoes Gloucester's earlier, equally futile invocation of the norms of the proper behavior of guests (Regan and Cornwall are in Gloucester's house): "I am your host./ With robbers' hands my hospitable favors/ You should not ruffle thus. What will you do?" (3.7.39–41). Even familial norms are rendered null in the face of the angry power of the sovereign, for the most terrifying notice of Cornwall's power as sovereign is surely the fact that Cornwall sends Edmund out of the room so that he can torture his father more freely: "Edmund, keep you our sister company. The revenges we are bound to take upon your traitorous father are not fit for your beholding" (3.7.6–9). And at the moment his second eye is taken, Gloucester calls out for his son Edmund, only to be told the terrible truth:

SERVANT: O, I am slain. My lord, you have one eye left
                 To see some mischief on him. O!
CORNWALL: Lest it see more, prevent it. Out, vile jelly!
                 Where is thy luster now?
GLOUCESTER: All dark and comfortless. Where's my son Edmund?

Edmund, enkindle all the sparks of nature
To quit this horrid act.

REGAN: Out, treacherous villain!
Thou call'st on him that hates thee. It was he
That made the overture of thy treasons to us,
Who is too good to pity thee. (3.7.82–91)

Humanist critics sometimes imagine that the point of staging torture, of forcing spectators to view the wrathful mistreatment of Gloucester's body, is to appeal to some sense of collective solidarity as human beings. But Shakespeare seems instead to use the scene to teach spectators a kind of shocked passivity before the spectacle of angry power, which shreds any pretense of shared norms with the power to indict sovereign power from the outside, as it were. The play knows what liberal critics do not know; namely, that all there is is power and that human rights are only contingent norms backed by pure will. This is the truth that Cornwall represents, as against Gloucester's continuing nostalgia for a political order supposedly rooted in something other than arbitrary will.[19]

As always, by insisting that state power is, at its core, nothing but wrath, Shakespeare unveils the "true" nature of instituted state power, but in doing so he also opens the door to a transformed way of relating to state power. This path is revealed insofar as the spectacle of torture is transformed into a theatrical spectacle. At the same time that Gloucester's theatrically mangled face marks the fact that he has become flesh, it also serves as the engine of a transformed relation to audience members, who must face that face and feel the flesh within. There is a strange pleasure in audience members watching and identifying with the tortured body of Gloucester, a pleasure that Rocklin, for one, connects to adolescent cruelty (as in dismembering flies).[20] As much as spectators may wish to help Gloucester at the level of following the story—in which he is a good character whose sufferings are undeserved—at the level of the theatrical spectacle, audience members can feel some perverse desire to see Shakespeare and the play go all the way in staging cruelty, something that is paradoxically connected to the way in which Shakespeare invites audience members to feel their way into the body that is being tortured.[21] Reduced to (or exposed as) flesh, Gloucester (or perhaps it would be better to say "ex-Gloucester") comes to seem like an everyman, a locus of identification, structurally exposed to a form of sovereign power to which spectators know that they, too, are exposed.[22] As theater, the torture scene, like so many other scenes of violence in the Shakespeare canon, has a strange, luminous quality to it. That is because it points to a transformed foundation for common life; namely, the flesh that is the precondition of any functioning sovereign power, and that Cornwall makes visible by losing his temper on the body of Gloucester.

Inside the play, the point of exposing Gloucester's body to raw sovereign power is to undermine his socio-symbolic identity in favor of revealing the flesh that lies beneath any such identity. Gloucester is stripped of his socio-symbolic identities in the play (as earl, as father) and he comes to recognize himself instead as nothing but flesh. And this stripping is, in turn, the precondition for the strange reunion he experiences with his son, Edgar, who has also been stripped of his traditional identity, and with whom Gloucester engages in a kind of denatured mime-play. As with the Lear–Cordelia relationship that I will discuss later, there is a persistent tension in the Edgar–Gloucester relationship between relating at the level of socio-symbolic identities (father and son, earl and heir) and relating at the level of the phenomenologically experienced body. This tension seems central to Shakespeare's project and I would suggest accounts for the otherwise puzzling fact that Edgar does not disclose himself to Gloucester for most of the play, and never does so on the stage. Such a self-revelation would resolve the tension that Shakespeare is interested in maintaining in favor of a relationship driven by stable symbolic identities.

When Edgar first sees his father in the wilderness, he says, "I cannot daub it further" (4.1.54). Edgar means that he cannot maintain the "Mad Tom" role he is playing. The blood emitted by Gloucester's empty eyes provokes him: "Bless thy sweet eyes, they bleed" (4.1.56), and what they provoke is tears, the same tears that Edgar also shed when confronted with the spectacle of the raving Lear. Gloucester's bleeding rings provoke answering fluids from his son, even when an official reunion of "father" and "son" is deferred. And from this point on, there is an insistently and weirdly corporeal quality to the way Edgar manages and even manipulates his (ex)father who is now utterly at his (ex) son's mercy. They touch physically without touching symbolically, as it were, and their ability to do so is mediated by the theatricality of their gestural interactions.

The gestural theatricality of the Gloucester–Edgar relationship is most insistently on display in the "Dover Cliff" sequence, when Gloucester asks Edgar to lead him to the cliffs so that he can commit suicide.[23] The premise leads to much physical business on the stage—the two bodies pull and tug along until they arrive at the make-believe Dover, where Gloucester engages in a pratfall, followed by a physical revival at the hands of Edgar. Lawrence connects this thwarted suicide to the other thwarted suicides in the play, reading them in light of Emmanuel Lévinas's claim that it is the exposure to death, the ability to die, that is the basis for an ethical relation between self and other, since it makes the self open to something utterly non-self, something utterly Other to the self. Lawrence argues that by foreclosing the possibility of suicide, the play takes away an open relation to the alienness of death.[24] However, insofar as the blocked suicides seem to foreground an unvanquishable life within that cannot be eradicated, the experience of such an unvanquishable life within the self seems to be the basis for an ethical relation that cannot be reduced to the recognition of (and respect for) socio-symbolic identities.

For Gloucester, the suspension of the narrative-theatrical frame achieved by the "practical joke" of the Dover Cliff sequence puts his body in a state of suspended animation, in which it can neither be "in" character nor leave character behind through suicide. After he fails to kill himself, Edgar tries to persuade Gloucester that his life is charmed and that he has been saved by an intervention of the gods. This does not cure Gloucester of his despair (as Edgar had hoped, saying "Why I do trifle thus with his despair/ Is done to cure it" [4.6.33–34]), so much as make him determined to experience that despair to the death. Gloucester says the option of suicide was yet some comfort:

> Is wretchedness deprived that benefit
> To end itself by death? 'Twas yet some comfort
> When misery could beguile the tyrant's rage
> And frustrate his proud will. (4.6.61–64)

Gloucester puts his situation in terms of subjection to a tyrant's power; where he had hoped to escape the sovereign power that is apparently inscribed in the very structure of the universe and its gods, he now sees that there is no escape, and that his flesh is doomed to live:

> Henceforth I'll bear
> Affliction till it do cry out itself
> "Enough, enough," and die. (4.6.75–77)

Gloucester recognizes a persistent fleshly life within himself, and he is determined now to experience this fleshly life even in its most extreme manifestation.

At the same time, the fact that Gloucester cannot commit suicide is also a fact about the medium, the theater, in which a strange, ineradicable life within the character is aligned with the life that emanates from another dimension, the dimension of the real world in which characters are really actors playing parts. The theatricality of the medium, and the use of theatricality for building a life of the flesh, is what the sub-plot seems designed to show. When they arrive at Dover, Edgar paints a striking picture of cliffs, and Shakespeare makes a point of not clearly signaling to the audience that this description is false. To the extent that the audience is taken in by Edgar's deception and narrative, they have the same jarring experience of waking up that Gloucester has. An ironic note of practical joking enters the play here, and under its pressure the whole scene of pratfalls and rolling on the ground takes on a strangely unserious quality.

Jan Kott notes the "foolish" component to this scene, which he connects to a long tradition of comic clowning on the early modern stage.[25] It is no surprise that it should be Kott, with his attention to absolutist political power (albeit of the communist rather than the monarchical variety), who recognizes something subversive in this scene's gestural work. However, whereas Kott explains this subversive force as a Bahktinian refusal of seriousness, I see it instead as an alternative form of life, in which persons relate to one another in ways that bypass the category of the person itself. Here, the illusion of the theater is used to pull the audience into a corporeal mime show between the two bodies of two actors on the stage engaging in a ritual histrionics of gesture, which points to a connection between these characters that flourishes beyond the rules of the plot and therefore beyond characterization. Looking at this sequence "outside" of the narrative frame may seem a perverse response on the part of an audience, and yet it is hard to see the Dover Cliff sequence as aiming to do anything but invite audiences to relate to the spectacle in precisely this way.[26]

IV.   Lear and Cordelia

When it comes to the life of the flesh that I have been describing in this book, the line between the dystopian and the utopian is a thin one. I want to end now with the relationship that embodies this dichotomy most overwhelmingly, that between Lear and Cordelia. Like Edgar and Gloucester, the Lear–Cordelia relationship moves from dissolution in conventional social terms to a renewed though murky basis of love founded on shared, mutual recognition of what remains of the person who has been condemned by state power.

The play opens with the question of whether the Lear–Cordelia relationship will be defined and regulated by socio-symbolic identities— what Cordelia calls her "bond" with Lear. When Cordelia refuses to declare her love for Lear, he disowns her:

> Here I disclaim all my paternal care,
> Propinquity, and property of blood,
> And as a stranger to my heart and me
> Hold thee from this forever. (1.1.114–117)

Stanley Cavell famously sees this as a moment at which Lear is overwhelmed by empiricist skepticism about the mind of the other ("But goes thy heart with this," [1.1.103] a dumbfounded Lear asks after Cordelia refuses to flatter him), which leads him to refuse to acknowledge the other. From Cavell's perspective, Shakespeare here is diagnosing a characteristically modern predicament, and Cavell contextualizes this predicament within the history of philosophy. However, the play seems to go out of its way to align the shattering of the matrix by which persons can relate to one another with the cracking of the structure of sovereignty that Lear embodies. In doing so, of course, the play seems to suggest that one of the essential functions of sovereign power is to grant and define the identities by which persons can relate to each other, without encountering the corrosive skepticism that Cavell describes. When Cordelia says "I love your majesty/ According to my bond, no more nor less" (1.1.91–92), this is obviously not reassuring to Lear, yet it reveals the truth of socially sanctioned love—it can never be rooted in anything other than socially recognized characteristics, and these characteristics in turn require sovereign power to anchor them (Lear never ceases to be king in Cordelia's eyes).[27]

Yet beyond or beneath this socially sanctioned and symbolically vectored love—once Lear has divested Cordelia of her social role, once he has divested himself of his social role—another experience of love becomes possible, one rooted in an ambivalent and sometimes disabling experience of the body—of the flesh—as unhinged from the symbolic attributes of the person. Beneath social identities (and acted characters) there is only flesh, a flesh that turns out to be capable of an experience of love that has nothing to do with the social identities of the persons involved.

The "restored" relationship between Lear and Cordelia in Acts 4 and 5 contains the same irreducible tension between a legible socio-symbolic tie and a radically bodily or corporeal bond that also marks

the Gloucester–Edgar relationship. When Lear and Cordelia are first reunited, Cordelia does try to give Lear back his old social identity; she has
him dressed and treats him as a king and a father, and Lear recognizes
Cordelia as his daughter (while at the same time recognizing Kent for
the first time since he banished him).[28]

> Methinks I should know you, and know this man [i.e., Kent];
> Yet I am doubtful, for I am mainly ignorant
> What place this is; and all the skill I have
> Remembers not these garments; nor I know not
> Where I did lodge last night. Do not laugh at me,
> For, as I am a man, I think this lady
> To be my child Cordelia. (4.7.66–72)

But by the time Lear produces the name and the family bond ("my child
Cordelia"), he has made it clear that his grasp of personal and relational
identities has been transformed dramatically. The relationship into
which Lear and Cordelia enter at the end of the play is born not of a
(late) recognition by Lear that Cordelia is the good daughter, but rather
of the displacement of both Lear and Cordelia from the family roles
they once inhabited.

The alternative sociability that arises beyond their socio-symbolic
identities is most emblematically visible when Lear and Cordelia are
taken prisoner, subjected jointly to the leveling power of sovereign
force, and led off to jail. Cordelia somewhat desperately continues to
frame Lear as a father and a king, but Lear disavows this social identity
in favor of a transformed experience of self and of its connection with
another:

CORDELIA: We are not the first
> Who with best meaning have incurred the worst.
> For thee, oppressèd king, I am cast down,
> Myself could else outfrown false fortune's frown.
> Shall we not see these daughters and these sisters?

LEAR: No, no, no, no. Come, let's away to prison.
> We two alone will sing like birds i'th' cage.
> When thou dost ask me blessing, I'll kneel down
> And ask of thee forgiveness; so we'll live,
> And pray, and sing, and tell old tales, and laugh
> At gilded butterflies, and hear poor rogues
> Talk of court news, and we'll talk with them too,

> Who loses and who wins, who's in, who's out,
> And take upon's the mystery of things
> As if we were God's spies; and we'll wear out
> In a walled prison packs and sects of great ones
> That ebb and flow by th' moon. (5.3.3–19)

Lear disavows the traditional familial and social hierarchy that Cordelia attempts to reassert; when she asks for his blessing, he will kneel with her and ask forgiveness. In the context of Renaissance family politics, this is a shocking disavowal of status for a father in relation to his daughter. Yet that is just the point: Lear no longer views Cordelia as his daughter, and he no longer views himself as her father. Rather, it is a relationship based on performatively stripping the self of its socio-symbolic status. Nor is it (merely) a matter of reversing roles here; what Lear seems to engineer is an interpersonal union based on the paradoxically shared absence of socio-symbolic status indicated physically (even physiologically) by the image he paints of two kneeling bodies facing each other in a cage. The bond Lear imagines here is radically apart from the normal human social world and its conceptions of social identity and human dignity. It arises out of their joint exposure to state power, and their conscious recognition of this fact. In their very bodies they testify to the power of the state that has taken them into its custody, but they testify as well to the resistance to state power lying in the corporeal lump that always remains outside the calculations of power and is displayed at the end of the play in the tableau of Lear holding Cordelia's dead body, desperately wishing to find life in it: "And my poor fool is hanged. No, no, no life./ Why should a dog, a horse, a rat have life,/ And thou no breath at all?" (5.3.312–314). When he relates Cordelia's life to that of a dog and a rat, it is not a "human" life that he seeks to find in Cordelia so much as a "bare life," which he had found only after ceasing to see her as a daughter and himself as a father and a king.

In the final theatrical tableau Shakespeare stages, it is precisely this fleshly life that we still see, insofar as the bodies of Lear and Cordelia are, in some sense, "undead," they quiver (probably perceptibly as they lie on the stage); the lines of eros and corporeal bonding continue (virtually) to tie them together. The lines of family solidarity are in play here, but only as a kind of virtual matrix that the bodies deliberately transcend. Commenting on the force of a final tableau of dead bodies in a variety of Shakespeare's plays in her book *The Early Modern Corpse and Shakespeare's Theater*, Zimmerman examines the force of dead bodies on the stage in light of the Protestant reformation's emphasis on avoiding idolatry. More importantly for my argument here, she also uses Benjamin's idea of the *Trauerspiel*, in which the human desire for transcendence is balanced by recognition of the sheer material corporeality of the body that never adequately carries meaning. That is where *King Lear* ends up: with raw matter that is animated and yet is not fully captured by the sovereign power that imposes stable socio-symbolic identities. By the end of the play, the force of Lear's displacement from his social identity as king and father, and the force of Cordelia's displacement, is so great that the bond joining them is not a "natural" bond of familial love. Indeed, if this were nothing more than a father–daughter reunion, it would be deprived of the haunting theatrical force that it has. In the love that joins Lear who was once a father and Cordelia who was once a daughter, in a love born of a profound sense of separation from the competition and status hierarchies of the social world, Shakespeare gestures toward a kind of love founded on the recognition of that ambivalent, luminescent substrate of social identity that I term the life of the flesh.

In my discussion of *King Lear*, I have drawn attention to moments in which spectators enter into a transformed relation to the play, in which the socio-symbolic identities of the characters in the play are suspended or exceeded through ritual, transformative violence—gruesomely displayed on the stage in the case of Gloucester's torture, jokingly displayed in the case of the Dover Cliff sequence, ambivalently displayed in the final tableau of (socially) dead but (biologically) living bodies with which the play ends. At such moments, spectators are ejected from a character-driven and narratological relation to the play, and instead relate to it as a way of putting bodies (mere flesh that points back to socio-symbolic identities that are in crisis) into motion with other bodies in ways that exceed the sanctioned, normative modes of interpersonal relation between socio-symbolic persons. Again and again, this Artaudian development—in the direction of ritual violence, spectacle, farce, and, one could almost say, regenerative dance—is explicitly located by the play in the unsettling exposure to sovereign power.[29] Seen in this light, the relationship between the ex-king and his ex-daughter, and that between tortured Gloucester and outlawed Edgar, take their place in a whole series of self-consciously theatrical and fleshly clusters of characters that I have examined in this book—Marc Antony and Caesar;

Brutus and Cassius and Pindarus; Angelo and Isabella; Escalus and Pompey; Claudio and the duke; Othello, Desdemona, Iago, Emilia, and Cassio. Together, these relationships sketch out the geometry of a fleshly life that has passed through sovereign power only to emerge transmogrified, luminous, transcendent.

Epilogue: The Afterlife of the Life of the Flesh

Recovering the specific morphologies of the "life of the flesh" described and enacted in Shakespeare's theater is a contribution to historical phenomenology, to our understanding of the experience of living in early modern England and of encountering the sovereign power of the nation-state at the moment of its birth. Yet it is also a utopian resource, helping us to rethink and reimagine some of the most basic assumptions of political modernity, including the relationship between persons, bodies, and the political community and the possibilities for resistance to state power.[1] The specific ways in which the life of the flesh appears in this book are essentially and inescapably caught up with a historically specific experience of being subjected to the sovereign power of the new political form of the nation-state. At the same time, the structural opening that Shakespeare's plays identify—a mode of resistance that uses subjection to sovereign power against itself to energize new forms of life together, founded on a new experience of the bodily self—carries a lesson that applies in other times and places. Shakespeare's vision is not unprecedented or radically eccentric, and analogues to the early modern life of the flesh that I have examined in this book can also be triggered by crises within very different structures of sovereign power in very different historical contexts, albeit in ways that reflect the historically variable ways in which sovereign power seizes its subjects. My hope is that the analytical terms I develop here for analyzing the life of the flesh in Shakespeare's plays can be used to bring into view other "scenes" from a history of the life of the flesh. In that sense, the particular, historically situated life of the flesh that I catalog in this book is an example of what Bordwell, in a very different context, calls a "contingent universal," an experience whose underlying structure appears not necessarily but contingently, though it does so in

124

a way that is repeated even across very different cultural and historical contexts (Bordwell and Carroll, eds. 94).

The question of the historical boundaries of Shakespeare's life of the flesh is one of the central concerns of Julie Taymor's brilliant and disturbing 1999 film adaptation of *Titus Andronicus*. I argue that this film transposes the life of the flesh from the particular early modern political-discursive universe that I have examined in this book into the modern political domain. If Shakespeare wrote at the dawn of the era of the nation-state, and focused on the discursive underbelly of this new form of sovereign power, then Taymor's *Titus* transposes Shakespeare's vision into the era of massively powerful corporate states uneasily caught up in the forces of globalization.

Read within the terms of early modern political discourse, the written play of *Titus Andronicus* stages a version of the same conflict between civic republicanism and absolutism that Shakespeare uses to energize the life of the flesh in all of his plays. The debate between civic republicanism and absolutism appears, for example, in the conflict between Saturninus's hereditary claim to power and Bassianus's appeal to virtue and popular will as a check on tyranny. The character of Titus attempts to straddle this discursive divide. On the one hand, he looks like a kind of civic republican, in that his power is rooted in military virtue and personal honor, which gives him an independent power base separate from the emperor. However, on the other hand, Titus has an exaggerated respect for authority and therefore throws his support behind Saturninus. Once Saturninus is appointed as emperor, he and his new wife Tamora increasingly assert precisely the kind of unchecked sovereign power against which the civic republican Bassianus warns, and Titus and his family are increasingly the objects of that unchecked sovereign power. Saturninus's raw power of life and death over his subjects leads to increasingly gruesome bodily violations, which, however, always carry the philosophical weight of Shakespeare's project of touching a life beyond the defined personhood presided over by functioning sovereign power.

Taymor updates the early modern conflict between absolutism and a critical civic republicanism by setting her film in the context of a 1930s Italian fascism and thereby evoking the ghost of the Holocaust. As Taymor notes in an interview, "I keep using the Holocaust because it's the biggest event of our century—it can be twisted and manipulated" (Deluca and Lindroth 31).[2] However, the 1930s Italian context is also supplemented by imagery and styles from other times and places, ranging from 1920s Weimar culture to contemporary teenage goth and video game culture. Taymor's historical collage adverts to the forces of globalization, which render all local boundaries permeable. Yet this historical collage style also universalizes the context of 1930s fascism and the Holocaust, making them seem less historically contained to a place and time long ago and more a blueprint of all modern political formations. As Agamben has argued, quite controversially, the fascist state is not the exception to modern democratic political orders that liberal political theorists would like it to be, but is, rather, the rule in an era in which states pay lip service to the sacred rights of the person even as, in practice, they make a mockery of liberal personhood. This is precisely what Taymor's historically unmoored mise en scène suggests.[3]

Taymor's recasting of the play in terms of an historically unlocalized form of sovereign power accounts for the strange relevance her film seems to have to the issues of state power raised by the 9/11 terrorist attacks, even though the film was made before these attacks. Some critics have sought to explain the film's seeming relevance to 9/11 by focusing on the issue of racial and ethnic otherness raised by the Goths, who are at once outside and inside Rome.[4] Nevertheless, what is more germane is Taymor's insistent focus on the raw reality of state power. After all, the so-called war on terrorism has had the salutary effect of giving the lie to the bland liberal fantasy that persons have inalienable rights, by making us aware of the ways in which the body is inescapably subjected to sovereign power. In fact, the war on terror has made it seem increasingly obvious that "rights" occur only in the framework of a sovereign state that can choose to grant or withhold those rights.

Taymor seems to endorse precisely this Schmittian starting point, and her goal is the same as Shakespeare's; namely, to stay with the body as her characters dive into the very heart of raw state power. The strategy of staying with the body as it is transfigured through an encounter with sovereign power accounts for the most distinctive visual feature of Taymor's film, its campy and gruesome violence. But as in Shakespeare's play, this violence gains philosophical weight by remaining dialectically tied to the issue of state power.

The two critics who have addressed the relationship between the visual spectacle of corporeal violence and the political frame of Taymor's film most effectively are Richard Burt and Peter S. Donaldson. In a brilliant discussion, Burt concludes that the character of Titus is a failed anti-fascist resistance fighter.[5] However, rather than offering a realistic illustration of the political stance of resistance to fascism, Taymor's intention is to explore the effects—including, somewhat disturbingly, the utopian effects—of politically sponsored violence on bodies. This is the point that Donaldson makes when he suggests that Taymor believes that there is a necessary complicity linking political violence and her art. He writes that "for Taymor the intermingling of fascism and the roots and antecedents of her own art remain troubling, serving in *Titus* to suggest a kind of necessary complicity linking tragic art and the real-life violence it may once have been thought to refine or transcend."[6] For Donaldson, one emblem of the art that is founded on violence and cruelty occurs when Lucius gives Lavinia a beautiful prosthetic hand to remedy the dismemberment she has undergone at the hands of Tamora's sons. For Donaldson, the shattered body that is made beautiful is the preeminent emblem of the way Taymor wrings art from horror.

Seeing politically sponsored violence as the starting point for a form of art that offers a transformative vision of bodies destroyed and made new is the right framework for understanding Taymor's updated version of the life of the flesh. Taymor's film, like Shakespeare's plays, suggests that there is no way out of necessary subjection to state power, except by an intensified focus on the body as it becomes manifest through exposure to sovereign power. Early in the film, Titus and his family do attempt to *resist* sovereign power directly, but, as is always the case in Shakespeare's plays, this strategy of direct confrontation with power proves naïve. In the play as well as in the film, the strategy of resistance is replaced by a more tangential strategy, one of passing through sovereign power and allowing it to transform self and other. This transformative response to sovereign power is marked by an increasingly absurdist quality to the action, strikingly evident, for example, when Titus is presented with the severed hand and the heads of his two sons in a carnivaleque sideshow (in Taymor's brilliant updating); he bursts out laughing and then tells Lavinia to carry his severed hand between her teeth as he tucks the heads of his two sons under his own (now mutilated) arms. Thomas Cartelli and Katherine Rowe rightly see this as a transitional moment in the film, writing that "the ritualized nature of this scene echoes with crucial differences the earlier scene at the family mausoleum, as we watch the remaining Andonici gather together dismembered parts of their familial body as a first stage towards reinventing their relation-ship both to themselves and to the Roman state" (83). For Cartelli and Rowe, the tone of campy liberation that the film achieves here is rooted in a re-functioning of the symbols of Roman state power; they note that the "transition begins in their manipulation of the symbols that dominate Roman politics in the play: the heads and hands that figure martial and political authority" (82). To put the point slightly differ-ently, it is only once the Andronici are deprived of functional integration within the organs of the state that the components of their bodies, notably their heads and hands, are liberated to become emblems of new forms of subjective experience and interpersonal connection, based not on power within the Roman political order but on bodily exposure to that political order. As we watch Taymor's film, the powerlessness and vulnerability that first afflict Lavinia when she is raped and mutilated by Tamora's sons are progressively rendered universal in the Andonici family. The Andonici are increasingly subjected to amputation and dismemberment, but the savagery they experience has the effect of liberating them from state power by turning them into a strange, liminal form of depersonalized undeadness; they are victims of state power who have been victimized to the point of transcending the field of state power altogether. And the token of this victimized transcendence is the characters' and the film's growing inability or refusal to take state power seriously.

However, it is important to note that Taymor's absurdist violence is not unproblematically funny or merely entertaining. Taymor's violence is absurd, yet it always remains linked to the reality of the human body and its limitations, vulnerabilities, and finitude. In other words, unlike the escapist Hollywood action films that Taymor often criticizes, the violence depicted in her film remains bound by the reality of the body subjected to state power, a body that can really be damaged or killed, but that also offers a starting point for an ironic transcendence of state power. This ambivalent yoking together of surreal, transformative visions of the body subject to violence and a realistic acceptance of the body as the limited horizon for human life is what makes Taymor's film hard to watch at times, yet it is also what gives her stylized treatment of violence its philosophical weight as a species of the life of the flesh. As she notes in an interview, "*Titus...* is not just about violence; it's about how we make entertainment out of violence" (Bate). Taymor works hard to keep her film just this side of the line dividing transformative violence from the empty, disembodied, entertaining, or even funny spectacle that she associates with Hollywood.

Taymor's cinematic transposition of Shakespeare's conceptual universe suggests that the life of the flesh remains a political category for us today, though it no longer appears in the light of the (by now quaint) civic republican critique of absolute sovereignty. Rather, the life of the flesh appears through the framework of a globalized fascism that shatters the traditional liberal ideal of the sacred individual endowed with inalienable rights. Nor does the life of the flesh appear preeminently in the medium of theater, where the actual bodies of the actors play a fundamentally grounding role.[7] Rather, Taymor's film suggests that the life of the flesh appears today primarily in the purely visual realm of media such as cinema and the video games that her film so frequently echoes. And as much as Taymor's film offers a vision of what the life of the flesh looks like today, it also acts as a caution about the dangers that shadow a genuine engagement with the life of the flesh today. As I have suggested, Taymor's film is quite funny, but it is also wary of reducing the life of the flesh to mere comedy. The film implicitly warns that the life of the flesh is in danger of losing its political seriousness by becoming pure escapist fantasy, as occurs in many mainstream films as well as in the video game culture with which Taymor's film is sometimes associated.[8] The danger that serious engagement with the politically indexed life of the flesh faces today is, somewhat paradoxically, not too much respect for traditional liberal subjectivity but too little—a flippant escape into the world of video game violence and cinematic fantasy that is unmoored from the tidal forces of politics that endow Shakespeare's life of the flesh with its utopian seriousness.

Notes

Introduction

1. For a recent study in which Shakespeare is blamed for (and thus also credited with) the rise of xenophobic nationalism, see Levin and Watkins. For the most influential exposition of Shakespeare's role in paving the way for the nation-state, see Helgerson. For arguments that emphasize the role of literary culture in producing a collective national identity, see Dobson, and Cheney, *Shakespeare's Literary Authorship* as well as *Shakespeare, National Poet-Playwright*.
2. See Schmitt, *The Concept of the Political* and *Political Theology*.
3. For a nuanced effort to apply Schmitt's model to the American constitutional order, see Kahn.
4. For Foucault, "bio-politics" is a characteristic of late modernity, as opposed to the "classical" age of the nation-state. For Agamben, by contrast, bio-politics is characteristic of the entire history of Western politics. For Agamben, the only difference between the classical era of the nation-state and late modernity's shift to an explicitly bio-political orientation is that the state has ceased to veil its essentially bio-political orientation. For Agamben, in other words, the end of the classical era of the nation-state is marked not by the invention of bio-politics (as Foucault argues), but by the unveiling of the state's (essentially) bio-political orientation, a development emblematized by the concentration camp and the politicization of life in debates about issues like abortion and euthanasia.
5. It goes without saying that Agamben's focus is on the incomplete or provisional nature of any particular account of human nature, and on the ways in which the initial sovereign decision about human nature leaves traces within the resulting political order that unsettle its basic account of human nature. Colony explores the role of Heidegger's thought on Agamben's account of human and animal nature. Though he would disagree with some of the premises of my discussion, Lievens provides a useful discussion of how the idea of human nature functions in Schmitt's account.
6. Though the broader, bio-political perspective is anticipated by Schmitt's claim that the sovereign institutes the basic friend/enemy distinction, which, in its breadth, implies some concern with defending a whole way of life against what is perceived as antithetical ways of life. For a more psychoanalytic account of the psychic implications of sovereign power, see Pye.
7. Pierre Bourdieu's sociology is one of our most powerful theoretical models of the texture of subjective, relational, and cultural life, and a unified theory of the way the web of cultural, social, and relational life is structured (and, therefore, potentially destructured) by sovereign power would combine something of Agamben's perspective with Bourdieu's cultural sociology. One place where that combination might be prefigured is in John Guillory's discussion of the role of syllabi (in the context of state-mandated schooling)

in defining the literary canon that is, in turn, at the heart of sociologically legible cultural competition. For other treatments of the issue of how state power pervades and shapes cultural and social life, see Frey and essays in Steinmetz.

8. Though there is much to admire in her discussion, Lupton's *Citizen-Saints* suffers from the assumption of a civil society governed by social norms that exist separately from the exercise of sovereign power and that persist even in a state of emergency. Lupton writes: "Yet if Shakespeare's plays, especially his tragedies, are sundered by the lightning bolt of the monarch's caprice, his dramas, especially his comedies, are just as much concerned with the genesis, reestablishment, and renovation of social norms. Although some of this predilection can be accounted for generically, it is ultimately dispositional, temperamental, and even aesthetic. Shakespeare's normative orientation ultimately distinguishes him from Marlowe and from Milton" (6). In a comment on a previously published portion of Lupton's argument, "Othello Circumcised," Goldberg in *Tempest in the Caribbean* complains that she celebrates norms that exist separately from state power. In response, Lupton in *Citizen-Saints* affirms her intention to move "the discussion back toward the universal in response to the hegemony of the culturalist position in recent years. I hope that the current form of the chapter places additional emphasis on the political (as well as theological) traditions of universalism, and that my discussion of norms throughout the book indicates their creative rather than coercive character" (245 n. 8). Nevertheless, the relevant objection is not that the norms she posits are coercive, but rather that she posits norms (that spring from mysterious sources outside the exercise of sovereign power) in the first place. Lupton is also examining the persistent role of religious ideology in defining political communities (and demarcating insiders and outsiders), whereas I offer a predominantly secular framework. Hammill's *The Mosaic Constitution* offers an excellent account of early modern political theology that is also focused on the role of religious discourse in political community. For further elaboration of Hammill's and Lupton's position, see the introduction to Hammill and Lupton, eds. Yachnin attempts to broaden our understanding of what can count as "public" discourse beyond critically reasonable position-taking, but he also remains within the framework that assumes an autonomous civil society that is the kernel of a public sphere, and he argues that Shakespeare's basic goal is to provide a venue for public debate in the name of effecting change. For a basic statement of his position, see Yachnin and the introduction to Wilson and Yachnin, eds.

9. Though he is more focused on the French context, see also Engster.

10. See Gieskes.

11. Absolutist propaganda insisted, quite correctly in Schmitt's view, that the king was the bulwark of any rights and privileges his subjects might traditionally enjoy. As I shall go on to discuss at the end of Chapter 1 and throughout Chapter 2, the tension between the quasi-autonomous bureaucratic agencies of the state and the persistent, exceptional power of the king is most marked in the legal domain, where the apparatus of common law seems to run without any deference to the king but where its functioning is silently structured by the presence of an alternative system of justice—namely the prerogative equity courts, including the Chancellor's Court and Star

Chamber—which are explicitly seen as an expression of the king's absolute power.

12. Some critics and historians have seen early modern civic republicanism as a precursor of rights-based liberalism. It is certainly not that, in particular because it does not begin with a canon of individual rights on which a just state cannot infringe. Instead, civic republicanism is a spectrum of beliefs about the role and importance of consultation and the distribution of political power. Civic republican thought is often particularly interested in cultivating and celebrating public-mindedness, the willingness to pursue the public good rather than any private interest. Indeed, early modern civic republican thought tends to view any overdeveloped notion of private life that stands apart from public life as a danger to virtuous public-spiritedness. For civic republicanism, what is more important than any private pleasures, comforts, goals, or aspirations is the public life of political decision-making undertaken in conjunction with other public-minded men. By contrast, absolutism is more proto-liberal in its values, for it is comfortable with the notion of a private life since it imagines government as the province of specialized, administrative agencies anchored by the exceptional power of the king. The relative value of private and public life in absolutist and civic republican thought will return as a concern throughout this book.

13. This is the form of civic republicanism that Collinson describes in his influential account of the "monarchical republic" of Queen Elizabeth. In putting it this way, I am slightly understating the radicalism of the political formation Collinson describes. As he sees it, especially in response to the fear that Queen Elizabeth might be assassinated and leave no clear successor, the political agents he describes walk right up to the line of believing that king or queen is just one magisterial office among others, and that in the absence of a clear successor the political nation can name or elect a new king or queen to serve it.

14. In the early modern context, the radical version of civic republicanism tends to be associated with Protestant opponents to Catholic princes, who argued that magistrates and perhaps even citizens have a right to remove a king who does not serve the public interest.

15. For examples, see the discussion of civic republican historiography in Chapter 1.

16. Collinson has influentially argued for a view of Elizabethan political culture as a mixture of absolutist and republican elements. Yet even if absolutist and civic republican elements could coexist in practice, in theory civic republicanism undermines the "normalcy" of absolute power. This is precisely how Shakespeare uses civic republicanism in his plays. I am also drawing on Perry's discussion of favoritism as a way of understanding the prehistory of the conflict between prerogative power and republicanism that leads to the Civil War.

17. See Matheson.

18. In short, Contarini's Venice breaks with the transcendental, "miraculous" basis of sovereignty in absolutist thinking (through what J.G.A. Pocock describes as a movement toward a "secular time"). See Pocock, *The Machiavellian Moment*.

19. Contarini's account famously celebrates the institutional structures of Venice as an "artificial angel" that maintains and even creates public-minded virtue in its citizens who, in turn, uphold the republic. But if it is the institutional structures of the state that maintain or even create virtuous, public-minded citizens, then this gives rise to the question of where and when these institutions originated and who or what is responsible for maintaining them when they are threatened, questions Contarini cannot answer.

20. Looking at early modern civic republicanism with Shakespearean eyes, as it were, we notice that all early modern efforts to imagine a civic republican political order on a national scale are haunted by two characteristic breakdowns that point to the groundlessness of a theoretical effort to envision a political community not explicitly founded and backed by an arbitrary sovereign power that is prior to and outside the political community: (1) the impossibility of explaining the origin or foundational basis for a civic republican order; and (2) the impossibility of defining membership in the decision-making body. It is, in fact, difficult for early modern partisans of civic republicanism to set up a working republican model, or even to imagine a republic as anything other than a persistent state of emergency, as is the case in Milton's *The Ready and Easy Way* and Harrington's *Oceana*.

21. In other words, Shakespeare uses civic republicanism to teach the hard lesson of the Schmitt and Agamben approach to political life: that there is no way out of sovereign power, that sovereign power is the essential precondition of anything that might count as human life, that there is no form of personhood or subjectivity that is not fundamentally marked by sovereign power. De Wilde very helpfully emphasizes that for Schmitt (and Benjamin), the violence that institutes political order can also always shatter that order, but that there is no way out of this catch-22. He emphasizes that for Schmitt and for Benjamin, the role of the sovereign is one of infinite responsibility. Though I use different terminology, I am struck by de Wilde's notion of "desubjectivication" as the experience of being subject to the law without being a subject of the law. For de Wilde, this experience is especially prominent in apparent exceptions to the legal order that in fact reveal the rule of the legal order, and he cites Abu Ghraib as an example.

22. Jackson argues that despite the foundational effort to demarcate and cast out bare life, it nevertheless appears inside Western political orders as a model of the natural "good life" and as an object of repeated scapegoating. For Agamben himself, the Western political imaginary is haunted by the idea of a bare life that is both utterly beyond the pale of state-sanctioned existence and also utterly inside and even at the very heart of all structures of sovereign power.

23. Santner's notion of "creaturely life" provides one important analogue for the category I am attempting to articulate here. Though it is motivated by different concerns, I am also drawing on Shannon's discussion in *The Accomodated Animal* of a "cosmopoly" that is not marked by an absolute differentiation between human life and animal life. For discussion of the relation between human and animal life, see Chapter 4.

24. Notably, in the case of Negri, in the idea of "constitutive" power. The utopian streak to which I am pointing appears throughout Agamben's writing, see especially *The Coming Community*. Nancy, in *The Inoperative Community*, does

not contextualize this experience in terms of institutional structures of state power and thus does not indicate a path from here to there, save through the redeeming powers of the theoretical imagination. De la Durantaye notes the difficulty of concretely imagining the kind of normative community that Nancy posits, writing: "Is it possible to conceive of a community whose members share nothing but being?" (160). For a critique of the political effectiveness of alternative visions of community in Agamben and Nancy, see Elliot, who attacks the valuation of "radical passivity," as well as Norris. For a powerful critique of any politics founded on a positive valuation of "bare life," see Owens. In applying this theoretical vision to the early modern period, I am drawing on important theoretical work by Goldberg in *The Seeds of Things* as well as Kuzner.

25. See Gil, *Before Intimacy*. This view of sexuality as fundamentally at a tangent to other indices of social relationship is largely prefigured in Goldberg's groundbreaking *Sodometries*. In his more recent work, including *The Seeds of Things*, Goldberg has explored the social and political implications of his vision of sexuality, contextualizing it within the theoretical work of Agamben among other theorists.

26. See Gil, "The Deep Structure of Sexuality." My thought is also influenced by Marshall's important *The Shattering of the Self*, Kuzner's significant recent book on masochism in early modern literary culture, as well as Daniel's discussion and Hammill's response to it in "Converting Cruelty and Constituting Community in Shakespeare's Venice." See also Campana.

27. For a fuller discussion of the issue of whether Shakespeare and other imaginative writers are able to articulate political ideas that do not exist as such in political discourse, especially as this issue applies to civic republicanism, see the literature review I offer in the final section of Chapter 1.

28. To describe Shakespeare's distinctive use of humoral theory, I draw on important historicist studies of the early modern experience of humoral emotions. Among many excellent writings, I note the foundational work of Paster, Floyd-Wilson, Roach and, with an important corrective turn to stoicism, Schoenfeldt. Obviously, the body of criticism that has grown up around humoral theory in recent years is diverse and impressive. I engage with specific aspects of it in the chapters that follow, especially in the final section of Chapter 3.

29. I am echoing the introduction to Harvey, ed. On the materiality of voice, with especial attention to its ability to enter into other bodies, see Bloom.

30. Though his concerns are different than mine, I am struck by Weimann's use of the hybrid term "Actor-Character."

31. All Shakespeare quotations are from the Pelican edition, except as noted.

1   The Historical Conditions of Possibility of the Life of the Flesh: Absolutism, Civic Republicanism, and "Bare Life" in *Julius Caesar*

1. For one of the most influential applications of the notion of a public sphere to early modern culture, see Yachnin. Yachnin uses the Habermasian model even as he also criticizes and modifies it. For Habermas, an extra-state civil society

nurtures a purely human use of communicative rationality that transcends the framework of the nation-state and can therefore subject the state to reasoned critique from the outside. It is worth pointing out that Habermas himself, schooled as he is in the Hegelian dialectic, consistently foregrounds the ways in which civil society and the state are mutually constitutive, though this important nuance is often lost in applications of his basic model. Murakami offers a restatement of Habermas's model in the context of early modern theater performances. In *Ben Jonson's Theatrical Republics*, Sanders offers a careful account of the republican sympathies in Jonson's vision of the community defined by theatrical performances. In *Shakespeare's Imaginary Constitution*, Raffield argues that Shakespeare took advantage of what he sees as the theater's unique public space for political debate. Usefully, Raffield sees Shakespeare as staging the broadest theoretical debates, including the nature of unchecked prerogative power, which Raffield reconstructs very helpfully.

2. My argument that *Julius Caesar* is misaligned with the modern political imaginary that combines the nation-state with a structured, national civil society is influenced by Halpern's powerful discussion.

3. In making this claim, I am drawing on important work on early modern thought about the humors, notably including Paster; Floyd-Wilson; Schoenfeldt; and, somewhat differently, James. In advancing the claim that early modern humors can be seen as a social grammar of connections between bodies that stand in the place of functional social ties, including ties mediated by political frameworks, I draw on my own account of the role of emotions in early modern representations of sexuality. See Gil, *Before Intimacy*. For a more detailed account of the relation between contemporary historical work on the humors and the distinctive discourse of the life of the flesh that I recover in this book, see the last section of Chapter 3.

4. I draw the term "anti-systemic" from the title of the important study by Arrighi, Hopkins, and Wallerstein. Drawing on the world-systems perspective on economic history, these authors argue that twentieth-century anti-capitalist movements have been stuck in a catch-22, in which they seek to ameliorate the local effects of international capitalism by aiming to gain a measure of state power (through institutionalized trade union movements, for example) that paradoxically strengthens the nation-state, which is itself the key mechanism by which the capitalist world-system as a whole operates. In this context, Arrighi et al. examine modes of resistance and social organization that steer clear of affirming and even strengthening the administrative power of the nation-state, even as they challenge the power of international capital; it is such movements that they term "antisystemic." I aim to theorize an anti-systemic discourse of the life of the flesh that is spawned at the very historical moment when the nation-state form arrived on the scene of international capitalism.

5. This friction between rival political ideologies is resolved historically by the modern settlement in which the state is seen to guarantee certain rights within a unified, nationalized political field that pre-exists individual decisions about political allegiances; these rights, in turn, make possible certain kinds of political opposition. It is essentially this settlement (achieved in England through the Glorious Revolution) that is reflected and codified in Habermas's account of an oppositional public sphere.

6. It is as if the aristocratic self-conception of a virtue-oriented elite that constitutes the state is transposed onto the abstract, universal field conjured up by Caesar's leveling of local differences. In making the claim that "bare life" seems constitutive, I am drawing on Negri's important discussion. The early modern struggle to constitute power in the nation-state form foregrounds a level of constitutive power that appears as a pure ontological force.

7. Indeed, one important theoretical context for understanding Marc Antony's anti-political rage is Fanon's application of Sorel's program to the colonial context.

8. To some extent, the vision I recover here intersects with Smith's phenomenological account of the early modern theater, and it is certainly worth noting that Shakespeare represents Marc Antony as loving the theater. For the fullest statement of his phenomenological approach, see Smith, *Phenomenal Shakespeare.*

9. Obviously, gender complicates Portia's relationship to the conspirator's ideology of public life in important ways. For Portia, being inducted into the conspiracy seems like a powerful form of liberation from a domesticated and gendered role in the home, a liberation that she paradoxically completes with her spectacular suicide. In this context, see Marshall's discussion of Portia's self-mutilating turn against her gender identity in "Portia's Wound, Calphurnia's Dream." It is worth noting that Shakespeare consistently calls attention to the important role that women play in the life of the massed crowd, something to which I will return at several points in this study.

10. Leinwand also argues that new historicism has elided the space of the "middling sort" and he attempts to fill in the capabilities of the commercially active citizens. See *The City Staged* and "Shakespeare and the Middling Sort."

11. Hadfield, *Shakespeare and Republicanism* 53.

12. For a recent collection of essays exploring the implications of Collinson's argument, see McDiarmid, ed. For a sophisticated and thorough overview of the potency of republican humanism, see Peltonen.

13. For some historians, including Skinner, such a supplementary civic republicanism is not merely a historical artifact but is an inspiration for the present day, one that breaks with individualistic, rights-based neo-liberalism by emphasizing active participation in the civil domain and the preference for the collective good over the individual good. From this standpoint, civic republicanism is viewed as (nothing more than) a portable reservoir of values that will motivate democratic subjects to become more active and involved in political life. To the extent that historians are motivated to recover a "usable" civic republicanism they are drawn to the vision of an early modern civic republicanism that is built on the assumption of a civil society that can act as a basis for the active involvement of an informed citizenry, but that does not inquire into the political origin of that civil society. As Sullivan notes, this amounts to aligning early modern civic republicanism with a communitarianism that (naïvely) assumes the community as an unproblematic starting point for historical analysis and for politics. Skinner himself makes this point, but Sullivan especially associates it with Sandel. For the complete discussion see Sullivan 6–9.

14. As Pocock argues in *The Machiavellian Moment.* The view that in general there is no meaningful civic republicanism worthy of the name in England before

the Civil War dovetails with the view that Shakespeare does not champion civic republicanism in his plays. For this view, see the introduction in Armitage, Condren, and Fitzmaurice, eds. See also Worden.

15. On the one hand, even this definition of liberty could issue in a limited form of political resistance, for example the defense of supposed natural rights; this tendency is what leads Sullivan to see civic republicanism as containing a strain of proto-liberal, quasi rights-based individualism within it. However, the neo-Roman conception of liberty could also be the starting point for a much more radical form of civic republicanism defined by a direct engagement with the issue of sovereignty.

16. See Norbrook, *Writing the English Republic*, especially the introduction; and Hadfield, *Shakespeare and Republicanism*. For an explicit defense of literary discourse's ability to articulate political ideals that do not appear in official political discourse, see O'Brien. For a powerful account of the way in which republican ideas shaped the self-conception of the author, with Marlowe as the test case, see Cheney, *Marlowe's Republican Authorship*.

17. Hadfield, "Republicanism in Sixteenth- and Seventeenth-Century Britain" 112.

18. For the argument that Shakespeare saw the history of Rome not as a reservoir of civic republican values but as a pessimistic account of political agency, see Cherniak. I see Shakespeare as neither pro nor con, but as playing the two sides against each other to lay bare the basic structure of sovereign power.

19. Pocock, *The Ancient Constitution and the Feudal Law* 51.

20. Because of this divorce from morality, Raffield, in "The Inner Temple Revels," argues that common lawyers sometimes perceived the need to ground their profession in something other than commercial skills.

21. Coke writes, "causes which concern the life or inheritance or goods or fortunes of subjects are not to be decided by natural reason, but by the artificial reason and judgment of law." Quoted in White 48.

22. I do not focus on parliament, partly because I see it as essentially the law-making mechanism of prerogative power, though that is obviously a contested position in the early modern era. I see the discursive conflict between absolutism and civic republicanism as undercutting any easy belief in a public that is represented in parliament. Insofar as I am skeptical of the ideology of parliamentary representation, my framework dovetails with Oliver's, though he sees Shakespeare himself as fundamentally focused on parliament only to undercut its pretensions to being broadly representative, whereas I see Shakespeare as not falling for the red herring of parliamentary discourse in the first place. For a useful account of the ideology of parliamentary representation rooted in the most material practices by which parliamentary business was conducted, see Kyle.

23. There is sometimes tension between the apparent claims of natural law and simple obedience to the positive law ratified by the sovereign, especially when the individual's reason is supposed capable of discovering natural law. However, as White puts it, "there was a skeptical and resistant tradition dating from Calvin and summated by Hobbes, suggesting that after the Fall Natural Law existed, not, as Aquinas held, in the human mind and heart, but in God's will and the sovereign's fiat" (White xi).

24. Baker 11–20.

25. In addition to Baker's standard account, see also Plucknett; Dickinson. Literary critics often emphasize that equity courts had their origin in church courts. See, for example, Cormack, among many others.
26. White 46. White's quotation is from Ogilvie 40.
27. The relationship between absolutism and natural rights is quite complicated, since republicans could claim to be defending natural rights, while kings could claim to be the true source of natural law in the face of the decay of human reasoning capacities from within a Christian understanding of the fall. The theory of equity as rooted in the king's conscience has a long discursive history, beginning with Christopher St. German, who affirmed the role of the king's conscience in providing for a true justice in his "dyalogue in Englysshe, bytwyxt a Doctour of Dyuynyte, and a student in the lawes of Englande" (first published in 1530). Though he defended the customary laws of England, Sir John Fortescue also understood the king to have a natural capacity to understand and embody true justice, a view he influentially articulated in *De laudibus legum* (published in an English translation in 1567). For a good account of St. German's thought, see Zurcher, Chapter 5; Eppley; White 2–4. Coke articulated his views in the *Institutes of the lawes of England*.
28. In their famous debate, Thomas Egerton, King James's Chancellor, defended the king's right to assert his conscience against Chief Justice Coke's arguments for the autonomy of common law against the equity courts. The preeminence of Chancery over common law courts was established in 1616, when James removed Coke from his position as Chief Justice of the common law Court of King's Bench, after his clash with Ellesmere, the Lord Chancellor.

2   The Life of the Condemned: The Autonomous Legal System and the Community of the Flesh in *Measure for Measure*

1. "These letters at fit time deliver me," the duke asks Friar Peter, "Go call at Flavius' house,/ And tell him where I stay; give the like notice/ To Valencius, Rowland, and to Crassus,/ And bid them bring the trumpets to the gate,/ But send me Flavius first" (4.5.1–10). These characters have played no role in the play thus far and they play no role in the conclusion of the play either. Their purpose is apparently only to provide a visual emblem of the duke acting through a public of presumably like-minded men, and the classical names of these friends seem to confirm that they are rooted in a classical, republican imaginary. Returning to the city gates, the duke will come not as a tyrant but as the first among a group of equals. For a very different understanding of the play, see Rackley, who claims that the play illustrates how a prince who lacks absolute power must opt for a social contract vision of the political community. See also Shuger.
2. Casting the play as an expression of the ideology of divine monarchy, Andrew Barnaby and Joan Wry argue that *Measure for Measure* shows King James as trying to absorb divine authority. However, they do also see some "blowback" when Christian ideals of valuing the spirit over the letter of the law bite back.
3. Similarly, for Jensen, the point of the play is that beneath "justice" is nothing but political will. She calls this recognition "deep politics" and argues that the

Machiavellian point of the play is to conjure up chaos so that people will be happy to have a prince reasserting absolute power at the end.

4. Pittion offers a good discussion of the way in which the technical language of the play affirms the professional community of lawyers. He reviews legal education at a time when it was only barely professionalized and anyone could claim to be a legal consultant. The Inns of Court fostered a mix of formal and informal social interaction designed to breed a sense of shared habitus. Many of the essays in Archer, Goldring, and Knights, eds. are especially attuned to the issue of legal professionalization at the Inns, especially Raffield. For a useful discussion of professionalization in a range of professions including the law, see Gieskes. Drawing on Bourdieu's notion of "fields," Gieskes argues that the "professional field" emerges first around the need by the court for new bureaucratic administrators. For him, a professional field defines itself as providing important services and regulating itself (through training, ethics, and discipline). Gieskes emphasizes the straightforward opposition between sovereign power and supposedly self-regulating professions, whereas I emphasize the sometimes disruptive symbiosis of the two institutions. Sokol and Sokol offer a good account of how the legal profession is made up of a web of "institutions, practices and procedures." For an account that sees early modern literary texts (including *Measure for Measure*) as appealing to an emerging public sphere and seeking to foster a sense of equity and justice in readers, see Visconsi. For an important related discussion see also Hanson.

5. The evidence for the influence of "moot courts" (staged at the Inns of Court or even in coffee houses) on Shakespeare's plotting in *Measure for Measure* is reviewed by Cunningham, "Opening Doubts Upon the Law," and more fully in *Imaginary Betrayals*. Cunningham notes that moot cases often involved convoluted situations concerning marriages, death, heirs, and property, and she notes that the process of reasoning them through would help to build a sense of a community in possession of collective, proverbial legal frameworks.

6. Discussing the formal properties of the "disguised ruler" sub-genre, Cohen makes the important point that delegation of power to a failed subordinate emphasizes the necessity of the ruler's personal fiat. For Cohen, the debate between common law and mercy thus gives way to a different question: the personal fitness of the person who wields power over the law. Cohen also argues that, formally, *Measure for Measure* moves from romantic comedy (which captures Elizabeth's strategy of concealing her power) to the disguised ruler genre (associated with James's more overt [and male] power). For Cohen, the conflict between different expectations and conventions of these genres accounts for the play's seeming incoherence. See "From Mistress to Master" and the slightly revised version in *Shakespeare and Historical Formalism*. Of course, its incoherence is also partly due to its textual history, which is reviewed by G. Taylor.

7. Angelo himself seems to confirm the equation of law and sovereign will when he issues the proclamation to which Pompey refers in Act 1. We do not hear the proclamation and do not know what it says, but it seems unlikely that Shakespeare imagines Angelo announcing a new law, since the duke says the biting statutes have all been on the books "these fourteen years."

It seems more likely that Angelo's proclamation announces the seemingly redundant fact that henceforth the laws will in fact be applied;that is, that henceforth Angelo intends to apply the laws. The play makes the same point in Act 2, when Escalus rhetorically asks Pompey—the pimp of the play—if prostitution is legal. Attempting to make a joke out of the situation, Pompey answers with "if the law would allow it," to which Escalus replies both that prostitution is against existing positive law and that this law will in fact be applied in this instance: "But the law will not allow it, Pompey, nor it shall not be allowed in Vienna" (2.1.216–218). This is a comic (but comic-serious) illustration of Schmitt's anti-liberal theory that a positive legal code depends on an extra-legal will, a sovereign authority who says that in fact the law applies here.

8. This argument is made, for example, by Beauregard in "Shakespeare on Monastic Life," in which he argues that Shakespeare uses the Thomistic taxonomy of virtues and vices and that he emphasizes the ultimate aim of moral actions, so that even "bad" actions can be good if undertaken for a good purpose (as with the bed trick). In general, Beauregard sees Shakespeare actively revising the explicitly anti-Catholic polemic of his sources for the play, an argument he develops most fully in *Catholic Theology in Shakespeare's Plays*. There, Beauregard places the play's attack on the abuse of royal authority (and thus Erastianism) in the context of a lingering Catholic culture in England.

9. Dickinson tracks the confusion between a Christian notion of "mercy" (in which everyone is forgiven regardless of the circumstances or causes) and the "secular" legal concept of equity, which takes causes and circumstances into account. For Dickinson, the secular legal notion of equity comes from Aristotle's claim (in the *Nicomachean Ethics*) that laws always take the form of the universal, but that in applying the laws, one should take particular circumstances into account as if the initial lawgiver were still there to take them into account. For Dickinson, Aristotle essentially sees equity as a "corrective," and Dickinson also quotes Bodin (predictably) on the need for equity as a corrective to the mechanical application of law. Panther discusses how *Measure for Measure* can be used in contemporary American law school classes to teach the messiness of the law's application to real human situations.

10. In part, I draw on Cormack's discussion of the historical background. Cormack emphasizes the jurisdictional conflict between English common law courts on the one hand and ecclesiastical, equity, and the High Court of Admiralty on the other. Fortier notes that John Selden opposed the idea of equity because he wanted to defend the inviolable power of common law over a judge's conscience. By contrast, James's chancellor, Lord Ellesmere, defended equity as royal prerogative rooted in the king's conscience (in turn rooted in the supposed Law of God). In this debate, "equity" could refer either to the spirit as opposed to the letter of the law or to conscience regardless of what the law says. See also Platt.

11. For a thorough account of Coke's artificial reasoning in contrast to the kind of reasoning undertaken in equity courts, see Skulsky.

12. It is worth noting that at the end of the play, Isabella articulates the same common law principle as Angelo does here when she begs that Angelo be

pardoned for attempting to rape her, since he was not able to act on his intention: "His act did not o'ertake his bad intent,/ And must be buried but as an intent/ That perished by the way. Thoughts are no subjects,/ Intents but merely thoughts" (5.1.449–452). Since intents are merely thoughts, and "thoughts are no subjects" to the legal system, she argues that the legal system has no purchase on Angelo.

13. See, for example, Lockey.

14. Claudio's seizure is also registered as an arbitrary act of will by the community of onlookers, including the unnamed gentlemen, Lucio, the pimp Pompey, and Mistress Overdone. The "people" gathered on the streets of Vienna all react defensively to the imposition of new laws, for, like Claudio, they instinctively believe that the law is nothing but Angelo's will. In fact, the experience of being subject to a radically incomprehensible law has the effect of generating a certain collective tenacity of life.

15. Flanigan notes the view that prunes conferred protection against syphilis in his broad discussion of the regulation of sex as a test for royal power. He argues that the early modern English state attempted to take control of sexuality away from church courts, which were lenient, often resorting only to public shaming, and were for this reason called "bawdy courts" by puritan critics. He notes that the construction of Bridewell prison marked a real acceleration of secular control over sexuality, but also describes the Bridewell scandal of 1602, in which the prison was handed over to undertakers who essentially turned it into a house of prostitution. This scandal seems to be one of the relevant contexts on which Shakespeare drew for *Measure for Measure*. For a fascinating discussion of the records of the Bridewell prison, see Griffiths. Among other interesting points Griffiths makes is that Shakespeare's jokes about inept constables notwithstanding, there is in fact evidence of powerful policing through an interlacing network of constables, warders, watchmen, beadles, deputy aldermen, and marshals. Griffiths notes that in 1643 a square mile of London had an average of 800 officers, as compared to 304 in 2000–01. The assertion that the power of the state was in fact quite able to touch many of its subjects helps to make plausible my claim that Shakespeare is interested in examining the (shared) experience of subjection to state power.

16. Huston Diehl parallels Isabella's argument, claiming that the play discloses a sense of universal shame that the play cannot absolve because only God can. She quotes Calvin's *Institutes* on the law as a mechanism that makes people guilty rather than preventing them from being guilty. For a feminist counteraccount that frames Isabella's commitment to abstract moral principles no matter the consequences as a source of a personal autonomy that ultimately saves her from being defined by men, see Kamaralli. Kamaralli notes that in Shakespeare's sources, a novella by Cinthio and Whitstone's play about the same story, Isabella and Angelo end up marrying. For a good discussion of the radical implications of the Christian framework that Isabella applies here, see Magedanz.

17. Gross writes that "Angelo's discovery of an alien life within himself, within his own language, reads as both monstrous and human. His desire not only wounds him, but provokes a kind of nameless terror, a terror that at once drives him apart from humanity and restores him to it" (Gross 78–79).

The drive away from the legally codified person or role (justice and petitioner, sovereign and sister of condemned) to the body stripped, as it were, of socio-symbolic identity is highlighted by the otherwise inexplicable, submerged puns on testicles (or stones) that Isabella starts throwing out when she offers to bribe Angelo "not with fond sicles of the tested gold,/ Or stones .../ ...but with true prayers" (2.2.149–151). It is as if the language itself "breeds sense" here.

18. The same is true of Isabella. Behnegar argues that the lax moral background of the play energizes an explosion of a new moral severity exemplified by Angelo and Isabel that can, paradoxically, be converted into sexuality. For him, the point of the play is to suggest that "sexuality is not a sufficient basis for community" (156), a sentiment with which I agree to the extent that I see the relationship between Isabella and Angelo as prefiguring a new form of corporeal connection that is not, strictly speaking, a community of persons.

19. Widmayer argues that early modern magistrates were seen as using their personal discretion to enforce statues of personal conduct (especially against bastardy) more strictly than the law required. For that reason, they depended on personal reputation for virtue and when they were deposed (which happened frequently) they were often publicly humiliated (as Angelo is at the end of the play). For Widmayer, the duke is an old aristocrat (lenient, but also grand and personally lax), whereas Angelo is a new godly magistrate.

20. Burks argues that accounts of martyrdom and torture in Protestant propaganda influenced Renaissance and Restoration drama, and, more specifically, that Foxe's account of Anne Askew's interrogation influences Shakespeare's account of Angelo and Isabella's relationship.

21. To some extent I see Isabella's perversity as an instance of the kind of resistance that K. Schwarz describes, in which there is a transgressive potential in the perfect inhabitation of normative rules, especially for women. Her important discussion of consent is quite enabling for my discussion.

22. I am treating the scene as an Artaudian performance that breaks with mere representation to highlight the gestural reality of the actors themsleves. For a remarkable effort to apply Artaud's comments on characters as "animated hieroglyphics," see Kunin, "Decoration, Modernism, Cruelty."

23. The version of *Measure for Measure* we have was significantly reworked by Thomas Middleton, and it is likely that many of the prison scenes are by his hand. For a discussion of the role of Middleton in producing the play, see Jowett.

24. Zaller argues that the natural life that appears in the prison calls into question the nature and limits of political authority as such.

25. Of course, the staged attempt to execute Barnardine only heightens his strange, ineradicable, fleshly status, since he declines to accompany the executioner Abhorson and his new helper Pompey, saying simply, "Away, you rogue, away! I am sleepy" (4.3.27–28). Relatedly, when Claudio is taken to prison, the disguised duke counsels him to accept and even to welcome the death sentence to which he has been subjected. "Be absolute for death," says the Duke, "either death or life/ Shall thereby be the sweeter" (3.1.5–6). Like Isabella in her argument with Angelo, the duke here frames the legal state of condemnation that Claudio has been subjected to as universal, and

argues for a stoical acceptance of death-within-life. For the duke, Claudio's legal subjection brings to light the death that lies within the heart of life, and the effect is a world-weariness that seems to take away Claudio's will to live. However, the speech also discloses a kind of freedom in accepting legal condemnation, a freedom in escaping from any wish to be spared. The duke's speech suggests that the life of condemnation contains the possibility of a transformed experience of the flesh together.

26. Bernthal offers a good discussion of the unveiling scene.

27. In some sense, the civic republican "community" that the duke engineers is paralleled or even mirrored by the "community" of the flesh that Angelo (inadvertently) sparks. The duke's extreme touchiness about Lucio's slanders is easier to understand once we understand that for the duke, what is at stake is the nature of the public life itself, and his desire to remain above and outside the fleshly life of Vienna.

28. The conclusion of *Measure for Measure* returns the political order to the foundational moment when sovereign power is first instituted by drawing a line between life that is sanctioned and life that is not.

3 Unsettling the Civic Republican Order: The Face of Sovereign Power and the Fate of the Citizen in *Othello*

1. According to Magnusson, what annoys Iago about Cassio is that he can profit from words that would not do Iago any good, because he is not socially positioned to reap benefits from them. Magnusson argues that Iago engages in "re-ranking" behavior. She also argues that for Iago, Othello is an outsider who is not quite at ease in the market of public speech in Venice and who therefore overcompensates, thus creating bombast, as suggested when he tells Roderigo that Othello's speech is marked by "bombast circumstance/ Horribly stuffed with epithets of war" (1.1.13–14). Berry argues that class resentment is at odds with and yet underpins military hierarchy in ways that provoke the action of the play.

2. For Saunders, Iago has specific goals, though goals that take the regular work of cultural competition to murderous extremes. Saunders argues that Iago is the embodiment of Norbert Elias's sociological account of the civilizing process, and that he wants to purge himself and Venice of everything that is alien—women, desire, blackness itself. Within a humoral framework, the bad ideas that Iago feeds to Othello will fill his head with excrement. Saunders argues that the play diagnoses a historical moment when racial hatred is already present, but without a developed racial ideology; it is therefore structured by deep fantasies about the difference between civility and barbarism, cleanliness (and self-control) and dirt (and lack of self-control). In Iago's final silence, Saunders, like me, sees the sign of his having gotten what he wanted, though for Saunders that means he has finally been purged and is therefore empty. Similarly, Raatzsch argues that Iago represents a pathologically extreme determination to separate himself from other characters and the concerns that typify human relations: "The difference between Iago and others is, for Iago, the quintessential boundary... for him there is no essential difference between the different kinds of things, human and nonhuman, that are not himself" (73).

3. To put it in a slightly different way, for Iago, Othello is the veiled, absolute power that anchors Venetian political culture, and unsettling Othello is therefore a way of unsettling the whole political space that is the precondition for the orderly distribution of sociological attributes that define personhood within a symbolic order.

4. In a similar vein, Logan argues that Iago represents an increasingly disenfranchised or alienated subjectivity in the face of the economic and imperial agendas of the state. Logan is interested in the homology between the domestic sphere and the political sphere, and makes the interesting point that the state's projects are aligned with Desdemona's empowerment.

5. Along the same lines, see Schalwyk's application of Hegel's master–slave dialectic to argue that because of his inferior position, Iago has the self-awareness that Othello lacks.

6. Othello's supposed racial otherness notwithstanding, therefore, we can say that Iago is the true alien, the existential outsider, because it is he who reveals that all socio-symbolic identity is the contingent product of contingent political will, and that when this will shows its foundation in violence, social identities come unglued and break down.

7. For a full discussion of the historiography on civic republicanism, see the final section of Chapter 1.

8. The community exists in time, constantly threatened with the possibility of decay from within or attack from without, and when confronted with such a danger it is the citizens themselves who must collectively find a way to survive, rather than handing their collective fate over to a divine monarch whose will is law.

9. For a useful account that sees Shakespeare as committed to the civic republican institutions of Venice, see Matheson. Matheson makes the important point that Othello embodies traditional absolutist values and uses the language of love for political loyalty. For an interesting recent discussion of civic republicanism and masochism, see Hammill, "Converting Cruelty and Constituting Community in Shakespeare's Venice: A Response to Drew Daniel."

10. Contarini notes that Venice made it illegal for a citizen to command more than 25 soldiers in order to keep an internal armed interest from developing, something that Contarini (and Machiavelli) thought caused the downfall of Rome when Julius Caesar returned with his army. Thus, the Venetians hire mercenaries, which is what opens the door to the role Othello plays within the constitutional order that seems to exclude him.

11. One consequence of the endogamous foundation of the constitutional order is a persistent hint that the Venetian aristocrats take themselves to be racially different from non-Venetians, notably including the foreign mercenaries who defend the ancient constitutional order. The ways in which a notion of race affects how the character of Othello is represented have obviously been a major source of interest for scholars, but if race means an understanding of insuperable, "biological" difference between human beings—something like species difference—then we can surely say that the Venetian aristocrats are in the vanguard of racial thinking, insofar as Venice is defined by the fantasy of a hermetically sealed, blood-mediated in-group. For the classic argument about the way the play equates racial difference with gender

difference, see Newman, who argues that there is an analogous monstrosity in women and black men. For an important related account, see Callaghan's chapter on *Othello*. She argues that blackface was related to the white face that represented female beauty in boy actors, and claims that the use of cosmetics elicited hostility from contemporaries because it represented an assertion of control by women over their own cultural image. For a powerful recent discussion of race in the play, see Bovilsky.

12. In a sense, the state-affirmed intimacy of Othello and Desdemona is simply a continuation of the face-to-face ties between members of the Venetian in-group that define and constitute the republican order.

13. I discuss how this idea is translated into cinematic style in Orson Welles's film of the play. See Gil, "Avant-garde Technique."

14. In an argument that is interestingly antithetical to mine, Bristol argues that the Othello–Desdemona marriage is a carnivalesque inversion of social norms, and that Iago is the agent of social convention who engineers a public shaming to put them back in their places.

15. Relatedly, Zamir argues that there are two forms of subjectivity, one biography centered and the other being oriented, and that Othello has the first and Desdemona the second. For Zamir, Desdemona's love of Othello threatens to reduce him to a biography-centered subjectivity, which he rebels against by choosing to believe Iago's deceptions.

16. The culture of civic republicanism notwithstanding, what stands between Venice and the Turk is the sheer will of Othello, and the absolute power of life and death over Venetian and Cypriot subjects that he embodies. In Cyprus, Iago's goal is to reveal what Venice wants to conceal; namely, the presence within the constitutional order of Venice of an exception in the form of Othello, who represents pure will, the raw assertion of the power of life and death. Iago brings this dimension to the fore, and that opens the door to a somewhat confused and indeterminate state in which the relation between the rulers and the ruled is dissolved, and new connections between self and other become possible. In the state of exception, there is no obvious difference between a person and bare life. What the state of exception that Iago triggers in Cyprus means is a state where people experience connections via an intensified experience of the flesh. For an account that assumes that the Turks are truly alien (rather than emphasizing the role of the sovereign in affirming an existential border where there would otherwise be none), see Lupton, "Othello Circumcised," and the expanded version in *Citizen-Saints*. Lupton argues that Shakespeare can imagine a universal brotherhood that crosses the white/black divide, but that he can do so only by reemphasizing the difference between the different monotheistic religions.

17. Roderigo is here advised to see shame as a positive rather than a negative experience. Fernie argues that what drives the play is not jealousy, but a primal shame that replicates itself and spreads between male characters.

18. For an interesting account of the final scene of murder as arising out of an aggravated defense of individualism (rather than a crisis in sovereign power), see D. Cohen, who argues that the frantic individualism released in the tragedies takes its most horrific but logical endpoint in the right of an individual to kill another individual who stands in his way. Cohen sees

Othello's individualism as bound up with the struggle to totally dominate Desdemona's individualism. R. Schwartz (50–54) sees Desdemona's murder as a sacrifice.

19. I was first drawn to thinking about this image by Aebischer's discussion, which goes on to note Desdemona and Emilia's peculiar vocalness in the final scene.

20. Cassio reports of Roderigo that "even but now he spake,/ After long seeming dead – Iago hurt him,/ Iago set him on" (5.2.327–329).

21. In her chapter on *Othello*, Floyd-Wilson argues that the play reflects a historical process in which geo-humoralism is gradually replaced by racialism. Other important inaugural figures in the humoral studies movement have been Smith and (with greater attention to the presence of a countervailing stoical principle) Schoenfeldt. See also the essays in Paster, Rowe, and Floyd-Wilson, eds.

22. From a phenomenological standpoint, the emotions are the effect of a primordial interconnectedness between self and other, a primordial experience that is always in some sense falsified when it is elaborated into a theory. The early modern writers on the passions register but also falsify this primordial state of affairs in elaborating their theoretical picture of a separable self that is exposed to the world, but that is also made of the same stuff as the world. One of the things that humoral *theory* does is to insert the phenomenologically primordial knowledge into a context in which the humors and passions will signify and function within a social imaginary. The goal of early modern humoral theorists is to make people legible within a certain social and even political framework.

23. It is for this reason that so many of the treatises on the passions are written by religious figures interested in preaching: they wished to plug into the passions as the effective site of their intervention, but they also wished to understand the passionate self as the center of a cosmic battle.

24. In her account, Paster argues that the play is structured, in part, by the humoral framework that sees pre-marital girls as suffering from greensickness caused by a thickening of the blood, which can supposedly only be cured by marriage, since the friction of sex creates bodily heat that thins the fluids. Thus, the humoral cure is aligned with the social imperative to marry and have children. Paster says that in *Othello*, Desdemona follows this pattern, which would have been recognizable to early modern theatergoers.

4 Life Outside the Law: Torture and the Flesh in *King Lear*

1. In the other plays I have examined, this stripping of sovereign power is accomplished by exposing sovereign power to the corrosive acid of civic republicanism. In *King Lear* there is a hint of civic republicanism, insofar as the break-up of the kingdom divides up the basis for autonomous political authority or power. In place of a single, unified structure of sovereignty, there is a competition between centers of power, each grounded in its own power base in land and arms. And as with the other plays I have discussed, rather than founding a new, functional political order in which competing

power centers balance each other out, this multiplication of power bases reveals absolute sovereignty as nothing but force, the power to impose one's will on others. Dubrow connects Lear's initial act of resignation (and the ensuing action in the play) to the evolving law of property in the period. She notes that Lear asserts his sovereign power in disregarding any preexisting law about inheritance and the transfer of property to heirs. However, no character in the opening scene evokes any sense of preexisting norms or rules governing property transfer; even Kent, despite his associations with feudal traditions, sees Lear's actions not as legally bad but only as morally bad. Dubrow also discusses the way in which Cordelia and Regan displace Gloucester from his house. They are bad guests who pry their host out, but at the same time they are sovereigns who technically own all the land. She argues that ultimately Shakespeare is drawn to the language of hospitality as a way of bringing the focus back to persons taking care of each other, bypassing disputes and the radical uncertainty of land ownership. Cooley also highlights the legal issues that subtend *King Lear*. He notes that the character of Kent is invented by Shakespeare; in the precursor play, the comparable character is Perillus. The new name points to the distinctive land law of Kent, which is based on gavelkind, or divisibility of inheritance, dating from the pre-Norman era. Cooley argues that Shakespeare is representing and defending the ideology of the common law practice of primogeniture, but noting challenges, such as the famous case of a Kentish gentleman, Brian Annesley, who wanted to settle his estate on a daughter named Cordelia. For another sophisticated account of the context of inheritance law in *King Lear*, see Restivo.

2. In view of the Jacobean fantasy that the king's word is law, by uttering the self-canceling speech act "I am not a king," Lear challenges sovereignty as such. For a vital account of self-canceling speech acts by kings, see Lemon. After Lear resigns (or says he does), his very body is a discursive provocation. To the good characters Lear always remains king; to the bad characters he is a mere man. And yet, both ways of seeing Lear are ultimately strategies for containing what he really represents, which is a wound within the fabric of a particular, structured form of social life presided over by functioning sovereign power. In an article with some interesting formulations, Brayton says that Lear is presiding over his own symbolic death, fossilizing himself into the political order that succeeds.

3. In *On the Psychotheology of Everyday Life*, Santner argues that Rosenzweig's version of Jewish thought contains something very similar to Badiou's thinking on St. Paul; namely, a drive away from a society where people are all parts fitting into a whole to a conception of the self radically freed of any social predicates encountering another self also so freed. Santner is operating in a psychoanalytic framework, and thinks that the self always has an excess in it that is bound up with the fantasies that glue it into the existing social world. He is interested in the moments in Jewish thought where that fantasy is suspended and a radical experience of the self-as-alien opens to other selves-as-aliens.

4. I am drawing on the excellent discussion in Shannon's "Poor, Bare, Forked." For an account of the play that sees the human as essentially reducible to the animal, see Hoefele.

5. For an account that sees *Lear* as a political satire attacking the inequalities of early modern England, see Heinemann, who argues that the play, especially the quarto version, represents a radical attack on the massive inequality between rich and poor. For Heinemann, the Q mock trial parodies the very idea of securing justice in such an unjust society. This perspective is the object of a persuasive attack by Kronenfeld, who argues that critics have misunderstood key words in *Lear* that come from an Anglican discourse on charity that is ultimately meant to affirm inequality. For an account of the radical potential in the religious language appearing in *Lear*, see Young as well as Strier's discussion of the play.

6. As I will go on to discuss later, this is also a "theater" problem, insofar as the actor's body may begin to "show through" the character's costume. For a detailed discussion of how the actor represents himself even as he also represents the character, and of how those processes may be at odds, see the introduction to Weimann and Bruster, eds. They contain the radicalism of their insight by arguing that Shakespeare is able to construct "deep character" out of the fact that the corporeal person who speaks on the stage is neither that which is signified by the text nor by the body on the stage, but something in between. For Womack, by contrast, the disconnect between the actor and the character is something that Shakespeare highlights in the play. Womack argues that in the wilderness, the clothes characters wear are disrupted as theatrical signs in the way that, he believes, the fool's costume always is disrupted, signifying a role and a non-role at the same time. His basic claim is that the fool and Tom are only barely mimetic characters; they are also allegorical negations, like the character "nobody" of the earlier word-riddle play that Womack describes.

7. That this experience is "cross-cultural," being a feature of absolute monarchy as a political formation, is suggested by Forcione's account of Lope de Vega's *El Villano en su Rincon* and *El Rey Don Pedro o El Infanzon de Illescas*, together with Cervantes's *Viaje del Parnasso* and Velasquez's "Las Meninas," as revealing the phantasmagoric emptiness at the heart of royal self-presentation. For Forcione, these texts reveal the organic body of the king beneath the fictions of power.

8. For a sometimes suggestive account of the indeterminate states of the bodies of actors when they switch roles on stage, and on how such indeterminate states can be characterized by a kind of corporeal autonomy, see E. Sanders.

9. For a very suggestive account of Lear-as-actor, as well as the potentially redemptive experience of the audience, see Cartwright's chapter on *King Lear*.

10. For the passages that appear only in Q I use the Orgel and Braunmuller edition, which prints the F and the Q versions separately.

11. For an interesting account of incest as enabling, especially for women and women writers, see Quilligan.

12. For an interesting personal reflection on the emotion-laden experience of watching *King Lear*, see Smith, "Speaking What We Feel about *King Lear*." He examines two competing models of memory in early modern thought: the spacial, in which memory is like a storeroom where static ideas are held; and the fluid, in which memory is like a liquid whose motion is altered by stored experiences. He associates the second with feeling and the first with

facts and associates these two, respectively, with the "feel" and "ought" of Albany/Edgar's closing line in the play. The most useful part of the discussion is Smith's emphasis on "feeling" in the play itself—Lear wishes that Regan will feel what it is to have an ungrateful child, and he himself wants to feel what the poor feel; after Gloucester is blinded he says he sees "feelingly." I see these characters groping for a new way of understanding interpersonal ties beyond the stable socio-symbolic identities defined in the *dramatic personae*. Smith also situates the emotion-laden experience of watching the play within theater history, arguing that a theater performance is a concrete moment in space-time that cannot be translated into another medium, since narrative description or even video eliminates the interaction with audience altogether. He makes reference to how the actor elicits a passion within him- or herself and through physical movement communicates that passion to the audience; for the audience to remember the play is therefore not merely cerebral but physiological.

13. For another account that discovers an Artaudian dimension in theatrical displays of bodies as a kind of residue of the early modern re-emphasis on verbal rhetoric, see Hawkes.

14. In part, Artaud is drawing on the complex interplay between the Apollonian and the Dionysian in Nietzsche's philosophy of art. Like the Dionysian, the gestural theater cannot appear except through an Apollonian mask. The nature of the Apollonian mask is what I attempt to specify historically; I root it in a sovereign decision about the nature and experience of identity and community.

15. For an account suggesting that the Essex rebellion plays a role in Shakespeare's depiction of Cornwall, see Rubinstein.

16. There is, of course, an analogous moment in *Othello*, namely when Othello returns after the first riot and only manages to restore order by losing his temper and threatening to start killing people at random. For another important discussion of the status of torture in the early modern context, see Brownlow's description of the notorious figure of Richard Topcliffe, who presided over many instances of torture and execution (especially of suspected Catholic agents) and seems to have gotten direct warrants to do so from the queen. Like Rocklin, Brownlow notes that torture was always based on prerogative, since it was illegal from the common law perspective. Thus, when Topcliffe was present at a bloody spectacle, he represented Elizabeth's sovereign power.

17. For Traub, the play provides a genealogy of the modern concepts of norms and the normal, especially an abstract universal humanity and common nature.

18. For an important discussion of how vexed the status of service could be in the early modern era, see Schalwyk.

19. This way of putting it only highlights the logical endpoint of White's claim that the play stages a particularly naked form of the conflict between natural law and positive law (185).

20. For a discussion of the literary historical context of Shakespeare's decision to put the torture of Gloucester on the stage, see Groves's account of medieval mystery plays as games that involve fictional identities and plots. One of the primary games in the mystery play tradition is to treat Christ as an animal,

which is a model for how Regan and Cornwall treat Gloucester. Gloucester also refers to himself as a blinded bear, which was one form bear baiting could take. For an account of the blinding as a symbolic castration, a loss of a symbolic personhood, see Halio.

21. In his discussion of the play, Pechter diagnoses a desire for vengeance in audience members, a desire for justice, that always rebounds to the self, and the lesson, for the characters inside the play as well as for the audience outside, is to resist this impulse. Pechter is interested in how the play sets up an expectation of a happy ending or of justice, and then systematically defeats that expectation, by doing so (he argues) punishing the audience. He says that Gloucester is careful and prudential, but when he is spurred to angry, vengeful action, he is immediately defeated. In a larger sense, what is ultimately defeated by the play, in Pechter's view, is nothing less than the desire to impose meaning or to make sense of things, even the sense of an ending.

22. Nunne claims that the audience "shares" the pain of the blinding on the stage because it relies on its eyes to see this scene.

23. For a vital discussion of the Dover Cliff sequence, see Goldberg, "Perspectives."

24. Lawrence argues that Lear wants to impose a meaning on his death by making the heavens (and indeed the whole world) apocalyptically reflect his inner state. For Lawrence, this is a Heideggerian moment in which Lear is trying to choose the terms of his own death.

25. In his chapter on *King Lear* and *Endgame*, Kott argues that Shakespeare offers a reduction *ad absurdum* of the human condition. For Kott, man is just man, trying to impose meaning on his suffering, trying in that sense to find redemption, but ultimately doomed to die in meaninglessness. This is highlighted by the "pantomime" (as Kott sees it) of Gloucester's attempted suicide. Kott describes Gloucester as ending up doing a somersault on the ground, which is to say that he and Edgar finally engage in clowning around, a kind of staged buffoonery, and he connects it to other absurd gestures in the play, like Lear asking that his pinching shoe to be taken off.

26. In the final act of the play, Edgar does report that he had a reunion with his father in which he revealed himself, but it is significant that Shakespeare—who shows us everything in this most painfully visual of plays—withholds a staged scene and instead has it reported, along with the death that this revelation caused. Edgar's attempt to reassert his and his father's traditional identities has the effect of foregrounding the dislodged flesh, the heart that is overwhelmed with extremes of passion, and that it is the business of the play to bring to the fore.

27. In making this speech, Cordelia also aligns Lear's status as father with his status as king, and by refusing to declare her love she defends a world where identities are guaranteed by a firmly structured form of sovereign power, and where human relationships are mediated by such anchored socio-symbolic identities—where love is always according to a bond, a socially defined form of connection between socially defined selves.

28. Lawrence also notes that Kent is essentially returning from the grave at the "reunion" and that Lear should properly be horrified at this undead man. Earlier, of course, Lear has suggested that in seeing Cordelia he has been awakened from the dead: "You do wrong to take me out of the grave" (4.7.45).

29. As with *Measure for Measure*, the end of *King Lear* attempts to restore sovereign order, albeit in a half-hearted way. Albany invites Edgar and Kent to "Rule in this realm, and the gored state sustain" (5.3.327). However, like other Shakespeare tragedies, the play pairs this effort to reassert functioning sovereignty with the spectacle of a pile of bodies that remind the audience of the life of the flesh that the play has rendered bare and that it cannot fully recontain.

Epilogue: The Afterlife of the Life of the Flesh

1. Implied here is an important methodological point, which is that I decline to view Shakespeare as merely symptomatic of larger forces at work in his culture. Rather, I view him as thinking through the major discourses at play in his historical context, and as using his art to stage an alternative that escapes from—even as it is also conditioned by—the historical culture in which he worked.
2. In the same interview, Taymor also notes the influence of Luchino Visconti's 1969 film *The Damned*, about the rise of the Nazis, and of Leni Riefenstahl's style, especially in regard to the scene of Titus's army entering the Coliseum.
3. Agamben's main statement is *Remnants of Auschwitz*. For an overview of the controversy about whether the Holocaust should be understood as a one-of-a-kind historical event or as a type, see de la Durantaye.
4. See, for example, Fedderson and Richardson.
5. See Burt's "Shakespeare and the Holocaust."
6. Taymor herself says precisely this is an interview with Pizzello: "I think you need to stop that moment to highlight the way we create art out of violence, or masterpieces out of torture" (Pizzello 68).
7. In fact, the fascist and Holocaust context was absent from the off-Broadway play that Taymor produced before she directed the film. McCandless argues that the play is morally superior to the film precisely in bracketing and estranging the violence—through theatrical *Verfremdungs* effects—whereas the film, for him, is complicit in the violence, especially against women, that it also appears to condemn. However, the explicit introduction of the fascist political context in the film is inseparable from the distinctively filmic project of putting the life of the flesh on display, something that is less and less a part of theater (which is, of course, limited by the respect for the physical persons of the actors).
8. At the same time, Taymor also aims to avoid the equal and opposite danger of violence that is so viscerally affecting that it allows no room for imaginative transcendence.

Bibliography

Aebischer, Pascale. *Shakespeare's Violated Bodies: Stage and Screen Performances.* New York: Cambridge University Press, 2004.

Agamben, Giorgio. *The Coming Community.* Trans. Michael Hardt. Minneapolis: University of Minnesota Press, 1993.

Agamben, Giorgio. *Homo Sacer: Sovereign Power and Bare Life.* Trans. Daniel Heller-Roazen. Stanford, CA: Stanford University Press, 1998.

Agamben, Giorgio. *Remnants of Auschwitz: The Witness and the Archive.* Trans. Daniel Heller-Roazen. New York: Zone Books, 2002.

Alexander, Catherine M.S., ed. *Shakespeare and Politics.* New York: Cambridge University Press, 2004.

Archer, Elizabeth Jayne, Elizabeth Goldring, and Sarah M. Knights, eds. *The Intellectual and Cultural World of the Early Modern Inns of Court.* Manchester: Manchester University Press, 2011.

Archer, John Michael. *Citizen Shakespeare: Freemen and Aliens in the Language of the Plays.* NewYork: Palgrave Macmillan, 2005.

Armitage, David, ed. *British Political Thought in History, Literature and Theory, 1500–1800.* New York: Cambridge University Press, 2006.

Armitage, David, Conal Condren, and Andrew Fitzmaurice, eds. *Shakespeare and Early Modern Political Thought.* New York: Cambridge University Press, 2009.

Arrighi, Giovanni, Terence K. Hopkins, and Immanuel Wallerstein. *Antisystemic Movements.* London: Verso, 1989.

Artaud, Antonin. "On the Balinese Theater." *The Theater and Its Double.* Trans. Mary C. Richards. New York: Grove Press, 1966.

Artaud, Antonin. *The Theater and Its Double* in *Collected Works.* Trans. Victor Corti. Vol. 4. London: Calder & Boyars, 1974.

Badiou, Alain. *Saint Paul: The Foundation of Universalism.* Trans. Ray Brassier. Stanford, CA: Stanford University Press, 2003.

Baker, J.H. *An Introduction to English Legal History.* New York: Oxford University Press, 2005.

Ball, Terence, James Farr, and Russell L. Hanson, eds. *Political Innovation and Conceptual Change.* Cambridge: Cambridge University Press, 1989.

Barnaby, Andrew and Joan Wry. "Authorized Versions: *Measure for Measure* and the Politics of Biblical Translation." *Renaissance Quarterly* 51 (1998): 1225–1254.

Bate, Jonathan. "A Shakespeare Tale Whose Time Has Come." *New York Times.* January 2, 2000. http://www.nytimes.com/2000/01/02/movies/film-a-shakespeare-tale-whose-time-has-come.html?pagewanted=all&src=pm, accessed April 23, 2013.

Beauregard, David N. *Catholic Theology in Shakespeare's Plays.* Newark: University of Delaware Press, 2008.

Beauregard, David N. "Shakespeare on Monastic Life: Nuns and Friars in *Measure for Measure.*" Taylor and Beauregard, eds. 311–35.

Behnegar, Nasser. "The Political and Theological Psychology of Shakespeare's *Measure for Measure*," *Interpretation* 29 (2001–02): 153–69.

Berry, Ralph. *Tragic Instance: The Sequence of Shakespeare's Tragedies*. Newark: University of Delaware Press, 1999.

Bernthal, Craig. "Staging Justice: James I and the Trial Scenes of *Measure for Measure*." *Studies in English Literature* 32 (1992): 247–269.

Bersani, Leo. *The Freudian Body: Psychoanalysis and Art*. New York: Columbia University Press, 1986.

Blanchot, Maurice. *The Unavowable Community*. Trans. Pierre Joris. Barrytown, NY: Station Hill Press, 1983.

Bloom, Gina. *Voice in Motion: Staging Gender, Shaping Sound in Early Modern England*. Philadelphia: University of Philadelphia Press, 2007.

Bodin, Jean. *On Sovereignty: Four Chapters from The Six Books of the Commonwealth*. Ed. and trans. Julian H. Franklin. New York: Cambridge University Press, 1992.

Bordwell, David and Noël Carroll, eds. *Post-Theory: Reconstructing Film Studies*. Madison: University of Wisconsin Press, 1996.

Bourdieu, Pierre. *Distinction: A Social Critique of the Judgment of Taste*. Trans. Richard Nice. Cambridge, MA: Harvard University Press, 1984.

Bovilsky, Lara. *Barbarous Play: Race on the English Renaissance Stage*. Minneapolis: University of Minnesota Press, 2008.

Brayton, Dan. "Angling in the Lake of Darkness: Possession, Dispossession and the Politics of Discovery in *King Lear*." *ELH* 70 (2003): 399–426.

Bristol, Michael. *Carnival and Theater: Plebeian Culture and the Structure of Authority in Early Modern England*. London: Methuen, 1985.

Brownlow, Frank. "Richard Topcliffe: Elizabeth's Enforcer and the Representation of Power in *King Lear*." Kezar, ed. 161–178.

Burks, Deborah G. *Horrid Spectacle: Violation in the Theater of Early Modern England*. Pittsburgh, PA: Duquesne University Press, 2003.

Burt, Richard, ed. *Shakespeare after Mass Media*. New York: Palgrave, 2002.

Burt, Richard. "Shakespeare and the Holocaust: Julie Taymor's *Titus* is Beautiful, or Shakesploi Meets (the) Camp." Burt, ed. 295–329.

Callaghan, Dympna. *Shakespeare without Women: Representing Gender and Race on the Renaissance Stage*. New York: Routledge, 2000.

Campana, Joseph. *The Pain of Reformation: Spenser, Vulnerability, and the Ethics of Masculinity*. New York: Fordham University Press, 2012.

Cartelli, Thomas and Katherine Rowe. *New Wave Shakespeare on Screen*. Malden, MA: Polity Press, 2012.

Cartwright, Kent. *Shakespearean Tragedy and Its Double: The Rhythms of Audience Response*. University Park: Pennsylvania State University Press, 1991.

Cavell, Stanley. *Disowning Knowledge: In Seven Plays of Shakespeare*. New York: Cambridge University Press, 2003.

Cerasano, S.P., ed. *Medieval and Renaissance Drama in England*. Cranbury, NJ: Associated University Presses, 2007.

Cheney, Patrick G. *Shakespeare, National Poet-Playwright*. New York: Cambridge University Press, 2004.

Cheney, Patrick G. *Shakespeare's Literary Authorship*. Cambridge: Cambridge University Press, 2008.

Cheney, Patrick G. *Marlowe's Republican Authorship: Lucan, Liberty, and the Sublime*. New York: Palgrave Macmillan, 2009.

Cherniak, Warren L. *The Myth of Rome in Shakespeare and His Contemporaries*. Cambridge: Cambridge University Press, 2011.

Clayton, Tom, Susan Brock, and Vicente Fores, eds. *Shakespeare and the Mediterranean: The Selected Proceedings of the International Shakespeare Association Congress, Valencia, 2001*. Newark: University of Delaware Press, 2004.

Cohen, Derek. *Shakespeare's Culture of Violence*. New York: St. Martin's Press, 1993.

Cohen, Stephen. "From Mistress to Master: Political Transition and Formal Conflict in *Measure for Measure*." *Criticism* 41 (1999): 431–464.

Cohen, Stephen. *Shakespeare and Historical Formalism*. Aldershot: Ashgate, 2007.

Coke, Sir Edward. *The Institutes of the lawes of England*. London, 1628–1648.

Collinson, Patrick. "The Monarchical Republic of Queen Elizabeth I." Guy, ed. 110–134.

Colony, Tracy. "Before the Abyss: Agamben on Heidegger and the Living." *Continental Philosophy Review* 40 (2007): 1–16.

Condren, Conal. "Unfolding 'the properties of government': The Case of *Measure for Measure* and the History of Political Thought." Armitage, Condren, and Fitzmaurice, eds. 157–175.

Contarini, Gaspar. *The Commonwealth and Government of Venice*. Trans. Lewes Lewkenor. London, 1599.

Cooley, Ronald W. "Kent and Primogeniture in *King Lear*." *SEL* 48 (2008): 327–348.

Cormack, Bradin. *A Power to Do Justice: Jurisdiction, English Literature, and the Rise of Common Law, 1509–1625*. Chicago: University of Chicago Press, 2008.

Croteau, Melissa and Carolyn Jess-Cooke, eds. *Apocalyptic Shakespeare*. Jefferson, NC: McFarland, 2009.

Cunningham, Karen. *Imaginary Betrayals: Subjectivity and the Discourses of Treason in Early Modern England*. Philadelphia: University of Pennsylvania Press, 2002.

Cunningham, Karen. "Opening Doubts upon the Law: *Measure for Measure*." Dutton and Howard, eds. 316–332.

Cunningham, Karen and Constance Jordan, eds. *Shakespeare and the Law*. New York: Palgrave Macmillan, 2007.

Daniel, Drew. "'Let Me Have Judgment, and the Jew His Will': Melancholy Epistemology and Masochistic Fantasy in *The Merchant of Venice*." *Shakespeare Quarterly* 61:2 (2000): 206–234.

de la Durantaye, Leland. *Giorgio Agamben: A Critical Introduction*. Stanford, CA: Stanford University Press, 2009.

Deluca, Maria and Mary Lindroth. "Mayhem, Method, Madness: An Interview with Julie Taymor." *Cinéaste* 25:3 (2000), 30.

Derrida, Jacques. "The Theater of Cruelty and the Closure of Representation." *Writing and Difference*, trans. Alan Bass. Chicago: University of Chicago Press, 1978. pp. 292–317.

DeVries, Hent and Lawrence E. Sullivan, eds. *Political Theologies: Public Religions in a Post-Secular World*. New York: Fordham University Press, 2006.

de Wilde, Marc. "Violence in the State of Exception: Reflections on Theologico-Political Motifs in Benjamin and Schmitt." DeVries and Sullivan, eds. 188–200.

Dickinson, John W. "Renaissance Equity in *Measure for Measure*." *Shakespeare Quarterly* 13 (1962): 275–285.

Diehl, Huston. "'Infinite Space': Representation and Reformation in *Measure for Measure*." *Shakespeare Quarterly* 49 (1998): 393–410.

Dobson, Michael. *The Making of the National Poet: Shakespeare, Adaptation and Authorship, 1660–1769*. Oxford: Oxford University Press, 1992.

Donaldson, Peter S. "Game Space/Tragic Space: Julie Taymor's *Titus*." Hodgdon and Worthen, eds. 457–477.

Dubrow, Heather. "'They took from me the use of mine own house': Land Law in Shakespeare's *Lear* and Shakespeare's Culture." Kezar, ed. 81–98.

Dutton, Richard and Jean E. Howard, eds. *A Companion to Shakespeare's Works, Volume IV: The Poems, Problem Comedies, Late Plays*. Malden, MA: Blackwell, 2003.

Elliot, Brian. "Community and Resistance in Heidegger, Nancy and Agamben." *Philosophy & Social Criticism* 37 (2011): 259–271.

Engster, Daniel. *Divine Sovereignty: The Origins of Modern State Power*. DeKalb: Northern Illinois University Press, 2001.

Eppley, Daniel. *Defending Royal Supremacy and Discerning God's Will in Tudor England*. Aldershot: Ashgate, 2007.

Erne, Lukas and Margaret Jane Kidnie, eds. *Textual Performances: The Modern Reproduction of Shakespeare's Drama*. New York: Cambridge University Press, 2004.

Fanon, Franz. *The Wretched of the Earth*. Trans. Constance Farrington. New York: Grove, 1963.

Fedderson, Kim and J. Michael Richardson. "*Liberty's Taken*, or How "captive women may be cleansed and used": Julie Taymor's *Titus* and 9/11." Croteau and Jess-Cooke, eds. 70–89.

Fernie, Ewan. *Shame in Shakespeare*. New York: Routledge, 2002.

Flanigan, Tom. "What to Do about Bawds and Fornicators: Sex and Law in *Measure for Measure* and Tudor/Stuart England." *Journal of the Wooden O Symposium* 3 (2003): 36.

Floyd-Wilson, Mary. *English Ethnicity and Race in Early Modern Drama*. New York: Cambridge University Press, 2003.

Forcione, Alban K. *Majesty and Humanity: Kings and Their Doubles in the Political Drama of the Spanish Golden Age*. New Haven, CT: Yale University Press, 2009.

Fortescue, Sir John. *A learned commendation of the politique laws of Englande*. London, 1567.

Fortier, Mark. *The Culture of Equity in Early Modern England*. Farnham: Ashgate, 2005.

Foucault, Michel. *History of Sexuality*. Trans. Robert Hurley. New York: Pantheon Books, 1978.

Frey, Anne. *British State Romanticism: Authorship, Agency, and Bureaucratic Nationalism*. Stanford, CA: Stanford University Press, 2009.

Gieskes, Edward. *Representing the Professions: Administration, Law and Theater in Early Modern England*. Newark: University of Delaware Press, 2006.

Gil, Daniel Juan. *Before Intimacy: Asocial Sexuality in Early Modern England*. Minneapolis: University of Minnesota Press, 2005.

Gil, Daniel Juan. "Avant-garde Technique and the Visual Grammar of Sexuality in Orson Welles's Shakespeare Films." *Borrowers and Lenders: The Journal of Shakespeare and Appropriation* 1 (Fall 2005).

Gil, Daniel Juan. "The Deep Structure of Sexuality: War and Masochism in *Henry IV, part 2*." Menon, ed. 114–120.

Goldberg, Jonathan. "Perspectives: Dover Cliff and the Conditions of Representation." Zimmerman, ed. 155–166.

Goldberg, Jonathan. *The Seeds of Things: Theorizing Sexuality and Materiality in Renaissance Representations*. New York: Fordham University Press, 2009.

Goldberg, Jonathan. *Sodometries: Renaissance Texts, Modern Sexualities.* New York: Fordham University Press, 2010.

Goldberg, Jonathan. *Tempest in the Caribbean.* Minneapolis: University of Minnesota Press, 2004.

Griffiths, Paul. *Lost Londons: Change, Crime, and Control in the Capital City, 1550–1660.* Cambridge: Cambridge University Press, 2008.

Gross, Kenneth. *Shakespeare's Noise.* Chicago: University of Chicago Press, 2001.

Groves, Beatrice. "Now wole I a newe game begynne": Staging Suffering in *King Lear*, the Mystery Plays and Grotius's *Christus Patiens.*" Cerasano, ed. 136–150.

Guillory, John. *Cultural Capital: The Problem of Literary Canon Formation.* Chicago: University of Chicago Press, 1995.

Guy, John, ed. *The Tudor Monarchy.* New York: Arnold, 1997.

Habermas, Jürgen. *The Structural Transformation of the Public Sphere: An Inquiry into a Category of Bourgeois Society.* Trans. Frederick Lawrence. Cambridge, MA: MIT Press, 1989.

Hadfield, Andrew. *Shakespeare and Republicanism.* New York: Cambridge University Press, 2005.

Hadfield, Andrew. "Republicanism in Sixteenth- and Seventeenth-Century Britain." Armitage, ed. 111–128.

Halio, Jay. "Gloucester's Blinding." *Shakespeare Quarterly* 43:2 (Summer, 1992): 221–223.

Halper, Louise. "*Measure for Measure*: 'Law, Prerogative, Subversion.'" *Cardozo Studies in Law and Literature* 13 (2001): 221–264.

Halpern, Richard. *Shakespeare among the Moderns.* Ithaca, NY: Cornell University Press, 1997.

Hammill, Graham. "Converting Cruelty and Constituting Community in Shakespeare's Venice: A Response to Drew Daniel." *Shakespeare Quarterly* 61:2 (Summer 2010), 234–240.

Hammill, Graham. *The Mosaic Constitution: Political Theology and Imagination from Machiavelli to Milton.* Chicago: University of Chicago Press, 2012.

Hammill, Graham and Julia Reinhard Lupton, eds. *Political Theology and Early Modernity.* With an afterword by Etienne Balibar. Chicago: University of Chicago Press, 2012.

Hanson, Elizabeth. "*Measure for Measure* and the Law of Nature." Cunningham and Jordan, eds., pp. 249–265.

Harrington, James. *The common-wealth of Oceana.* London, 1656.

Harvey, Elizabeth D., ed. *Sensible Flesh: On Touch in Early Modern Culture.* Philadelphia: University of Pennsylvania Press, 2002.

Hawkes, Terence. *Shakespeare's Talking Animals: Language and Drama in Society.* London: Edward Arnold, 1973.

Heinemann, Margot. "'Demystifying the Mystery of State': *King Lear* and the World Upside Down." *Shakespeare Survey* 44 (1992): 75–83.

Helgerson, Richard. *Forms of Nationhood: The Elizabethan Writing of England.* Chicago: University of Chicago Press, 1992.

Hodgdon, Barbara and W.B. Worthen, eds. *A Companion to Shakespeare and Performance.* Malden, MA: Blackwell, 2005.

Hoefele, Andreas. *Stage, Stake, and Scaffold: Humans and Animals in Shakespeare's Theatre.* Oxford: Oxford University Press, 2011.

Holland, Peter, ed. *Writing about Shakespeare*. New York: Cambridge University Press, 2005.

Holland, Peter, ed. *Shakespeare, Memory and Performance*. New York: Cambridge University Press, 2006.

Jackson, Ken. "'Is It God or the Sovereign Exception?': Giorgio Agamben's *Homo Sacer* and Shakespeare's *King John*." *Religion & Literature* 38 (2006): 85–100.

James, Susan. *Passion and Action: The Emotions in Seventeenth-Century Philosophy*. New York: Oxford University Press, 1997.

Jensen, Pamela K. "Vienna Vice: Invisible Leadership and Deep Politics in Shakespeare's *Measure for Measure*." Murley and Sutton, eds. 105–54.

Jowett, John. "Addressing Adaptation: *Measure for Measure* and *Sir Thomas More*." Erne and Kidnie, eds. 63–76.

Kahan, Jeffrey, ed. *King Lear: New Critical Essays*. New York: Routledge, 2008.

Kahn, Paul W. *Political Theology: Four New Chapters on the Concept of Sovereignty*. New York: Columbia University Press, 2012.

Kamaralli, Anne. "Writing about Motive: Isabella, the Duke and Moral Authority." Holland, ed. 48–59.

Kezar, Denis, ed. *Solon and Thespis: Law and Theater in the English Renaissance*. Notre Dame, IN: University of Notre Dame Press, 2007.

Kott, Jan. *Shakespeare Our Contemporary*. Trans. Boleslaw Taborski. London: Methuen, 1967.

Kronenfeld, Judy. King Lear *and the Naked Truth: Rethinking the Language of Religion and Resistance*. Durham, NC: Duke University Press, 1998.

Kunin, Aaron. "Characters Lounge." *Modern Language Quarterly: A Journal of Literary History* 70 (2009): 291–317.

Kunin, Aaron. "Decoration, Modernism, Cruelty." *Modernism/Modernity* 17 (2010): 87–107.

Kuzner, James. *Open Subjects: English Renaissance Republicans, Modern Selfhoods, and the Virtue of Vulnerability*. Edinburgh: Edinburgh University Press, 2011.

Kyle, Chris R. *Theater of State: Parliament and Political Culture in Early Stuart England*. Stanford, CA: Stanford University Press, 2012.

Laplanche, Jean. *Life and Death in Psychoanalysis*. Trans. Jeffrey Mehlman. Baltimore, MD: Johns Hopkins University Press, 1976.

Lawrence, Sean. "The Difficulty of Dying in *King Lear*." *ESC* 31 (December 2005): 35–52.

Leinwand, Theodore B. *The City Staged: Jacobean City Comedy 1603–13*. Madison: University of Wisconsin Press, 1986.

Leinwand, Theodore B. "Shakespeare and the Middling Sort." *Shakespeare Quarterly* 44 (1993): 284–303.

Lemon, Rebecca. *Treason by Words: Literature, Law, and Rebellion in Shakespeare's England*. Ithaca, NY: Cornell University Press, 2006.

Lesser, Zachary and Benedict S. Robinson, eds. *Textual Conversations in the Renaissance: Ethics, Authors, Technologies*. Burlington, VT: Ashgate, 2006.

Levin, Carol and John A. Watkins, *Shakespeare's Foreign Worlds: National and Transnational Identities in the Elizabethan Age*. Ithaca, NY: Cornell University Press, 2009.

Lievens, Matthias. "Carl Schmitt's Two Concepts of Humanity." *Philosophy & Social Criticism* 36 (2010): 917–934.

Lockey, Brian. *Law and Empire in English Renaissance Literature*. New York: Cambridge University Press, 2006.

Logan, Sandra. "Domestic Disturbance and the Disordered State in Shakespeare's *Othello*." *Textual Practice* 18 (2004): 351–375.

Lupton, Julia Reinhard. "Othello Circumcised: Shakespeare and the Pauline Discourse of Nations." *Representations* 57 (Winter 1997): 73–89.

Lupton, Julia Reinhard. *Citizen-Saints: Shakespeare and Political Theology*. Chicago: University of Chicago Press, 2005.

Magedanz, Stacy. "Public Justice and Private Mercy in *Measure for Measure*." *SEL* 44 (Spring 2004): 317–332.

Magnusson, Lynne. *Shakespeare and Social Dialogue: Dramatic Language and Elizabethan Letters*. New York: Cambridge University Press, 1999.

Marshall, Cynthia. "Portia's Wound, Calphurnia's Dream: Reading Character in Julius Caesar Source." *English Literary Renaissance* 24 (1994): 471–488.

Marshall, Cynthia. *The Shattering of the Self*. Baltimore, MD: Johns Hopkins University Press, 2002.

Matheson, Mark. "Venetian Culture and the Politics of Othello." Alexander, ed. 169–184.

McCandless, David. "A Tale of Two Tituses: Julie Taymor's Vision on Stage and Screen." *Shakespeare Quarterly* 53 (2002): 487–511.

McDiarmid, John F., ed. *The Monarchical Republic of Early Modern England*. Burlington, VT: Ashgate, 2007.

Menon, Medhavi, ed. *Shakesqueer*. Durham, NC: Duke University Press, 2011.

Milton, John. *The readie and easie way to establish a free commonwealth and the excellence therof compar'd with the inconveniences and dangers of readmitting kingship in this nation*. London, 1660.

Murakami, Ineke. *Moral Play and Counterpublic: Transformations in Moral Drama, 1465–1599*. New York: Routledge, 2011.

Murley, John A. and Sean D. Sutton, eds. *Perspectives on Politics in Shakespeare*. New York: Lexington Books, 2006.

Nancy, Jean-Luc. *The Inoperative Community*. Ed. Peter Connor, trans. Peter Connor, Lisa Garbus, Michael Holland, and Simon Sawhney. Minneapolis: University of Minnesota Press, 1991.

Nancy, Jean-Luc. *Being Singular Plural*. Trans. Robert Richardson and Anne O'Byrne. Stanford, CA: Stanford University Press, 2000.

Negri, Antonio. *Insurgencies: Constituent Power and the Modern State*. Trans. Maurizia Boscagli. Minneapolis: University of Minnesota Press, 1999.

Newman, Karen. "'And wash the Ethiop White': Femininity and the Monstrous in *Othello*." Reprinted in Newman, *Essaying Shakespeare*. Minneapolis: University of Minnesota Press, 2009.

Norbrook, David. *Writing the English Republic: Poetry, Rhetoric and Politics, 1627–1660*. New York: Cambridge University Press, 1999.

Norris, Andrew. "Jean-Luc Nancy on the Political after Heidegger and Schmitt." *Philosophy & Social Criticism* 37 (10/2011): 899–913.

Nunne, Hillary M. *Staging Anatomies: Dissection and Spectacle in Early Stuart Tragedy*. Aldershot: Ashgate, 2005.

O'Brien, Karen. "Poetry and Political Thought: Liberty and Benevolence in the Case of the British Empire c. 1680–1800. Armitage, ed. 168–190.

Ogilvie, Sir Charles. *The King's Government and the Common Law 1471–1641*. Oxford: Oxford University Press, 1958.

Oliver, Arnold. *The Third Citizen: Shakespeare's Theater and the Early Modern House of Commons*. Baltimore, MD: Johns Hopkins University Press, 2007.

Owens, Patricia. "Reclaiming 'Bare Life'? Against Agamben on Refugees." *International Relations* 23 (12/2009): 567–582.

Panther, Penelope. "Measured Judgments: Histories, Pedagogies, and the Possibility of Equity." *Law and Literature* 14 (2002): 489–543.

Paster, Gail Kern. *The Body Embarrassed: Drama and the Disciplines of Shame in Early Modern England*. Ithaca, NY: Cornell University Press, 1993.

Paster, Gail Kern, Katherine Rowe, and Mary Floyd-Wilson, eds. *Reading the Early Modern Passions: Essays in the Cultural History of Emotion*. Pennsylvania: University of Pennsylvania Press, 2004.

Pechter, Edward. "On the Blinding of Gloucester." *ELH* 45 (1978): 181–200.

Peltonen, Markku. *Classical Humanism and Republicanism in English Political Thought 1570–1640*. New York: Cambridge University Press, 1995.

Perry, Curtis. *Literature and Favoritism in Early Modern England*. Cambridge: Cambridge University Press, 2006.

Pittion, Jean-Paul. "Borrowing the Language of Lawyers: The Rhetoric of the Law in Shakespeare's Comedies." *Journal de la Renaissance* 1 (2000): 189–204.

Pizzello, Stephen. "From Stage to Screen: Theatrical Director Julie Taymor Reimagines Her Radical Stage Version of *Titus Andronicus* for the Cinema." *American Cinematographer* 81 (2000): 64–73.

Platt, Peter G. "'Much More the Better for Being a Little Bad,' or, Gaining by Relaxing: Equity and Paradox in *Measure for Measure*." Lesser and Robinson, eds. 45–68.

Plucknett, Theodore. *A Concise History of the Common Law*. London: Butterworth, 1940.

Pocock, J.G.A. *The Ancient Constitution and the Feudal Law*. Cambridge: Cambridge University Press, 1987. (Reissue of the 1957 edition)

Pocock, J.G.A. *The Machiavellian Moment: Florentine Political Thought and the Atlantic Republican Tradition*. Princeton, NJ: Princeton University Press, 1975.

Pye, Christopher. *The Regal Phantasm: Shakespeare and the Politics of Spectacle*. New York: Routledge, 1990.

Quilligan, Maureen. *Incest and Agency in Elizabeth's England*. Philadelphia: University of Philadelphia Press, 2005.

Raatzsch, Richard. *The Apologetics of Evil: The Case of Iago*. Princeton, NJ: Princeton University Press, 2009.

Rackley, Erika. "Judging Isabella: Justice, Care and Relationships in *Measure for Measure*." Raffield and Watt, eds. 65–80.

Raffield, Paul. *Shakespeare's Imaginary Constitution: Late-Elizabethan Politics and the Theatre of Law*. Portland, OR: Hart, 2010.

Raffield, Paul. "The Inner Temple Revels (1561–62) and the Elizabethan Rhetoric of Signs: Legal Iconography at the Early Modern Inns of Court." Archer et al., eds. 32–50.

Raffield, Paul and Gary Watt, eds. *Shakespeare and the Law*. Portland, OR: Hart, 2008.

Restivo, Giuseppina. "Inheritance in the Legal and Ideological Debate of Shakespeare's *King Lear*." Raffield and Watt, eds. 159–172.

Roach, Joseph. *The Player's Passion: Studies in the Science of Acting.* Newark: University of Delaware Press, 1985.

Rocklin, Edward L. "The Smell of Morality: Performing Torture in *King Lear* 3.7." Kahan, ed. 297–325.

Rubinstein, Frankie. "Speculating on Mysteries: Religion and Politics in *King Lear.*" *Renaissance Studies* 16:2 (2002): 234–262.

Saint German, Christopher. *Hereafter foloweth a dyalogue in Englysshe, bytwyxt a Doctour of DyuyNYte, and a student in the lawes of Englande.* London, 1530.

Sandel, Michael. *Democracy's Discontent: America in Search of a Public Philosophy.* Cambridge, MA: Harvard University Press, 1996.

Sanders, Eve Rachelle. "The Body of the Actor in *Coriolanus.*" *Shakespeare Quarterly* 57 (2006): 387–412.

Sanders, Julie. *Ben Jonson's Theatrical Republics.* New York: Palgrave Macmillan, 1998.

Santner, Eric L. *On the Psychotheology of Everyday Life.* Chicago: University of Chicago Press, 2001.

Santner, Eric L. *On Creaturely Life: Rilke, Benjamin, Sebald.* Chicago: University of Chicago Press, 2006.

Saunders, Ben. "Iago's Clyster: Purgation, Anality, and the Civilizing Process." *Shakespeare Quarterly* 55 (Summer 2004): 148–176.

Schalwyk, David. *Shakespeare, Love and Service.* New York: Cambridge University Press, 2008.

Schoenfeldt, Michael. *Bodies and Selves in Early Modern England: Physiology and Inwardness in Spenser, Shakespeare, Herbert and Milton.* New York: Cambridge University Press, 1999.

Schmitt, Carl. *The Concept of the Political.* Trans. George Schwab. Chicago: University of Chicago Press, 1996.

Schmitt, Carl. *Political Theology: Four Chapters on the Concept of Sovereignty.* Trans. George Schwab. Chicago: University of Chicago Press, 2005.

Schmitt, Carl. *Constitutional Theory.* Trans. Jeffrey Seitzer. Durham, NC: Duke University Press, 2008.

Schwarz, Kathryn. *What You Will: Gender, Contract, and Shakespearean Social Space.* Philadelphia: University of Pennsylvania Press, 2011.

Schwartz, Regina. *Sacramental Poetics and the Dawn of Secularism: When God Left the World.* Stanford, CA: Stanford University Press, 2008.

Shakespeare, William. *The Arden Shakespeare Complete Works.* Ed. Richard Proudfoot, Ann Thompson, and David Scott Kastan. New York: Arden Shakespeare, 2001.

Shakespeare, William. *The Complete Pelican Shakespeare.* Ed. Stephen Orgel and A. R. Braunmuller. New York: Penguin, 2002.

Shannon, Laurie. *Sovereign Amity: Figures of Friendship in Shakespeare Contexts.* Chicago: University of Chicago Press, 2002.

Shannon, Laurie. "Poor, Bare, Forked: Animal Sovereignty, Human Negative Exceptionalism, and the Natural History of *King Lear.*" *Shakespeare Quarterly* 60:2 (Summer 2009): 168–196.

Shannon, Laurie. *The Accommodated Animal: Cosmopolity in Shakespearean Locales.* Chicago: University of Chicago Press, 2012.

Shell, Mark. *The End of Kinship: Measure for Measure, Incest, and the Ideal of Universal Siblinghood.* Baltimore, MD: Johns Hopkins University Press, 1995.

Shuger, Deborah Kuller. *Political Theologies in Shakespeare's England: The Sacred and the State in* Measure for Measure. New York: Palgrave, 2001.

Skinner, Quentin. *Liberty before Liberalism.* New York: Cambridge University Press, 1998.

Skulsky, Harold. "Pain, Law and Conscience in *Measure for Measure.*" *Journal of the History of Ideas* 25 (1964): 147–168.

Smith, Bruce R. *Phenomenal Shakespeare.* Malden, MA: Wiley-Blackwell, 2010.

Smith, Bruce R. "Speaking What We Feel about *King Lear.*" Holland, ed., *Shakespeare, Memory and Performance.* 23–42.

Smith, Thomas. *De Republica Anglorum.* London, 1583.

Sokol, B.J. and Mary Sokol. *Shakespeare, Law and Marriage.* New York: Cambridge University Press, 2003.

Sommerville, J.P. "English and Roman Liberty in the Monarchical Republic of Early Stuart England." McDiarmid, ed. 201–216.

Sorel, Georges. *Reflections on Violence.* Trans. T.E. Hulme and J. Roth, intro. Edward A. Shils. New York: Dover, 2004.

Steinmetz, George, ed. *State/Culture: State-Formation after the Cultural Turn.* Ithaca, NY: Cornell University Press, 1999.

Strier, Richard. *Resistant Structures: Particularity, Radicalism, and Renaissance Texts.* Berkeley: University of California Press, 1995.

Sullivan, Vickie B. *Machiavelli, Hobbes and the Formation of a Liberal Republicanism in England.* New York: Cambridge University Press, 2004.

Taylor, Dennis and David Beauregard, eds. *Shakespeare and the Culture of Christianity in Early Modern England.* New York: Fordham University Press, 2003.

Taylor, Gary. "Shakespeare's Mediterranean *Measure for Measure.*" Clayton et al., eds. 243–269.

Traub, Valerie. "The Nature of Norms in Early Modern England: Anatomy, Cartography, *King Lear.*" *South Central Review* 26 (Spring–Summer 2009): 42–81.

van Gelderen, Martin and Quentin Skinner, eds. *Republicanism: A Shared European Heritage.* 2 vols. New York: Cambridge University Press, 2005.

Visconsi, Elliot. *Lines of Equity: Literature and the Origins of Law in Later Stuart England.* Ithaca, NY: Cornell University Press, 2008.

Weimann, Robert. "The Actor-Character Is 'Secretly Open' Action: Doubly Encoded Personation on Shakespeare's Stage." Yachnin and Slights, eds. 177–196.

Weimann, Robert and Douglas Bruster, eds. *Shakespeare and the Power of Performance: Stage and Page in the Elizabethan Theater.* Cambridge: Cambridge University Press, 2008.

White, R.S. *Natural Law in English Renaissance Literature.* New York: Cambridge University Press, 1996.

Widmayer, Martha. "'To Sin in Loving Virtue': Angelo of *Measure for Measure.*" *Texas Studies in Literature and Language* 49 (2007): 155–180.

Wilson, Bronwen and Paul Yachnin, eds. *Making Publics in Early Modern Europe: People, Things, Forms of Knowledge.* New York: Routledge, 2009.

Womack, Peter. "Nobody, Somebody and *King Lear.*" *NTQ* 23 (August 2007): 195–207.

Worden, Blair. "Republicanism, Regicide and Republic: The English Experience." van Gelderen and Skinner, eds. I, 307–327.

Yachnin, Paul. "Performing Publicity." *Shakespeare Bulletin* 28 (2010): 201–219.

Yachnin, Paul and Jessica Slights, eds. *Shakespeare and Character: Theory, History, Performance and Theatrical Persons.* New York: Palgrave Macmillan, 2009.

Young, R.V. "Hope and Despair in *King Lear:* The Gospel and the Crisis of Natural Law." Kahan, ed. 253–277.

Zaller, Robert. "'Send the Head to Angelo': Capital Punishment in *Measure for Measure.*" *The Upstart Crow* 24 (2004): 63–71.

Zamir, Tzachi. *Double Vision: Philosophy and Shakespearean Drama.* Princeton, NJ: Princeton University Press, 2007.

Zimmerman, Susan. *The Early Modern Corpse and Shakespeare's Theater.* Edinburgh: Edinburgh University Press, 2007.

Zimmerman, Susan, ed. and intro. *Shakespeare's Tragedies.* New York: St. Martin's, 1998.

Zurcher, Andrew. *Spenser's Legal Language: Law and Poetry in Early Modern England.* Rochester, NY: Boydell and Brewer, 2007.

Index

Note: "n." after a page reference refers to a note number on that page.

Absolutism, 6–9, 23–9, 43–4, 125–6
Aebischer, Pascale, 146 n.19
Agamben, Giorgio, 2–6, 10, 21–2,
  66–9, 126, 130 n.4, 130 n.5, 130
  n.7, 133 n.21, 133 n.24, 134 n.25,
  151 n.3
Althusser, Louis, 5
anti-politics, 1, 11, 28, 32, 69, 136 n.7
Archer, John Michael, 35–6
Armitage, David, 136 n.14
Arrighi, Giovanni, 135 n.4
Artaud, Antonin, 110–12, 142 n.22,
  149 n.13, 149 n.14

Badiou, Alain, 147 n.3
Baker, J.H., 137 n.24, 138 n.25
Bakhtin, Mikhail, 118
bare life: vs. the life of the flesh,
  10–11; in *Julius Caesar*, 22–8; and
  humors, 30–1; in *Othello*, 89, 145
  n.16; in *King Lear*, 101, 121
Barnaby, Andrew, 138 n.2
Bate, Jonathan, 128
Beauregard, David N., 140 n.8
Behnegar, Nasser, 142 n.18
Benjamin, Walter, 122
Berry, Ralph, 143 n.1
Bernthal, Craig, 143 n.26
Bersani, Leo, 12, 18–19
bio-politics, 2–5, 21–2, 130 n.4
Blanchot, Maurice, 11
Bloom, Gina, 134 n.29
Bodin, Jean, 140 n.9
Bordwell, David, 124–5
Bourdieu, Pierre, 68–9, 130 n.7, 139 n.4
Bovilsky, Lara, 145 n.11
Brayton, Dan, 147 n.2
Bristol, Michael, 145 n.14
Brownlow, Frank, 149 n.16
Bruster, Douglas, 148 n.6

bureaucracy, and sovereign power,
  7, 44
Burks, Deborah G., 142 n.20
Burt, Richard, 126–7, 151 n.5

Callaghan, Dympna, 145 n.11
Calvin, John, 141 n.16
Campana, Joseph, 134 n.26
cannibalism, 14, 17, 53–6
Cartelli, Thomas, 127–8
Cartwright, Kent, 148 n.9
Catholicism, 6
Cavell, Stanley, 119
Charles, King, 41
Cheney, Patrick G., 130 n.1, 137 n.16
Cherniak, Warren L., 137 n.18
civic republicanism: failure to define
  membership, 71–3, 133 n.20;
  critique of legal system, 7–9, 50–1;
  and state of emergency, 72, 133
  n.20; as political ideal, 68–9; in *Julius
  Caesar*, 23–8; in *King Lear*, 146 n.1;
  in *Measure for Measure*, 44–8; and
  communitarianism, 35–41
civil society, 4–6, 10, 20–2, 35–7, 105,
  131 n.8, 135 n.1, 136 n.13
Clausewitz, 16, 35
Cohen, Derek, 145 n.18
Cohen, Stephen, 139 n.6
Coke, Sir Edward, 39, 49, 112, 137
  n.21, 138 n.27, 138 n.28, 140 n.11
Collinson, Patrick, 36, 132 n.13, 132
  n.16, 136 n.12
Colony, Tracy, 130 n.5
common law, 4–5, 16–17, 20, 39–41,
  46–51, 66, 107, 112, 131, 137 n.20,
  138 n.28, 139 n.6, 140 n.10, 140
  n.12, 147 n.1, 149 n.16, see also
  legal system
communitarianism, 4, 39, 67, 136 n.13

Condren, Conal, 136 n.14
conscience, 40, 46–8, 138 n.27
constitutive power, 133 n.24
Contarini, Gaspar, 8–9, 71–4, 132
    n.18, 133 n.19, 144 n.10
Cooley, Ronald W., 147 n.1
Cormack, Bradin, 138 n.25, 140 n.10
Cunningham, Karen, 139 n.5

Daniel, Drew, 134 n.26
de la Durantaye, Leland, 134 n.24,
    151 n.3
Deluca, Maria, 125
Derrida, Jacques, 111
de Wilde, Marc, 133 n.21
Dickinson, John W., 138 n.25,
    140 n.9
Diehl, Huston, 141 n.16
disguised prince genre, 61, 139 n.6
Dobson, Michael, 130 n.1
Donaldson, Peter S., 126–7
Dubrow, Heather, 147

Elias, Norbert, 143 n.2
Elizabeth, Queen, 26, 36, 132 n.13,
    139 n.6, 149 n.16
Elliot, Brian, 134 n.24
emergency, 2–6, 11, 18, 37, 72, 82,
    131 n.8
emotions, 106, 146 n.22, 149 n.12;
    see also humors
Engster, Daniel, 131 n.9
Eppley, Daniel, 138 n.27
equity courts, 40–1, 46–50, 66, 107,
    131 n.11, 138 n.27, 140 n.9; see
    also legal system

Fanon, Franz, 136 n.7
Fedderson, Kim, 151 n.4
Fernie, Ewan, 145 n.17
Fitzmaurice, Andrew 136 n.14
Flanigan, Tom, 141 n.15
flesh: vs. bare life, 9–11; and theater,
    13–15; in *Julius Caesar*, 30–4; in
    Othello, 72–8; in *King Lear*, 103–5,
    112; in *Measure for Measure*, 52–7;
    in *Titus Andronicus*, 127–8
Floyd-Wilson, Mary, 18, 91–6, 134
    n.28, 135 n.3, 146 n.21, 146 n.26

Forcione, Alban K., 148 n.7
Fortescue, Sir John, 138 n.27
Fortier, Mark, 140 n.10
Foucault, Michel, 2–4, 130 n.4
Frey, Anne, 131 n.7

gender, 6, 9, 91, 136 n.9, 141 n.16,
    144 n.11
geo-humoralism, 91
Gieskes, Edward, 131 n.10, 139 n.4
Gil, Daniel Juan, 134 n.25, 134 n.26,
    135 n.3, 145 n.13
Goldberg, Jonathan, 131 n.8, 134
    n.24, 134 n.25, 150 n.23
Gramsci, Antonio, 5
Griffiths, Paul, 141 n.15
Gross, Kenneth, 141 n.17
Groves, Beatrice, 149 n.20
Guillory, John, 130 n.7

Habermas, Jürgen, 16, 20, 28, 35–6,
    134 n.1, 135 n.5
Hadfield, Andrew, 36–7, 136 n.11, 137
    n.16, 137 n.17
Halio, Jay, 150 n.20
Halper, Louise, 48–50, 135 n.2
Halpern, Richard, 135 n.2
Hammill, Graham, 131 n.8, 134 n.26,
    144 n.9
Hanson, Elizabeth, 139 n.4
Harrington, James, 133 n.20
Harrington, Sir John, 8
Harvey, Elizabeth D., 134 n.29
Hawkes, Terence, 149 n.13
Heinemann, Margot, 148 n.5
Helgerson, Richard, 130 n.1
historicism, 13, 125, 136 n.10
Hoefele, Andreas, 147 n.4
Hollywood, violence, 128
Hopkins, Terence K., 135 n.4
human nature, 4, 100–1, 130 n.5
human rights, 114–15
humors: and theater, 13–14; and
    corporeal connections, 17, 30–1,
    35, 54–6, 135 n.3; and selfhood,
    22, 54–5, 91–2, 95, 104, 146
    n.22; and sexuality, 60–1; vs.
    cognitive approach, 18, 90–7; and
    theatricality, 94–7

incest, 64, 99, 109, 148 n.11
Inns of Court, 139 n.4, 139 n.5

Jackson, Ken, 133 n.22
James, King, 6, 41–4, 48, 138 n.28, 138 n.2, 139 n.6
James, Susan, 135 n.3
Jensen, Pamela K., 138 n.3
Jowett, John, 142 n.23
Julius Caesar: overview, 15–16; absolutism vs. civic republicanism, 22–6; theatrical violence, 30–4; public sphere, 35–8
jury, 39, 49

Kahn, Paul W., 130 n.3
Kamaralli, Anne, 141 n.16
King Lear: overview, 18–19; sovereignty and identity, 99–103, 113–16; life of the flesh, 103–5, 112; theatricality, 106–8, 109–12, 116–18, 120–1; sexuality, 108–9
Kott, Jan, 118, 150 n.25
Kronenfeld, Judy, 148 n.5
Kunin, Aaron 110–11, 142 n.22
Kuzner, James, 134 n.24, 134 n.26
Kyle, Chris R., 137 n.22

Laplanche, Jean, 12, 18
Lawrence, Sean, 117, 150 n.24, 150 n.28
legal system: common law vs. prerogative 46, 140 n.9, 140 n.10; as organ of state power, 42–5; professionalization, 44, 137 n.20, 139 n.4; marriage, 64–6, 72–5, 77, 92, 139 n.4, 139 n.5; and national identity, 66; jury, 49; positive law vs. common law, 49; positive law vs. natural law, 137 n.23; and sexuality, 141 n.15; Inns of Court, 139 n.4, 139 n.5
Leinwand, Theodore B., 136 n.10
Lemon, Rebecca, 147 n.2
Levin, Carol, 130 n.1
Lévinas, Emmanuel, 117
liberalism, 132 n.12, 136 n.13, 137 n.15

Lievens, Matthias, 130 n.5
Lindroth, Mary, 125
Lockey, Brian, 141 n.13
Logan, Sandra, 144 n.3
love, and social identity, 28–9, 75, 99, 118–19, 122
Lupton, Julia Reinhard, 5–6, 131 n.8, 145 n.16

Magedanz, Stacy, 141 n.16
Magnusson, Lynne, 69, 143 n.1
marriage, 64–6, 72–5, 77, 92, 139 n.4, 139 n.5
Marshall, Cynthia, 134 n.26, 136 n.9
masochism, 12–13, 18, 58–61, 134 n.26, 144 n.9
Matheson, Mark, 132 n.17, 144 n.9
McCandless, David, 151 n.7
McDiarmid, John F., 136 n.12
Measure for Measure: overview, 16–17; legal system, 42–8; mercy as deconstructive lever, 50–1; life of the flesh, 52–7; sexuality, 57–61; prison, 62–3; marriage, 65–6
Middleton, Thomas, 142 n.23
Milton, John, 66, 133 n.20
monarchomachs, 36
Murakami, Ineke, 135 n.1

Nancy, Jean-Luc, 11, 133 n.24
Negri, Antonio, 11, 133 n.24, 136 n.6
Newman, Karen, 145 n.11
Norbrook, David, 37, 137 n.16
norms, 5, 19, 39–41, 55, 60, 68, 114–15, 131 n.8
Norris, Andrew, 134 n.24
Nunne, Hillary M., 150 n.22

O'Brien, Karen, 137 n.16
Oliver, Arnold, 137 n.22
Othello: overview, 17–18; appeal of civic republicanism, 68–9; Bourdieuvian symbolic economy, 69–70; Contarini, 71–2; Othello as sovereign, 72; sexuality, 73–6, 85–7; theatrical violence, 77–8, 83–4, 87–90; and humoralism, 90–7
Owens, Patricia, 134 n.24

Panther, Penelope, 140 n.9
Parker, Oliver, 88
Paster, Gail Kern, 18, 91–2, 134 n.28, 135 n.3, 146 n.24
Pechter, Edward, 150 n.21
Peltonen, Markku, 136 n.12
Perry, Curtis, 132 n.16
personhood: as grant of state power, 4, 12–13, 63–4, 102, 125–6, 133 n.21; undermined, 55, 85, 89–90, 102–4, 133 n.21; universal, 100–2; vs. animals, 100
Pittion, Jean-Paul, 139 n.4
Pizzello, Stephen, 151 n.6
Platt, Peter G., 140 n.10
Plucknett, Theodore, 138 n.25
Pocock, J.G.A., 39, 71, 132 n.18, 136 n.14, 137 n.19
positive law, see legal system
primogeniture, 147 n.1
prison: as model of community, 50–63, 84–8, 120–1; and theater, 14, 120–1; in *Measure for Measure*, 141 n.15, 142 n.23, 142 n.25; Bridewell scandal, 141 n.15
public sphere, 15–16, 20–3, 35, 131 n.8, 134 n.1
puritanism, 6, 36, 141 n.15
Pye, Christopher, 130 n.6

Quilligan, Maureen, 148 n.11

Raatzsch, Richard, 143 n.2
Rackley, Erika, 138 n.1
Raffield, Paul, 135 n.1, 137 n.20, 139 n.4
resistance theory, 36
Restivo, Giuseppina, 147 n.1
Richardson, Michael J., 151 n.4
rights, 132 n.12, 135 n.5, 137 n.15
rioting, 31–2, 76–85, 89–90
Roach, Joseph, 134 n.28
Rocklin, Edward L., 112–15, 149 n.16
Rowe, Katherine, 127–8
Rubinstein, Frankie, 149 n.15

Saint German, Christopher, 138 n.27
Sandel, Michael, 136 n.13

Sanders, Eve Rachelle, 148 n.8
Sanders, Julie, 135 n.1
Santner, Eric L., 98–9, 133 n.23, 147 n.3
Saunders, Ben., 143 n.2
scapegoat: in Agamben, 10, 133 n.22; as community, 53
Schalwyk, David, 144 n.5, 149 n.18
Schoenfeldt, Michael, 134 n.28, 135 n.3, 146 n.21
Schmitt, Carl, 2–8, 37, 39–40, 42, 45, 69, 82, 126, 130 n.2, 130 n.5, 130 n.6, 131 n.11, 133 n.21, 140 n.7
Schwarz, Kathryn, 142 n.21
Schwartz, Regina, 146 n.18
Selden, John, 39–40, 140 n.10
sexuality: and the life of the flesh, 11–12, 18–19, 81, 85, 108; and humors, 54–6, 60, 146 n.24; of sovereignty, 57–9, 86; and theatricality, 61, 108–9; and social intimacy, 11–12, 73–4, 85; private vs. public, 73–6; and community, 142 n.18; and masochism, 12–13, 18, 58–61, 134 n.26, 144 n.9
Shannon, Laurie, 133 n.23, 147 n.4
Shell, Mark, 64, 99
Shuger, Deborah Kuller, 138 n.1
Skinner, Quentin, 7, 37, 136 n.13
Skulsky, Harold, 140 n.11
Smith, Bruce R., 136 n.8, 146 n.21, 148 n.12
Smith, Sir Thomas, 112
Sokol, B.J. and Mary Sokol, 139 n.4
Sommerville, Johann P., 37
Sorel, Georges, 29
sovereignty: and the life of the flesh, 9–10; theories of, 2–7, 10, 35–41, 71–3; used against itself, 104; and communism, 118; and personhood, 4, 12–13, 63–4, 102, 125–6, 133 n.21; and democracy, 2; and sexuality, 57–9, 86
Spenser, Edmund, 8
Steinmetz, George, 131 n.7
Strier, Richard, 148 n.5
suicide, 33–5, 90, 116–18, 136 n.9, 150 n.25
Sullivan, Vickie B., 136 n.13, 137 n.15

Taylor, Gary, 139 n.6
Taymor, Julie, 19, 125–9
terrorism, 3, 89, 126
theatricality: overview, 12–15; and the
  life of the flesh, 106–7, 112, 122–2;
  and sexuality, 61, 107; gestural
  drama, 65, 111; and violence, 33,
  78, 84–5, 99–100, 110–12, 126–7;
  and audience response, 115–16
Titus Andronicus: civic republicanism
  and absolutism, 125; terrorism,
  126–7; life of the flesh, 127–8
torture, and theatricality, 14–15, 18,
  63, 87–90, 98, 109, 112–15, 122,
  142 n.20, 149 n.16, 149 n.20
Traub, Valerie, 149 n.17

violence, and theatricality, 14–15, 18,
  33, 63, 78, 84–5, 99–100, 110–12,
  126–7

Visconsi, Elliot, 139 n.4

Wallerstein, Immanuel, 135 n.4
Watkins, John A., 130 n.1
Weimann, Robert, 134 n.30, 148 n.6
White, R.S., 40, 137 n.23, 138 n.27,
  149 n.19
Widmayer, Martha, 142 n.19
Wilson, Bronwen, 131 n.8
Womack, Peter, 148 n.6
Worden, Blair, 137 n.14
Wry, Joan, 138 n.2

Yachnin, Paul, 131 n.8, 134 n.1
Young, R.V., 148 n.5

Zaller, Robert, 62, 142 n.24
Zamir, Tzachi, 145 n.15
Zimmerman, Susan, 122
Zurcher, Andrew, 138 n.27

CPSIA information can be obtained
at www.ICGtesting.com
Printed in the USA
BVHW041103070620
581047BV00013B/606